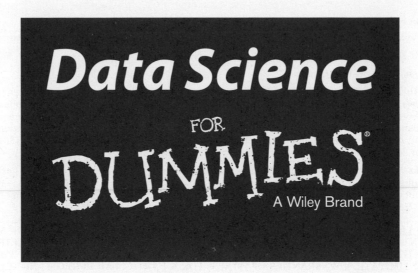

Data Science
FOR
DUMMIES®
A Wiley Brand

by Lillian Pierson

Foreword by Jake Porway
Founder and Executive Director of DataKind™

FOR
DUMMIES®
A Wiley Brand

Data Science For Dummies®

Published by: **John Wiley & Sons, Inc.,** 111 River Street, Hoboken, NJ 07030-5774, www.wiley.com

Copyright © 2015 by John Wiley & Sons, Inc., Hoboken, New Jersey

Published simultaneously in Canada

No part of this publication may be reproduced, stored in a retrieval system or transmitted in any form or by any means, electronic, mechanical, photocopying, recording, scanning or otherwise, except as permitted under Sections 107 or 108 of the 1976 United States Copyright Act, without the prior written permission of the Publisher. Requests to the Publisher for permission should be addressed to the Permissions Department, John Wiley & Sons, Inc., 111 River Street, Hoboken, NJ 07030, (201) 748-6011, fax (201) 748-6008, or online at http://www.wiley.com/go/permissions.

Trademarks: Wiley, For Dummies, the Dummies Man logo, Dummies.com, Making Everything Easier, and related trade dress are trademarks or registered trademarks of John Wiley & Sons, Inc. and may not be used without written permission. All other trademarks are the property of their respective owners. John Wiley & Sons, Inc. is not associated with any product or vendor mentioned in this book.

For general information on our other products and services, please contact our Customer Care Department within the U.S. at 877-762-2974, outside the U.S. at 317-572-3993, or fax 317-572-4002. For technical support, please visit www.wiley.com/techsupport.

Wiley publishes in a variety of print and electronic formats and by print-on-demand. Some material included with standard print versions of this book may not be included in e-books or in print-on-demand. If this book refers to media such as a CD or DVD that is not included in the version you purchased, you may download this material at http://booksupport.wiley.com. For more information about Wiley products, visit www.wiley.com.

Library of Congress Control Number: 2014955780

ISBN 978-1-118-4155-6 (pbk); ISBN 978-1-118-84145-7 (ebk); ISBN 978-1-118-84152-5

Manufactured in the United States of America

10 9 8 7 6 5 4 3 2 1

Contents at a Glance

Table of Contents

Part IV: Computing for Data Science............................ 215

Chapter 14: Using Python for Data Science......................217

Chapter 15: Using Open Source R for Data Science 239

Chapter 16: Using SQL in Data Science 255

Foreword

· ·

*W*e live in exciting, even revolutionary times. As our daily interactions move from the physical world to the digital world, nearly every action we take generates data. Information pours from our mobile devices and our every online interaction. Sensors and machines collect, store and process information about the environment around us. New, huge data sets are now open and publicly accessible.

This flood of information gives us the power to make more informed decisions, react more quickly to change, and better understand the world around us. However, it can be a struggle to know where to start when it comes to making sense of this data deluge. What data should one collect? What methods are there for reasoning from data? And, most importantly, how do we get the answers from the data to answer our most pressing questions about our businesses, our lives, and our world?

Data science is the key to making this flood of information useful. Simply put, data science is the art of wrangling data to predict our future behavior, uncover patterns to help prioritize or provide actionable information, or otherwise draw meaning from these vast, untapped data resources.

I often say that one of my favorite interpretations of the word "big" in Big Data is "expansive." The data revolution is spreading to so many fields that it is now incumbent on people working in all professions to understand how to use data, just as people had to learn how to use computers in the 80's and 90's. This book is designed to help you do that.

I have seen firsthand how radically data science knowledge can transform organizations and the world for the better. At DataKind, we harness the power of data science in the service of humanity by engaging data science and social sector experts to work on projects addressing critical humanitarian problems. We are also helping drive the conversation about how data science can be applied to solve the world's biggest challenges. From using satellite imagery to estimate poverty levels to mining decades of human rights violations to prevent further atrocities, DataKind teams have worked with many different nonprofits and humanitarian organizations just beginning their data science journeys. One lesson resounds through every project we do: The people and organizations that are most committed to using data in novel and responsible ways are the ones who will succeed in this new environment.

Just holding this book means you are taking your first steps on that journey, too. Whether you are a seasoned researcher looking to brush up on some data science techniques or are completely new to the world of data, *Data Science For Dummies* will equip you with the tools you need to show whatever you can dream up. You'll be able to demonstrate new findings from your physical activity data, to present new insights from the latest marketing campaign, and to share new learnings about preventing the spread of disease.

We truly are on the forefront of a new data age, and those that learn data science will be able to take part in this thrilling new adventure, shaping our path forward in every field. For you, that adventure starts now. Welcome aboard!

Jake Porway

Founder and Executive Director of DataKind™

Introduction

● ●

The power of big data and data science are revolutionizing the world. From the modern business enterprise to the lifestyle choices of today's digital citizen, data science insights are driving changes and improvements in every arena. Although data science may be a new topic to many, it's a skill that any individual who wants to stay relevant in her career field and industry needs to know.

Although other books dealing with data science tend to focus heavily on using Microsoft Excel to learn basic data science techniques, *Data Science For Dummies* goes deeper by introducing Python, the R statistical programming language, D3.js, SQL, Excel, and a whole plethora of open-source applications that you can use to get started in practicing data science. Some books on data science are needlessly wordy, with authors going in circles trying to get to a point. Not so here. Unlike books authored by stuffy-toned, academic types, I've written this book in friendly, approachable language — because data science is a friendly and approachable subject!

To be honest, up until now, the data science realm has been dominated by a few select data science wizards who tend to present the topic in a manner that's unnecessarily over-technical and intimidating. Basic data science isn't that hard or confusing. *Data science* is simply the practice of using a set of analytical techniques and methodologies to derive and communicate valuable and actionable insights from raw data. The purpose of data science is to optimize processes and to support improved data-informed decision making, thereby generating an increase in value — whether *value* is represented by number of lives saved, number of dollars retained, or percentage of revenues increased. In *Data Science For Dummies,* I introduce a broad array of concepts and approaches that you can use when extracting valuable insights from your data.

Remember, a lot of times data scientists get so caught up analyzing the bark of the trees that they simply forget to look for their way out of the forest. This is a common pitfall that you should avoid at all costs. I've worked hard to make sure that this book presents the core purpose of each data science technique and the goals you can accomplish by utilizing them.

About This Book

In keeping with the *For Dummies* brand, this book is organized in a modular, easy-to-access format. This format allows you to use the book as a practical guidebook and ad hoc reference. In other words, you don't need to read through, cover to cover. Just take what you want and leave the rest. I've taken great care to use real-world examples that illustrate data science concepts that may otherwise be overly abstract.

Web addresses and programming code appear in monofont. If you're reading a digital version of this book on a device connected to the Internet, you can click a web address to visit that website, like this: `www.dummies.com`.

Foolish Assumptions

In writing this book, I've assumed that readers are at least technical enough to have mastered advanced Microsoft Excel — pivot tables, grouping, sorting, plotting, and the like. Being strong in algebra, basic statistics, or even business calculus helps, as well. Foolish or not, it's my high hope that all readers have a subject-matter expertise to which they can apply the skills presented in this book. Since data scientists must be capable of intuitively understanding the implications and applications of the data insights they derive, subject-matter expertise is a major component of data science.

Icons Used in This Book

As you make your way through this book, you'll see the following icons in the margins:

The Tip icon marks tips (duh!) and shortcuts that you can use to make subject mastery easier.

Remember icons mark the information that's especially important to know. To siphon off the most important information in each chapter, just skim through these icons.

The Technical Stuff icon marks information of a highly technical nature that you can normally skip over.

The Warning icon tells you to watch out! It marks important information that may save you headaches.

Beyond the Book

This book includes the following external resources:

- ✔ **Data Science Cheat Sheet:** This book comes with a handy Cheat Sheet at www.dummies.com/cheatsheet/datascience. The Cheat Sheet lists helpful shortcuts, as well as abbreviated definitions for essential processes and concepts described in the book. You can use it as a quick-and-easy reference when doing data science.

- ✔ **Online articles on the practical application of data science:** This book has Parts pages that link to www.dummies.com, where you can find a number of articles that extend the topics covered. More specifically, these articles present best practices, how-to's, and case studies that exemplify the power of data science in practice. The articles are available on the book's Extras page (www.dummies.com/extras/datascience).

- ✔ **Updates:** I'll be updating this book on a regular basis. You can find updates on the Downloads tab of the book's product page. On the book's Extras page (www.dummies.com/extras/datascience), an article will either describe the update or provide a link to take readers to the Downloads tab for access to updated content. Any errata will appear in this section, as well.

Where to Go from Here

Just to reemphasize the point, this book's modular design allows you to pick up and start reading anywhere you want. Although you don't need to read cover to cover, a few good starter chapters include Chapters 1, 2, and 9.

Part I
Getting Started With Data Science

getting started
with

Data
Science

In this part . . .

✔ Get introduced to the field of data science.

✔ Define big data.

✔ Explore solutions for big data problems.

✔ See how a real-world businesses put data science to good use.

Chapter 1

Wrapping Your Head around Data Science

In This Chapter

▶ Defining data science

▶ Defining data science by its key components

▶ Identifying viable data science solutions to your own data challenges

*F*or quite some time now, we've all been absolutely deluged by data. It's coming off of every computer, every mobile device, every camera, and every sensor — and now it's even coming off of watches and other wearable technologies. It's generated in every social media interaction we make, every file we save, every picture we take, every query we submit; it's even generated when we do something as simple as get directions to the closest ice cream shop from Google.

Although data immersion is nothing new, you may have noticed that the phenomenon is accelerating. Lakes, puddles, and rivers of data have turned to floods and veritable tsunamis of structured, semi-structured, and unstructured data that's streaming from almost every activity that takes place in both the digital and physical worlds. Welcome to the world of *big data*!

If you're anything like me, then you may have wondered, "What's the point of all this data? Why use valuable resources to generate and collect it?" Although even one decade ago, no one was in a position to make much use of most of the data generated, the tides today have definitely turned. Specialists known as *data engineers* are constantly finding innovative and powerful new ways to capture, collate, and condense unimaginably massive volumes of data, and other specialists known as *data scientists* are leading change by deriving valuable and actionable insights from that data.

In its truest form, data science represents process and resource optimization. Data science produces *data insights* — insights you can use to understand and improve your business, your investments, your health, and even your lifestyle and social life. Using data science is like being able to see in the dark. For any goal or pursuit you can imagine, you can find data science methods to help you know and predict the most direct route from where you are to where you want to be — and anticipate every pothole in the road in between.

Seeing Who Can Make Use of Data Science

The terms data science and data engineering are often misused and confused, so let me start off right here by clarifying that these two fields are, in fact, separate and distinct domains of expertise. *Data science* is the practice of using computational methods to derive valuable and actionable insights from raw datasets. *Data engineering,* on the other hand, is an engineering domain that's dedicated to overcoming data-processing bottlenecks and data-handling problems for applications that utilize large volumes, varieties, and velocities of data. In both data science and data engineering, it's common to work with the following three data varieties:

- **Structured data:** Data that's stored, processed, and manipulated in a traditional relational database management system.

- **Unstructured data:** Data that's commonly generated from human activities and that doesn't fit into a structured database format.

- **Semi-structured data:** Data that doesn't fit into a structured database system, but is nonetheless structured by tags that are useful for creating a form of order and hierarchy in the data.

A lot of people think only large organizations that have massive funding are implementing data science methodologies to optimize and improve their business, but that's not the case. The proliferation of data has created a demand for insights, and this demand is embedded in many aspects of our modern culture. Data and the need for data insights are ubiquitous. Because organizations of all sizes are beginning to recognize that they're immersed in a sink-or-swim, data-driven, competitive environment, data know-how emerges as a core and requisite function in almost every line of business.

So, what does this mean for the everyday person? First off, it means that our culture has changed, and you have to keep up. It doesn't, however, mean that you must go back to school and complete a degree in statistics, computer science, or data science. In this respect, the data revolution isn't so different from any other change that's hit industry in the past. The fact is, in order to stay relevant, you only need to take the time and effort to acquire the skills that keep you current. When it comes to learning how to do data science, you can take some courses, educate yourself through online resources, read books like this one, and attend events where you can learn what you need to know to stay on top of the game.

Who can use data science? You can. Your organization can. Your employer can. Anyone who has a bit of understanding and training can begin using data insights to improve their lives, their careers, and the well-being of their businesses. Data science represents a change in the way you approach the world. People used to act and hope for an outcome, but data insights provide the vision people need to drive change and to make good things happen. You can use data insights to bring about the following types of changes:

- ✔ Optimize business systems and returns on investment (those crucial ROIs) for any measurable activity.

- ✔ Improve the effectiveness of sales and marketing initiatives — whether that be part of an organizational marketing campaign or simply a personal effort to secure better employment opportunities for yourself.

- ✔ Keep ahead of the pack on the very latest developments in every arena.

- ✔ Keep communities safer.

- ✔ Help make the world a better place for those less fortunate.

Looking at the Pieces of the Data Science Puzzle

To practice data science, in the true meaning of the term, you need the analytical know-how of math and statistics, the coding skills necessary to work with data, and an area of subject-matter expertise. Without subject-matter expertise, you might as well call yourself a mathematician or a statistician. Similarly, a software programmer without subject-matter expertise and analytical know-how might better be considered a software engineer or developer, but not a data scientist.

Because the demand for data insights is increasing exponentially, every area is forced to adopt data science. As such, different flavors of data science have emerged. The following are just a few titles under which experts of every discipline are using data science — Ad Tech Data Scientist, Director of Banking Digital Analyst, Clinical Data Scientist, Geo-Engineer Data Scientist, Geospatial Analytics Data Scientist, Retail Personalization Data Scientist, and Clinical Informatics Analyst in Pharmacometrics. Given the fact that it often seems you can't keep track of who's a data scientist without a scorecard, in the following sections I take the time to spell out the key components that would be part of any data science role.

Collecting, querying, and consuming data

Data engineers have the job of capturing and collating large volumes of structured, unstructured, and semi-structured *big data* — data that exceeds the processing capacity of conventional database systems because it's too big, it moves too fast, or it doesn't fit the structural requirements of traditional database architectures. Again, data engineering tasks are separate from the work that's performed in data science, which focuses more on analysis, prediction, and visualization. Despite this distinction, when a data scientist collects, queries, and consumes data during the analysis process, he or she performs work that's very similar to that of a data engineer.

Although valuable insights can be generated from a single data source, oftentimes the combination of several relevant sources delivers the contextual information required to drive better data-informed decisions. A data scientist can work off of several datasets that are stored in one database, or even in several different data warehouses. (For more on working with combined datasets, see Chapter 3.) Other times, source data is stored and processed on a cloud-based platform that's been built by software and data engineers.

No matter how the data is combined or where it's stored, if you're doing data science, you almost always have to *query* the data — write commands to extract relevant datasets from the data storage system, in other words. Most of the time, you use Structured Query Language (SQL) to query data. (Chapter 16 is all about SQL, so if the acronym scares you, jump ahead to that chapter right now.) Whether you're using an application or doing custom analyses by using a programming language such as R or Python, you can choose from a number of universally-accepted file formats. Those formats include

- ✔ **Comma-separated values (CSV) files:** Almost every brand of desktop and web-based analysis application accepts this file type, as do commonly-used scripting languages such as Python and R.

- ✔ **Scripts:** Most data scientists know how to use Python and R programming languages to analyze and visualize data. These script files end with the extensions `.py` and `.r`, respectively.

- ✔ **Application files:** Excel is useful for quick-and-easy, spot-check analyses on small- to medium-sized datasets. These application files have a `.xls or .xlsx` extension. Geospatial analysis applications such as ArcGIS and QGIS save with their own proprietary file formats (the `.mxd` extension for ArcGIS and the `.qgs` extension for QGIS).

> ✔ **Web programming files:** If you're building custom web-based data visualizations, then you may be working in D3.js — or, Data Driven Documents, a JavaScript library for data visualization. When working in D3.js, your work will be saved in `.html` files.

Making use of math and statistics

Data science relies heavily on a practitioner's math and statistics skills precisely because these are the skills needed in order to understand your data and its significance. The skills are also valuable in data science because you can use them to carry out predictive forecasting, decision modeling, and hypotheses testing.

Before launching into more detailed discussions on mathematical and statistical methods, it's important to stop right here and clearly explain the difference between the fields of math and statistics. Mathematics uses deterministic numerical methods and deductive reasoning to form a quantitative description of the world, while statistics is a form of science that's derived from mathematics, but that focuses on using a *stochastic* approach — an approach based on probabilities — and inductive reasoning to form a quantitative description of the world.

Applying mathematical modeling to data science tasks

Data scientists use mathematical methods to build decision models, to generate approximations, and to make predictions about the future. Chapter 7 presents some complex applied mathematical approaches that are useful when working in data science.

This book assumes that you've got a fairly solid skillset in basic math — it would be advantageous if you've taken college-level calculus or even linear algebra. I took great efforts, however, to meet readers where they are. I realize that you may be working based on a limited mathematical knowledge (advanced algebra or maybe business calculus), so I've tried to convey advanced mathematical concepts using a plain-language approach that's easy for everyone to understand.

Using statistical methods to derive insights

In data science, statistical methods are useful for getting a better understanding of your data's significance, for validating hypotheses, for simulating scenarios, and for making predictive forecasts of future events. Advanced statistical skills are somewhat rare, even among quantitative analysts, engineers, and scientists. If you want to go places in data science though, take some time to get up to speed in a few basic statistical methods, like linear regression, ordinary least squares regression, Monte Carlo simulations, and time series analysis. Each of these techniques is defined and described in Chapter 4's discussion on probability and statistics.

The good news is that you don't have to know everything — it's not like you need to go out and get a master's degree in statistics to do data science. You need to know just a few fundamental concepts and approaches from statistics to solve problems. (I cover several of these concepts and approaches in Chapter 4.)

Coding, coding, coding . . . it's just part of the game

Coding is unavoidable when you're working in data science. You need to be able to write code so that you can instruct the computer how you want it to manipulate, analyze, and visualize your data. Programming languages such as Python and R are important for writing scripts for data manipulation, analysis, and visualization, and SQL is useful for data querying. The JavaScript library D3.js is a hot new option for making really cool custom interactive web-based data visualizations.

Although coding is a requirement for data science, it really doesn't have to be this big scary thing people make it out to be. Your coding can be as fancy and complex as you want it to be, but you can also take a rather simple approach. Although these skills are paramount to success, you can pretty easily learn enough coding to practice high-level data science. I've dedicated Chapters 10, 14, 15, and 16 to helping you get up to speed in using D3.js for web-based data visualization, coding in Python and in R, and querying in SQL.

Applying data science to your subject area

There has been some measure of obstinacy from statisticians when it comes to accepting the significance of data science. Many statisticians have cried out, "Data science is nothing new! It's just another name for what we've been doing all along." Although I can sympathize with their perspective, I'm forced to stand with the camp of data scientists that markedly declare that data science is separate and definitely distinct from the statistical approaches that comprise it.

My position on the unique nature of data science is to some extent based on the fact that data scientists often use computer languages not used in traditional statistics and utilize approaches derived from the field of mathematics. But the main point of distinction between statistics and data science is the need for subject-matter expertise.

Due to the fact that statisticians usually have only a limited amount of expertise in fields outside of statistics, they're almost always forced to consult with a subject-matter expert to verify exactly what their findings mean and to decide the best direction in which to proceed. Data scientists, on the other hand, are required to have a strong subject-matter expertise in the area in which they're working. Data scientists generate deep insights and then use their domain-specific expertise to understand exactly what those insights mean with respect to the area in which they're working. The list below shows a few ways in which subject matter experts are using data science to enhance performance in their respective industries:

- ✔ Engineers use machine learning to optimize energy efficiency in modern building design.

- ✔ Clinical data scientists work on the personalization of treatment plans and use healthcare informatics to predict and preempt future health problems in at-risk patients.

- ✔ Marketing data scientists use logistic regression to predict and preempt *customer churn* (the loss or churn of customers from your product or service, to that of a competitor's, in other words) — more on decreasing customer churn is covered in Chapter 3 and Chapter 20.

- ✔ Data journalists scrape websites for fresh data in order to discover and report the latest breaking news stories (I talk more about data journalism in Chapter 18).

- ✔ Data scientists in crime analysis use spatial predictive modeling to predict, preempt, and prevent criminal activities (see Chapter 21 for all the details on using data science to describe and predict criminal activity).

- ✔ Data do-gooders use machine learning to classify and report vital information about disaster-affected communities for real-time decision support in humanitarian response, which you can read about in Chapter 19.

Communicating data insights

Another skill set is paramount to a data scientist's success (and may not be immediately obvious): As a data scientist, you must have sharp oral and written communication skills. If a data scientist can't communicate, all the knowledge and insight in the world will do nothing for your organization.

Data scientists need to be able to explain data insights in a way that staff members can understand. Not only that, they need to be able to produce clear and meaningful data visualizations and written narratives. Most of the time, people need to see something for themselves in order to understand. Data scientists must be creative and pragmatic in their means and methods of communication. (I cover the topics of data visualization and data-driven storytelling in much greater detail in Chapter 9 and Chapter 18.)

Getting a Basic Lay of the Data Science Landscape

Organizations and their leaders are still grappling with how to best use big data and data science. Most of them know that advanced analytics is positioned to bring a tremendous competitive edge to their organization, but very few have any idea about the options that are available or the exact benefits that data science can deliver. In the following sections, I introduce the major data science solution alternatives and the benefits that a data science implementation can deliver.

Exploring data science solution alternatives

When looking to implement data science across an organization, or even just across a department, three main approaches are available: You can build an in-house data science team, outsource the work to external data scientists, or use a cloud-based solution that can deliver the power of data analytics to professionals who have only a modest level of data literacy.

Building your own in-house team

Here are three options for building an in-house data science team:

- ✔ **Train existing employees.** This is a lower-cost alternative. If you want to equip your organization with the power of data science and analytics, then data science training can transform existing staff into data-skilled, highly specialized subject-matter experts for your in-house team.

- ✔ **Train existing employees and hire some experts.** Another good option is to train existing employees to do high-level data science tasks, and also bring on a few new hires to fulfill your more advanced data science problem-solving and strategy requirements.

✔ **Hire experts.** Some organizations try to fill their requirements by hiring advanced data scientists or fresh graduates with degrees in data science. The problem with this approach is that there aren't enough of these people to go around, and if you do find someone who's willing to come onboard, he or she is going to have very high salary requirements. Remember, in addition to the math, statistics, and coding requirements, data scientists must also have a high level of subject matter expertise in the specific field where they're working. That's why it's extraordinarily difficult to find these individuals. Until universities make data-literacy an integral part of every educational program, finding highly specialized and skilled data scientists to satisfy organizational requirements will be nearly impossible.

Outsourcing requirements to private data science consultants

Many organizations prefer to outsource their data science and analytics requirements to an outside expert. There are two general routes: Outsource for the development of a comprehensive data science strategy that serves your entire organization, or outsource for piecemeal, individual data science solutions to specific problems that arise, or have arisen, within your organization.

Outsourcing for comprehensive data science strategy development

If you want to build an advanced data science implementation for your organization, you can hire a private consultant to help you with a comprehensive strategy development. This type of service is likely going to cost you, but you can receive tremendously valuable insights in return. A strategist will know about the options available to meet your requirements, as well as the benefits and drawbacks of each. With strategy in-hand and an on-call expert available to help you, you can much more easily navigate the task of building an internal team.

Outsourcing for data science solutions to specific problems

If you're not prepared for the rather involved process of comprehensive strategy design and implementation, you have the option to contract smaller portions of work out to a private data science consultant. This spot-treatment approach could still deliver the benefits of data science without requiring you to reorganize the structure and financials of your entire organization.

Leveraging cloud-based platform solutions

Some have seen the explosion of big data and data science coming from a long way off. Although it's still new to most, professionals and organizations in the know have been working fast and furious to prepare. A few organizations have expended great effort and expense to develop data science solutions that are accessible to all. Cloud applications such as IBM's Watson Analytics (www.ibm.com/analytics/watson-analytics) offers users code-free, automated data services — from cleanup and statistical modeling to analysis and data visualization. Although you still need to understand the statistical, mathematical, and substantive relevance of the data insights, applications such as Watson Analytics can deliver some powerful results without requiring users to know how to write code or scripts.

If you decide to use cloud-based platform solutions to help your organization reach its data science objectives, remember that you'll still need in-house staff who are trained and skilled to design, run, and interpret the quantitative results from these platforms. The platform will not do away with the need for in-house training and data science expertise — it will merely augment your organization so that it can more readily achieve its objectives.

Identifying the obvious wins

Through this book, I hope to show you the power of data science and how you can use that power to more quickly reach your personal and professional goals. No matter the sector in which you work, acquiring data science skills can transform you into a more marketable professional. The following is just a small list of benefits that data science and analytics deliver across key industry sectors:

- **Benefits for corporations, small and medium-sized enterprises (SMEs), and e-commerce businesses:** Production-costs optimization, sales maximization, marketing ROI increases, staff-productivity optimization, customer-churn reduction, customer lifetime-value increases, inventory requirements and sales predictions, pricing-model optimization, fraud detection, and logistics improvements

- **Benefits for governments:** Business-process and staff-productivity optimization, management decision-support enhancements, finance and budget forecasting, expenditure tracking and optimization, and fraud detection

- **Benefits for academia:** Resource-allocation improvements, student performance management improvements, drop-out reductions, business-process optimization, finance and budget forecasting, and recruitment ROI increases

Chapter 2

Exploring Data Engineering Pipelines and Infrastructure

There's a lot of hype around big data these days, but most people don't really know or understand what it is or how they can use it to improve their lives and livelihoods. This chapter defines the term *big data*, explains where big data comes from and how it's used, and outlines the roles that data engineers and data scientists play in the big data ecosystem. In this chapter, I introduce the fundamental big data concepts that you need in order to start generating your own ideas and plans on how to leverage big data and data science to improve your life and business workflow.

Defining Big Data by Its Four Vs

Big data is data that exceeds the processing capacity of conventional database systems because it's too big, it moves too fast, or it doesn't fit the structural requirements of traditional database architectures. Whether data volumes rank in the terabyte or petabyte scales, data engineering solutions must be designed to meet requirements for the data's intended destination and use.

When you're talking about regular data, you're likely to hear the words *kilobyte* or *gigabyte* used — 10^3 and 10^9 bytes, respectively. In contrast, when you're talking about big data, words like *terabyte* and *petabyte* are thrown around — 10^{12} and 10^{15} bytes, respectively. A *byte* is an 8-bit unit of data.

Four characteristics (*the four Vs*) define big data: volume, velocity, variety, and value. Since the four Vs of big data are continually growing, newer, more innovative data technologies must continuously be developed to manage big data problems.

Whenever you're in doubt, use the 4V criteria to determine whether you have a big-data or regular-data problem on your hands.

Grappling with data volume

The lower limits of big data volumes range between a few terabytes, up to tens of petabytes, on an annual basis. The volume numbers by which a big data set is defined have no upper limit. In fact, the volumes of most big data sets are increasing exponentially on a yearly basis.

Handling data velocity

Automated machinery and sensors are generating high-velocity data on a continual basis. In engineering terms, *data velocity* is data volume per unit time. Big data velocities range anywhere between 30 kilobytes (K) per second up to even 30 gigabytes (GB) per second. High-velocity, real-time data streams present an obstacle to timely decision making. The capabilities of data-handling and data-processing technologies often limit data velocities.

Dealing with data variety

Big data makes everything more complicated by adding unstructured and semi-structured data in with the structured datasets. This is called *high-variety data*. High-variety data sources can be derived from data streams that are generated from social networks or from automated machinery.

Structured data is data that can be stored, processed, and manipulated in a traditional relational database management system. This data can be generated by humans or machines, and is derived from all sorts of sources, from click-streams and web-based forms to point of sale transactions and sensors. *Unstructured data* comes completely unstructured — it's commonly generated from human activities and doesn't fit into a structured database format. Such data could be derived from blog posts, emails, and Word documents. *Semi-structured data* is data that doesn't fit into a structured database system, but is nonetheless structured by tags that are useful for creating a form of order and hierarchy in the data. Semi-structured data is commonly found in database and file systems. It can be stored as log files, XML files, or JSON data files.

Creating data value

In its raw form, most big data is *low value* — in other words, the value-to-data quantity ratio is low in raw big data. Big data is comprised of huge numbers of very small transactions that come in a variety of formats. These incremental components of big data produce true value only after they're rolled up and analyzed. Data engineers have the job of rolling it up and data scientists have the job of analyzing it.

Identifying Big Data Sources

Big data is being generated by humans, machines, and sensors everywhere, on a continual basis. Some typical sources include data from social media, financial transactions, health records, click-streams, log files, and the *internet of things* — a web of digital connections that joins together the ever-expanding array of electronic devices we use in our everyday lives. Figure 2-1 shows a variety of popular big data sources.

Figure 2-1:
A diagram of popular big data sources.

Grasping the Difference between Data Science and Data Engineering

Data science and data engineering are two different branches within the *big data paradigm* — an approach wherein huge velocities, varieties, and volumes of structured, unstructured, and semi-structured data are being captured, processed, stored, and analyzed using a set of techniques and technologies that is completely novel compared to those that were used in decades past.

Both are useful for deriving knowledge and actionable insights out of raw data. Both are essential elements for any comprehensive decision-support system, and both are extremely helpful when formulating robust strategies for future business management and growth. Although the terms *data science* and *data engineering* are often used interchangeably, they're definitely distinct domains of expertise. In the following sections, I introduce concepts that are fundamental to data science and data engineering, and then I show you the differences between how these two roles function in an organization's data processing system.

Defining data science

If *science* is a systematic method by which people study and explain domain-specific phenomenon that occur in the natural world, then you can think of *data science* as the scientific domain that's dedicated to knowledge discovery via data analysis.

 With respect to data science, the term *domain-specific* refers to the industry sector or subject matter domain that data science methods are being used to explore.

Data scientists use mathematical techniques and algorithmic approaches to derive solutions to complex business and scientific problems. Data science practitioners use its methods to derive insights that are otherwise unattainable. Both in business and in science, data science methods can provide more robust decision making capabilities. In business, the purpose of data science is to empower businesses and organizations with the data information that they need to optimize organizational processes for maximum efficiency and revenue generation. In science, data science methods are used to derive results and develop protocols for achieving the specific scientific goal at hand.

Data science is a vast and multi-disciplinary field. To truly call yourself a data scientist, you need to have expertise in math and statistics, computer programming, and your own domain-specific subject matter.

Using data science skills, you can do things like

- Use machine learning to optimize energy usages and lower corporate carbon footprints.
- Optimize tactical strategies to achieve goals in business and in science.
- Predict for unknown contaminant levels from sparse environmental datasets.
- Design automated theft and fraud prevention systems to detect anomalies and trigger alarms based on algorithmic results.
- Craft site-recommendation engines for use in land acquisitions and real estate development.
- Implement and interpret predictive analytics and forecasting techniques for net increases in business value.

Data scientists must have extensive and diverse quantitative expertise to be able to solve these types of problems.

Machine learning is the practice of applying algorithms to learn from and make automated predictions about data.

Defining data engineering

If *engineering* is the practice of using science and technology to design and build systems that solve problems, then you can think of *data engineering* as the engineering domain that's dedicated to overcoming data-processing bottlenecks and data-handling problems for applications that utilize big data.

Data engineers use skills in computer science and software engineering to design systems for, and solve problems with, handling and manipulating big data sets. Data engineers have experience working with and designing real-time processing frameworks and Massively Parallel Processing (MPP) platforms, as well as relational database management systems. They generally code in Java, C++, and Python. They know how to deploy Hadoop or MapReduce to handle, process, and refine big data into more manageably sized datasets. Simply put, with respect to data science, the purpose of data engineering is to engineer big data solutions by building coherent, modular, and scalable data processing platforms from which data scientists can subsequently derive insights.

Most engineered systems are *built systems* — systems that are constructed or manufactured in the physical world. Data engineering is different, though. It involves designing, building, and implementing software solutions to problems in the data world — a world that can seem pretty abstract when compared to the physical reality of the Golden Gate Bridge or the Aswan Dam.

Using data engineering skills, you can do things like

- ✔ Build large-scale Software as a Service (SaaS) applications.
- ✔ Build and customize Hadoop and MapReduce applications.
- ✔ Design and build relational databases and highly scaled distributed architectures for processing big data.
- ✔ Extract, transform, and load (ETL) data from one database into another.

Data engineers need solid skills in computer science, database design, and software engineering to be able to perform this type of work.

Software as a Service (SaaS) is a term that describes cloud-hosted software services that are made available to users via the Internet.

Comparing data scientists and data engineers

The roles of data scientist and data engineer are frequently completely confused and intertwined by hiring managers. If you look around at most position descriptions for companies that are hiring, they often mismatch the titles and roles, or simply expect applicants to do both data science and data engineering.

If you're hiring someone to help you make sense of your data, be sure to define your requirements very clearly before writing the position description. Since a data scientist must also have subject matter expertise in the particular area in which they work, this requirement generally precludes a data scientist from also having expertise in data engineering (although some data scientists do have experience using engineering data platforms). And if you hire a data engineer who has data-science skills, he or she generally won't have much subject-matter expertise outside of the data domain. Be prepared to call in a subject-matter expert to help him or her.

Because so many organizations combine and confuse roles in their data projects, data scientists are sometime stuck spending a lot of time learning to do the job of a data engineer, and vice versa. To get the highest-quality work product in the least amount of time, hire a data engineer to process your data and a data scientist to make sense of it for you.

Lastly, keep in mind that data engineers and data scientists are just two small roles within a larger organizational structure. Managers, middle-level employees, and organizational leaders also play a huge part in the success of any data-driven initiative. The primary benefit of incorporating data science and data engineering into your projects is to leverage your external and internal data to strengthen your organization's decision-support capabilities.

Boiling Down Data with MapReduce and Hadoop

Because big data's four Vs (volume, velocity, variety, and value) don't allow for the handling of big data using traditional relational database management systems, data engineers had to get innovative. To get around the limitations of relational database management systems, data engineers use the Hadoop data-processing platform (with its MapReduce programming paradigm) to boil big data down to smaller datasets that are more manageable for data scientists to analyze. As a distributed, parallel processing framework, MapReduce results in data processing speeds that are lightning-fast compared to those available through traditional methods.

In the following sections, I introduce you to the MapReduce paradigm, Hadoop data-processing platforms, and the components that comprise Hadoop. I also introduce the programming languages that you can use to develop applications in these frameworks.

Digging into MapReduce

MapReduce is a programming paradigm that was designed to allow parallel distributed processing of large sets of data, converting them to sets of tuples, and then combining and reducing those tuples into smaller sets of tuples. In layman's terms, MapReduce was designed to take big data and use parallel distributed computing to turn big data into little- or regular- sized data.

Parallel distributed processing refers to a powerful framework where mass volumes of data are processed very quickly by distributing processing tasks across clusters of commodity servers. With respect to MapReduce, *tuples* refer to key-value pairs by which data is grouped, sorted, and processed.

MapReduce jobs work via map and reduce process operation sequences across a distributed set of servers. In the *map task*, you delegate your data to key-value pairs, transform it, and filter it. Then you assign the data to nodes for processing. In the *reduce task*, you aggregate that data down to smaller sized datasets. Data from the reduce step is transformed into a standard *key-value format* — where the *key* acts as the record identifier and the *value* is the value that's being identified by the key. The clusters' computing nodes process the map and reduce tasks that are defined by the user. This work is done in accordance with the following two steps:

1. **Map the data.** The incoming data must first be delegated into key-value pairs and divided into fragments, which are then assigned to map tasks. Each *computing cluster* — a group of nodes that are connected to each other and perform a shared computing task — is assigned a number of map tasks, which are subsequently distributed among its nodes. Upon processing of the key-value pairs, intermediate key-value pairs are generated. The intermediate key-value pairs are sorted by their key values, and this list is divided into a new set of fragments. Whatever count you have for these new fragments, it will be the same as the count of the reduce tasks.

2. **Reduce the data.** Every reduce task has a fragment assigned to it. The reduce task simply processes the fragment and produces an output, which is also a key-value pair. Reduce tasks are also distributed among the different nodes of the cluster. After the task is completed, the final output is written onto a file system.

In short, you can quickly and efficiently boil down and begin to make sense of a huge volume, velocity, and variety of data by using map and reduce tasks to tag your data by (key, value) pairs, and then reduce those pairs into smaller sets of data through *aggregation operations* — operations that combine multiple values from a dataset into a single value. A diagram of the MapReduce architecture can be found in Figure 2-2.

If your data doesn't lend itself to being tagged and processed via keys, values, and aggregation, then map and reduce *generally* isn't a good fit for your needs.

If you're using MapReduce as part of a Hadoop solution, then the final output is written onto the *Hadoop Distributed File System* (HDFS). HDFS is a file system that includes clusters of commodity servers that are used to store big data. HDFS makes big data handling and storage financially feasible by distributing storage tasks across clusters of cheap commodity servers.

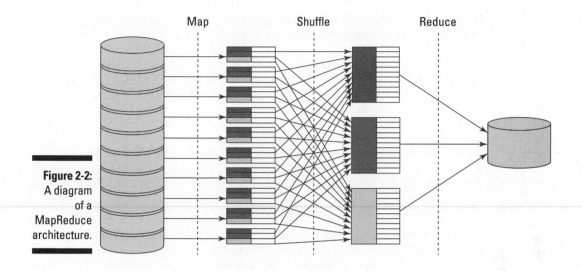

Figure 2-2:
A diagram
of a
MapReduce
architecture.

Understanding Hadoop

Hadoop is an open-source data processing tool that was developed by the Apache Software Foundation. Hadoop is currently the go-to program for handling huge volumes and varieties of data because it was designed to make large-scale computing more affordable and flexible. With the arrival of Hadoop, mass data processing has been introduced to significantly more people and more organizations.

Hadoop can offer you a great solution to handle, process, and group mass streams of structured, semi-structured, and unstructured data. By setting up and deploying Hadoop, you get a relatively affordable way to begin using and drawing insights from all of your organization's data, rather than just continuing to rely solely on that transactional dataset you have sitting over in an old data warehouse somewhere.

Hadoop is one of the most popular programs available for large-scale computing requirements. Hadoop provides a map-and-reduce layer that's capable of handling the data processing requirements of most big data projects.

Sometimes the data gets too big and fast for even Hadoop to handle. In these cases, organizations are turning to alternative, more-customized MapReduce deployments instead.

Hadoop uses clusters of commodity hardware for storing data. Hardware in each cluster is connected, and this hardware is comprised of *commodity servers* — low-cost, low-performing generic servers that offer powerful computing capabilities when run in parallel across a shared cluster. These commodity servers are also called *nodes*. Commoditized computing dramatically decreases the costs involved in handling and storing big data.

Hadoop is comprised of the following two components:

> ✔ **A distributed processing framework:** Hadoop uses Hadoop MapReduce as its distributed processing framework. Again, a *distributed processing framework* is a powerful framework where processing tasks are distributed across clusters of nodes so that large data volumes can be processed very quickly across the system as a whole.

> ✔ **A distributed file system:** Hadoop uses the Hadoop Distributed File System (HDFS) as its distributed file system.

The workloads of applications that run on Hadoop are divided among the nodes of the Hadoop cluster, and then the output is stored on the HDFS. The Hadoop cluster can be comprised of thousands of nodes. To keep the costs of input/output (I/O) processes low, Hadoop MapReduce jobs are performed as close to the data as possible. This means that the reduce tasks processors are positioned as closely as possible to the outgoing map task data that needs to be processed. This design facilitates sharing of computational requirements in big data processing.

Hadoop also supports hierarchical organization. Some of its nodes are classified as master nodes, and others are categorized as slaves. The master service, known as *JobTracker,* is designed to control several slave services. Slave services (also called *TaskTrackers*) are distributed one to each node. The JobTracker controls the TaskTrackers and assigns Hadoop MapReduce tasks to them. In a newer version of Hadoop, known as Hadoop 2, a resource manager called Hadoop YARN was added. With respect to MapReduce in Hadoop, YARN acts as an integrated system that performs resource management and scheduling functions.

Hadoop processes data in batch. Consequently, if you're working with real-time, streaming data, you won't be able to use Hadoop to handle your big data issues. This said, it's very useful for solving many other types of big data problems.

Seeing where Java, C++, and Python fit into your big data plans

You can program Hadoop using Java or Python. Hadoop supports programs that are written using a small Application Program Interface (API) in either of these languages. To run scripts and binaries in clusters' nodes in Hadoop, you have to use the Hadoop-specific string I/O convention. Also, Hadoop allows you to use abstracted forms of map and reduce. You can program these functions in Python and Lisp.

Identifying Alternative Big Data Solutions

Looking past Hadoop, you can see alternative big data solutions on the horizon. These solutions make it possible to work with big data in real-time or to use alternative database technologies to handle and process it. In the following sections, I introduce you first to the real-time processing frameworks, then the Massively Parallel Processing (MPP) platforms, and finally the NoSQL databases that allow you to work with big data outside of the Hadoop environment.

You should be aware of something referred to as ACID compliance, short for *A*tomicity, *C*onsistency, *I*solation, and *D*urability compliance. ACID compliance is a standard by which accurate and reliable database transactions are guaranteed. In big data solutions, most database systems are not ACID compliant, but this does not necessarily pose a major problem. That's because most big data systems use Decision Support Systems (DSS) that batch process data before that data is read out. *DSS* are information systems that are used for organizational decision-support. Non-transactional DSS demonstrate no real ACID compliance requirements.

Introducing real-time processing frameworks

Remember how Hadoop is a batch processor and can't process real-time, streaming data? Well, sometimes you might need to query big data streams in real-time . . . and you just can't do this sort of thing using Hadoop. In these cases, use a real-time processing framework instead. A *real-time processing framework* is — as its name implies — a framework that is able to process data in real-time (or near real-time) as that data streams and flows into the system. Essentially, real-time processing frameworks are the antithesis of the batch processing frameworks you see deployed in Hadoop.

Real-time processing frameworks can be classified into the following two categories:

- **Frameworks that lower the overhead of MapReduce tasks to increase the overall time efficiency of the system:** Solutions in this category include Apache Storm and Apache Spark for near–real-time stream processing.
- **Frameworks that deploy innovative querying methods to facilitate real-time querying of big data:** Some solutions in this category include Google's Dremel, Apache Drill, Shark for Apache Hive, and Cloudera's Impala.

Real-time, stream processing frameworks are quite useful in a multitude of industries — from stock and financial market analyses to e-commerce optimizations, and from real-time fraud detection to optimized order logistics. Regardless of the industry in which you work, if your business is impacted by real-time data streams that are generated by humans, machines, or sensors, then a real-time processing framework would be helpful to you in optimizing and generating value for your organization.

Introducing Massively Parallel Processing (MPP) platforms

Massively Parallel Processing (MPP) platforms can be used instead of MapReduce as an alternative approach for distributed data processing. If your goal is to deploy parallel processing on a traditional data warehouse, then an MPP may be the perfect solution.

To understand how MPP compares to a standard MapReduce parallel processing framework, consider the following. MPP runs parallel computing tasks on costly, custom hardware, whereas MapReduce runs them on cheap commodity servers. Consequently, MPP processing capabilities are cost restrictive. This said, MPP is quicker and easier to use than standard MapReduce jobs. That's because MPP can be queried using Structured Query Language (SQL), but native MapReduce jobs are controlled by the more complicated Java programming language.

Well-known MPP vendors and products include the old-school Teradata platform (www.teradata.com/), plus newer solutions like EMC²'s Greenplum DCA (www.emc.com/campaign/global/greenplumdca/index.htm), HP's Vertica (www.vertica.com/), IBM's Netezza (www-01.ibm.com/software/data/netezza/), and Oracle's Exadata (www.oracle.com/engineered-systems/exadata/index.html).

Introducing NoSQL databases

Traditional *relational database management systems* (RDBMS) aren't equipped to handle big data demands. That's because traditional relational databases are designed to handle only relational datasets that are constructed of data that's stored in clean rows and columns and thus are capable of being queried via Structured Query Language (SQL). RDBM systems are not capable of handling unstructured and semi-structured data. Moreover, RDBM systems simply don't have the processing and handling capabilities that are needed for meeting big data volume and velocity requirements.

This is where NoSQL comes in. NoSQL databases, like MongoDB, are non-relational, distributed database systems that were designed to rise to the big data challenge. NoSQL databases step out past the traditional relational database architecture and offer a much more scalable, efficient solution. NoSQL systems facilitate non-SQL data querying of non-relational or schema-free, semi-structured and unstructured data. In this way, NoSQL databases are able to handle the structured, semi-structured, and unstructured data sources that are common in big data systems.

NoSQL offers four categories of non-relational databases — graph databases, document databases, key-values stores, and column family stores. Since NoSQL offers native functionality for each of these separate types of data structures, it offers very efficient storage and retrieval functionality for most types of non-relational data. This adaptability and efficiency makes NoSQL an increasingly popular choice for handling big data and for overcoming processing challenges that come along with it.

There is somewhat of a debate about the significance of the name NoSQL. Some argue that NoSQL stands for *Not Only SQL*, while others argue that the acronym represents *Non-SQL databases*. The argument is rather complex and there is no real cut-and-dry answer. To keep things simple, just think of NoSQL as a class of non-relational database management systems that do not fall within the spectrum of RDBM systems that are queried using SQL.

Data Engineering in Action — A Case Study

A Fortune 100 telecommunications company had large datasets that resided in separate *data silos* — data repositories that are disconnected and isolated from other data storage systems used across the organization. With the goal of deriving data insights that lead to revenue increases, the company decided to connect all of its data silos, and then integrate that shared source with other contextual, external, non-enterprise data sources as well.

Identifying the business challenge

The company was stocked to the gills with all the traditional enterprise systems — ERP, ECM, CRM, you name it. Slowly, over many years, these systems grew and segregated into separate information silos — check out Figure 2-3 to see what I mean. Because of the isolated structure of their data systems, otherwise useful data was lost and buried deep within a mess of separate, siloed storage systems. Even if the company knew what data they had, it would be like pulling teeth to access, integrate, and utilize it. The company rightfully believed that this restriction was limiting their business growth.

To optimize their sales and marketing return on investments, the company wanted to integrate external, open datasets and relevant social data sources that would provide deeper insights about its current and potential customers. But to build such a 360 degree view of the target market and customer base, the company needed to develop a pretty sophisticated platform across which the data could be integrated, mined, and analyzed.

The company had the following three goals in mind for the project:

- Manage and extract value from disparate, isolated datasets.
- Take advantage of information from external, non-enterprise, or social data sources to provide new, exciting, and useful services that create value.
- Identify specific trends and issues in competitor activity, product offerings, industrial customer segments, and sales team member profiles.

Figure 2-3:
Different
data silos
being joined
together by
a common
join point.

Solving business problems with data engineering

To meet the company's goals, data engineers moved the company's datasets to Hadoop clusters. One cluster hosted the sales data, another hosted the human resources data, and yet another hosted the talent management data. Data engineers then modeled the data using the *linked data format* — a format that facilitates a joining of the different datasets in the Hadoop clusters.

After this big data platform architecture was put into place, queries that would have traditionally taken several hours to perform could be performed in a matter of minutes. New queries were generated after the platform was built, and these queries also returned efficient results within a few minutes' time.

Boasting about benefits

The following are some of the benefits that the telecommunications company now enjoys as a result of its new big data platform:

- ✔ **Ease of scaling:** Scaling is much easier and cheaper using Hadoop than it was with the old system. Instead of increasing capital and operating expenditures by buying more of the latest generation of expensive computers, servers, and memory capacity, the company opted to grow wider instead. They were able to purchase more hardware and add new commodity servers in a matter of hours, rather than days.

- ✔ **Performance:** With their distributed processing and storage capabilities, the Hadoop clusters deliver insights faster and produce more data insight for less cost.

- ✔ **High availability and reliability:** The company has found that the Hadoop platform is providing them with data protection and high availability while the clusters grow in size. Additionally, the Hadoop clusters have increased system reliability because of their *automatic failover* configuration — a configuration that facilitates an automatic switch to redundant, backup data handling systems in instances where the primary system might fail.

Chapter 3

Applying Data Science to Business and Industry

To the nerds and geeks out there, data science is interesting in its own right, but to most people, it's interesting only because of the benefits it can generate. Most business managers and organizational leaders couldn't care less about coding and complex statistical algorithms. They are, on the other hand, extremely interested in finding new ways to increase business profits by increasing sales rates and decreasing inefficiencies. In this chapter, I introduce the concept of business-centric data science, discuss how it differs from traditional business intelligence, and talk about how you can use data-derived business insights to increase your business' bottom line.

Incorporating Data-Driven Insights into the Business Process

The modern business world is absolutely deluged with data. That's because every line of business, every electronic system, every desktop computer, every laptop, every company-owned cellphone, and every employee is continually creating new business-related data as a natural and organic output of their work. This data is structured or unstructured, some of it is big and some of it is small, fast or slow; maybe it's tabular data, or video data, or spatial data, or data that no one has come up with a name for yet. But while there are many varieties and variations between the types of datasets produced, the challenge is only one — to extract data insights that add value to the organization when acted upon. In the following sections, I walk you through the challenges involved in deriving value from actionable insights that are generated from raw business data.

Benefiting from business-centric data science

Business is complex. Data science is complex. At times, it's easy to get so caught up looking at the trees that you forget to look for a way out of the forest. That's why, in all areas of business, it's extremely important to stay focused on the end goal. Ultimately, no matter what line of business you're in, true north is always the same — business profit growth. Whether you achieve that by creating greater efficiencies or by increasing sales rates and customer loyalty, the end goal is to create a more stable, solid profit-growth rate for your business. The following is a list of some of the ways that you can use business-centric data science and business intelligence to help increase profits:

- **Decrease financial risks.** A business-centric data scientist can decrease financial risk in ecommerce business by using time series anomaly detection methods for real-time fraud detection — to decrease Card-Not-Present fraud and to decrease incidence of account takeovers, to take two examples.

- **Increase the efficiencies of systems and processes.** This is a business systems optimization function that's performed by both the business-centric data scientist and the business analyst. Both use analytics to optimize business processes, structures, and systems, but their methods and data sources differ. The end goal here should be to decrease needless resource expenditures and to increase return on investment for justified expenditures.

- **Increase sales rates.** To increase sales rates for your offerings, you can employ a business-centric data scientist to help you find the best ways to upsell and cross-sell, increase customer loyalty, increase conversions in each layer of the funnel, and exact-target your advertising and discounts. It's likely that your business is already employing many of these tactics, but a business-centric data scientist can look at all data related to the business and, from that, derive insights that supercharge these efforts.

Deploying analytics and data wrangling to convert raw data into actionable insights

Turning your raw data into actionable insights is the first step in the progression from the data you've collected to something that actually benefits you. Business-centric data scientists use *data analytics* to generate insights from raw data.

Identifying the types of analytics

Listed below, in order of increasing complexity, are the four types of data analytics you'll most likely encounter:

- **Descriptive analytics:** This type of analytics answers the question, "What happened?" Descriptive analytics are based on historical and current data. A business analyst or a business-centric data scientist bases modern-day business intelligence on descriptive analytics.

- **Diagnostic analytics:** You use this type of analytics to find answers to the question, "why did this particular something happen?" or "what went wrong?" Diagnostic analytics are useful for deducing and inferring the success or failure of sub-components of any data-driven initiative.

- **Predictive analytics:** Although this type of analytics is based on historical and current data, predictive analytics go one step further than descriptive analytics. *Predictive analytics* involve complex model-building and analysis in order to predict a future event or trend. In a business context, these analyses would be performed by the business-centric data scientist.

- **Prescriptive analytics:** This type of analytics aims to optimize processes, structures, and systems through informed action that's based on predictive analytics — essentially telling you what you should do based on an informed estimation of what will happen. Both business analysts and business-centric data scientists can generate prescriptive analytics, but their methods and data sources differ.

Ideally, a business should engage in all four types of data analytics, but prescriptive analytics is the most direct and effective means by which to generate value from data insights.

Identifying common challenges in analytics

Analytics commonly pose at least two challenges in the business enterprise. First, organizations often have a very hard time finding new hires with specific skill sets that include analytics. Second, even skilled analysts often have difficulty communicating complex insights in a way that's understandable to management decision makers.

To overcome these challenges, the organization must create and nurture a culture that values and accepts analytics products. The business must work to educate all levels of the organization, so that management has a basic concept of analytics and the success that can be achieved by implementing them. Conversely, business-centric data scientists must have a very solid working knowledge about business in general and, in particular, a solid understanding of the business at hand. A strong business knowledge is one of the three main requirements of any business-centric data scientist — the other two being a strong coding acumen and strong quantitative analysis skills via math and statistical modeling.

Wrangling raw data to actionable insights

Data wrangling is another important portion of the work that's required to convert data to insights. To build analytics from raw data, you'll almost always need to use *data wrangling* — the processes and procedures that you use to clean and convert data from one format and structure to another so that the data is accurate and in the format analytics tools and scripts require for consumption. The following list highlights a few of the practices and issues I consider most relevant to data wrangling:

- **Data extraction:** The business-centric data scientist must first identify what datasets are relevant to the problem at hand, and then extract sufficient quantities of the data that's required to solve the problem. (This extraction process is commonly referred to as *data mining.*)

- **Data munging:** *Data munging* involves cleaning the raw data extracted through data mining, then converting it into a format that allows for a more convenient consumption of the data. (*Mung* began life as a destructive process, where you would convert something recognizable into something that was unrecognizable, thus the phrase *Mash Until No Good*, or MUNG.)

- **Data governance:** *Data governance standards* are standards that are used as a quality control measure to ensure that manual and automated data sources conform to the data standards of the model at hand. Data governance standards must be applied so that the data is at the right granularity when it's stored and made ready for use.

  Granularity is a measure of a dataset's level of detail. Data granularity is determined by the relative size of the sub-groupings into which the data is divided.

- **Data architecture:** IT architecture is key. If your data is isolated in separate, fixed repositories — those infamous *data silos* everybody complains about — then it's available to only a few people within a particular line of business. Siloed data structures result in scenarios where a majority of an organization's data is simply unavailable for use by the organization at large. (Needless to say, siloed data structures are incredibly wasteful and inefficient.)

If your goal is to derive the most value and insight from your organization's business data, then you should ensure that the data is stored in a central data warehouse and not in separate silos. (I discuss data warehouses in the "Looking at technologies and skillsets that are useful in business intelligence" section, later in this chapter.)

Taking action on business insights

After wrangling your data down to actionable insights, the second step in the progression from raw data to value-added is to take decisive actions based on those insights. In business, the only justifiable purpose for spending time deriving insights from raw data is that the actions should lead to an increase in business profits. Failure to take action on data-driven insights results in a complete and total loss of the resources that were spent deriving them, at no benefit whatsoever to the organization. An organization absolutely must be ready and equipped to change, evolve, and progress when new business insights become available.

What I like to call the *insight-to-action arc* — the process of taking decisive actions based on data insights — should be formalized in a written action plan and then rigorously exercised to affect continuous and iterative improvements to your organization — *iterative* because these improvements involve a successive round of deployments and testing to optimize all areas of business based on actionable insights that are generated from organizational data. This action plan is not something that should just be tacked loosely on the side of your organization, and then never looked at again.

To best prepare your organization to take action on insights derived from business data, make sure you have the following people and systems in place and ready to go:

- ✔ **Right data, right time, right place:** This part isn't complicated: You just have to have the right data, collected and made available at the right places and the right times, when it's needed the most.

- ✔ **Business-centric data scientists and business analysts:** Have business-centric data scientists and business analysts in place and ready to tackle problems when they arise.

- ✔ **Educated and enthusiastic management:** Educate and encourage your organization's leaders so that you have a management team that understands, values, and makes effective use of business insights gleaned from analytics.

✔ **Informed and enthusiastic organizational culture:** If the culture of your organization reflects a naivety or lack of understanding about the value of data, begin fostering a corporate culture that values data insights and analytics. Consider using training, workshops, and events.

✔ **Written procedures with clearly designated chains of responsibility:** Have documented processes in place and interwoven into your organization so that when the time comes, the organization is prepared to respond. New insights are generated all the time, but growth is achieved only through iterative adjustments and actions based on constantly evolving data insights. The organization needs to have clearly defined procedures ready to accommodate these changes as necessary.

✔ **Advancement in technology:** Your enterprise absolutely must keep up-to-date with rapidly changing technological developments. The analytics space is changing fast — very fast! There are many ways to keep up. If you keep in-house experts, you can assign them the ongoing responsibility of monitoring industry advancements and then suggesting changes that are needed to keep your organization current. An alternative way to keep current is to purchase cloud-based Software-as-a-Service (SaaS) subscriptions and then rely on SaaS platform upgrades to keep you up to speed on the most innovative and cutting-edge technologies.

When relying on SaaS platforms to keep you current, you're taking a leap of faith that the vendor is working hard to keep on top of industry advancements and not just letting things slide. Ensure that the vendor has a long-standing history of maintaining up-to-date and reliable services over time. Although you could try to follow the industry yourself and then check back with the vendor on updates as new technologies emerge, that is putting a lot of onus on you. Unless you're a data technology expert with a lot of free time to research and inquire about advancements in industry standards, it's better to just choose a reliable vendor that has an excellent reputation for delivering up-to-date, cutting-edge technologies to customers.

Distinguishing Business Intelligence and Data Science

Business-centric data scientists and business analysts who do business intelligence are like cousins. They both use data to work towards the same business goal, but their approach, technology, and function differ by measurable degrees. In the following sections, I define, compare, and distinguish between business intelligence and business-centric data science.

Defining business intelligence

The purpose of business intelligence is to convert raw data into business insights that business leaders and managers can use to make data-informed decisions. Business analysts use business intelligence tools to create decision-support products for business management decision making. If you want to build decision-support dashboards, visualizations, or reports from complete medium-sized sets of structured business data, then you can use business intelligence tools and methods to help you.

Business intelligence (BI) is comprised of

- **Mostly internal datasets:** By *internal,* I mean business data and information that's supplied by your organization's own managers and stakeholders.

- **Tools, technologies, and skillsets:** Examples here would include online analytical processing, ETL (*e*xtracting, *t*ransforming, and *l*oading data from one database into another), data warehousing, and information technology for business applications.

Looking at the kinds of data used in business intelligence

Insights that are generated in business intelligence (BI) are derived from standard-sized sets of structured business data. BI solutions are mostly built off of *transactional data* — data that's generated during the course of a transaction event, like data generated during a sale, or during a money transfer between bank accounts, for example. Transactional data is a natural byproduct of business activities that occur across an organization, and all sorts of inferences can be derived from it. You can use BI to derive the following types of insights:

- **Customer service data:** Possibly answering the question, "what areas of business are causing the largest customer wait times?"

- **Sales and marketing data:** Possibly answering the question, "which marketing tactics are most effective and why?"

- **Operational data:** Possibly answering the questions, "how efficiently is the help desk operating? Are there any immediate actions that must be taken to remedy a problem there?"

- **Employee performance data:** Possibly answering the questions, "which employees are the most productive? Which are the least?"

Looking at technologies and skillsets that are useful in business intelligence

To streamline BI functions, make sure that your data is organized for optimal ease of access and presentation. You can use multidimensional databases to help you. Unlike relational, or *flat* databases, *multidimensional databases* organize data into cubes that are stored as multi-dimensional arrays. If you want your BI staff to be able to work with source data as quickly and easily as possible, you can use multidimensional databases to store data in a cube, instead of storing the data across several relational databases that may or may not be compatible with one another.

This cubic data structure enables *Online Analytical Processing* (OLAP) — a technology through which you can quickly and easily access and use your data for all sorts of different operations and analyses. To illustrate the concept of OLAP, imagine that you have a cube of sales data that has three dimensions — time, region, and business unit. You can *slice* the data to view only one rectangle — to view one sales region, for instance. You can *dice* the data to view a smaller cube made up of some subset of time, region(s), and business unit(s). You can *drill down* or *up* to view either highly detailed or highly summarized data, respectively. And you can *roll up*, or total, the numbers along one dimension — to total business unit numbers, for example, or to view sales across time and region only.

OLAP is just one type of *data warehousing system* — a centralized data repository that you can use to store and access your data. A more traditional data warehouse system commonly employed in business intelligence solutions is a *data mart* — a data storage system that you can use to store one particular focus area of data, belonging to only one line of business in the enterprise. *Extract, transform, and load* (ETL) is the process that you'd use to extract data, transform it, and load it into your database or data warehouse. Business analysts generally have strong backgrounds and training in business and information technology. As a discipline, BI relies on traditional IT technologies and skills.

Defining business-centric data science

Within the business enterprise, data science serves the same purpose that business intelligence does — to convert raw data into business insights that business leaders and managers can use to make data-informed decisions. If you have large sets of structured and unstructured data sources that may or may not be complete and you want to convert those sources into valuable insights for decision support across the enterprise, call on a data scientist.

Business-centric data science is multi-disciplinary and incorporates the following elements:

- ✔ **Quantitative analysis:** Can be in the form of mathematical modeling, multivariate statistical analysis, forecasting, and/or simulations.

  The term *multivariate* refers to more than one variable. A multivariate statistical analysis is a simultaneous statistical analysis of more than one variable at a time.

- ✔ **Programming skills:** You need the necessary programming skills to both analyze raw data and make this data accessible to business users.

- ✔ **Business knowledge:** You need knowledge of the business and its environment so that you can better understand the relevancy of your findings.

Data science is a pioneering discipline. Data scientists often employ the scientific method for data exploration, hypotheses formation, and hypothesis testing (through simulation and statistical modeling). Business-centric data scientists generate valuable data insights, oftentimes by exploring patterns and anomalies in business data. Data science in a business context is commonly comprised of

- ✔ **Internal and external datasets:** Data science is flexible. You can create business data mash-ups from internal and external sources of structured and unstructured data fairly easily. (A *data mash-up* is combination of two or more data sources that are then analyzed together in order to provide users with a more complete view of the situation at hand.)

- ✔ **Tools, technologies, and skillsets:** Examples here could involve using cloud-based platforms, statistical and mathematical programming, machine learning, data analysis using Python and R, and advanced data visualization.

Like business analysts, business-centric data scientists produce decision-support products for business managers and organizational leaders to use. These products include analytics dashboards and data visualizations, but generally not tabular data reports and tables.

Looking at the kinds of data that are useful in business-centric data science

You can use data science to derive business insights from standard-sized sets of structured business data (just like BI) or from structured, semi-structured, and unstructured sets of big data. Data science solutions are not confined to transactional data that sits in a relational database; you can use data science to create valuable insights from all available data sources. These data sources include

- **Transactional business data:** A tried-and-true data source, transactional business data is the type of structured data used in traditional BI and includes management data, customer service data, sales and marketing data, operational data, and employee performance data.

- **Social data related to the brand or business:** A more recent phenomenon, the data covered by this rubric includes the unstructured data generated through emails, instant messaging, and social networks such as Twitter, Facebook, LinkedIn, Pinterest, and Instagram.

- **Machine data from business operations:** Machines automatically generate this unstructured data, like SCADA data, machine data, or sensor data.

The acronym SCADA refers to *S*upervisory *C*ontrol and *D*ata *A*cquisition. SCADA systems are used to control remotely operating mechanical systems and equipment. They generate data that is used to monitor the operations of machines and equipment.

- **Audio, video, image, and PDF file data:** These well-established formats are all sources of unstructured data.

Looking at the technologies and skillsets that are useful in business-centric data science

Since the products of data science are often generated from big data, cloud-based data platform solutions are common in the field. Data that's used in data science is often derived from data-engineered big data solutions, like Hadoop, MapReduce, and Massively Parallel Processing. (For more on these technologies, check out Chapter 2.) Data scientists are innovative, forward-thinkers who must often think outside-the-box in order to exact solutions to the problems they solve. Many data scientists tend toward open-source solutions when available. From a cost perspective, this approach benefits the organizations that employ these scientists.

Business-centric data scientists might use machine learning techniques to find patterns in (and derive insights from) huge datasets that are related to a line of business or the business at large. They're skilled in math, statistics, and programming, and they sometimes use these skills to generate predictive models. They generally know how to program in Python or R. Most of them know how to use SQL to query relevant data from structured databases. They are usually skilled at communicating data insights to end users — in business-centric data science, end users are business managers and organizational leaders. Data scientists must be skillful at using verbal, oral, and visual means to communicate valuable data insights.

Although business-centric data scientists serve a decision-support role in the enterprise, they're different from the business analyst in that they usually have strong academic and professional backgrounds in math, science, engineering, or all of the above. This said, business-centric data scientists also have a strong substantive knowledge of business management.

Summarizing the main differences between BI and business-centric data science

The similarities between BI and business-centric data science are glaringly obvious; it's the differences that most people have a hard time discerning. The purpose of both BI and business-centric data science is to convert raw data into actionable insights that managers and leaders can use for support when making business decisions.

BI and business-centric data science differ with respect to approach. Although BI can use forward-looking methods like forecasting, these methods are generated by making simple inferences from historical or current data. In this way, BI extrapolates from the past and present to infer predictions about the future. It looks to present or past data for relevant information to help monitor business operations and to aid managers in short- to medium-term decision making.

In contrast, business-centric data science practitioners seek to make new discoveries by using advanced mathematical or statistical methods to analyze and generate predictions from vast amounts of business data. These predictive insights are generally relevant to the long-term future of the business. The business-centric data scientist attempts to discover new paradigms and new ways of looking at the data to provide a new perspective on the organization, its operations, and its relations with customers, suppliers, and competitors. Therefore, the business-centric data scientist must know the business and its environment. She must have business knowledge to determine how a discovery is relevant to a line of business or to the organization at large.

Other prime differences between BI and business-centric data science are

- **Data sources:** BI uses only structured data from relational databases, whereas business-centric data science may use structured data and unstructured data, like that generated by machines or in social media conversations.

- **Outputs:** BI products include reports, data tables, and decision-support dashboards, whereas business-centric data science products either involve dashboard analytics or another type of advanced data visualization, but rarely tabular data reports. Data scientists generally communicate their findings through words or data visualizations, but not tables and reports. That's because the source datasets from which data scientists work are generally more complex than a typical business manager would be able to understand.

✓ **Technology:** BI runs off of relational databases, data warehouses, OLAP, and ETL technologies, whereas business-centric data science often runs off of data from data-engineered systems that use Hadoop, MapReduce, or Massively Parallel Processing.

✓ **Expertise:** BI relies heavily on IT and business technology expertise, whereas business-centric data science relies on expertise in statistics, math, programming, and business.

Knowing Who to Call to Get the Job Done Right

Since most business managers don't know how to do advanced data work themselves, it's definitely beneficial to at least know what type of problems are best-suited for a business analyst and what problems should be handled by a data scientist instead.

If you want to use enterprise data insights to streamline your business so that its processes function more efficiently and effectively, then bring in a business analyst. Organizations employ business analysts so that they have someone to cover the responsibilities associated with requirements management, business process analysis, and improvements-planning for business processes, IT systems, organizational structures, and business strategies. Business analysts look at enterprise data and identify what processes need improvement. They then create written specifications that detail exactly what changes should be made for improved results. They produce interactive dashboards and tabular data reports to supplement their recommendations and to help business managers better understand what is happening in the business. Ultimately, business analysts use business data to further the organization's strategic goals and to support them in providing guidance on any procedural improvements that need to be made.

In contrast, if you want to obtain answers to very specific questions on your data, and you can obtain those answers only via advanced analysis and modeling of business data, then bring in a business-centric data scientist. Many times, a data scientist may support the work of a business analyst. In such cases, the data scientist might be asked to analyze very specific data-related problems and then report the results back to the business analyst to support him in making recommendations. Business analysts can use the findings of business-centric data scientists to help them determine how to best fulfill a requirement or build a business solution.

Exploring Data Science in Business: A Data-Driven Business Success Story

Southeast Telecommunications Company was losing many of its customers to *customer churn* — the customers were simply moving to other telecom service providers. Because it's significantly more expensive to acquire new customers than it is to retain existing customers, Southeast's management wanted to find a way to decrease their churn rates. So, Southeast Telecommunications engaged Analytic Solutions, Inc. (ASI), a business-analysis company. ASI interviewed Southeast's employees, regional managers, supervisors, front-line employees, and help-desk employees. After consulting with personnel, they collected business data that was relevant to customer retention.

ASI began examining several years' worth of Southeast's customer data to develop a better understanding of customer behavior and why some people left after years of loyalty, while others continued to stay on. The customer datasets contained records for the number of times a customer had contacted Southeast's help desk, the number of customer complaints, and the number of minutes and megabytes of data each customer used per month. ASI also had demographic and personal data (credit score, age, and region, for example) that was contextually relevant to the evaluation.

By looking at this customer data, ASI discovered the following insights. Within the one-year time interval before switching service providers

- Eighty-four percent of customers who left Southeast had placed two or more calls into its help desk in the nine months before switching providers.

- Sixty percent of customers who switched showed drastic usage drops in the six months prior to switching.

- Forty-four percent of customers who switched had made at least one complaint to Southeast in the six months prior to switching. (The data showed significant overlap between these customers and those who had called into the help desk.)

Based on these results, ASI fitted a logistic regression model to the historical data in order to identify the customers who were most likely to churn. With the aid of this model, Southeast could identify and direct retention efforts at the customers that they were most likely to lose. These efforts helped Southeast improve its services by identifying sources of dissatisfaction; increase returns on investment by restricting retention efforts to only those customers at risk of churn (rather than all customers); and most importantly, decrease overall customer churn, thus preserving the profitability of the business at large.

What's more, Southeast didn't make these retention efforts a one-time thing: The company incorporated churn analysis into its regular operating procedures. By the end of that year, and in the years since, they've seen a dramatic reduction in overall customer churn rates.

Part II

Using Data Science to Extract Meaning from Your Data

For more on mining data using data science, check out
www.dummies.com/extras/datascience.

In this part . . .

✔ Explore the importance of probability and statistics for data science.

✔ Master the basics of clustering and classification.

✔ Work with nearest neighbor algorithms.

✔ Examine how modeling works with data science.

Chapter 4

Introducing Probability and Statistics

Statistical methods are not the big and scary things many people try to make them out to be. In data science, the need for statistical methods is simply a fact of life, but it's nothing to get too alarmed over. Although you have to get a handle on as much statistics as you need to solve the problem at hand, you don't need to go out and get a degree in the field.

Contrary to what many pure statisticians would have you believe, the data science field is not the same thing as the statistics field. A data scientist is someone who has substantive knowledge of one or several fields and uses statistics, math, coding, and strong communication skills to help her tease out, understand, and communicate data insights that lie within raw datasets related to her field of expertise. Statistics is a vital component of this formula, but not more vital than the others. In this chapter, I introduce you to the basic ideas behind probability, regression, Monte Carlo simulation, and time series analysis.

Introducing the Fundamental Concepts of Probability

Probability is one of the most basic and fundamental concepts in statistics. To even get started in making sense of your data by using statistics, you need to be able to identify something as basic as whether you're looking at *descriptive* or *inferential* statistics. What's more, you need a firm grasp of the basics behind random variables, expectations, and probability distributions. The following sections cover all of these concepts.

Exploring the relationship between probability and inferential statistics

A *statistic* is a result that's derived from performing a mathematical operation on numerical data. In general, you use statistics in decision making. You also tend to encounter statistics of two distinct flavors:

- ✔ **Descriptive statistics:** As the name implies, descriptive statistics focus on providing you with a description that illuminates some characteristic of your numerical dataset.

- ✔ **Inferential statistics:** Rather than focusing on pertinent descriptions of your dataset, inferential statistics carve out a smaller section of the dataset and attempt to deduce something significant about the larger dataset. Use this type of statistics to get information about some real-world measure in which you're interested.

It's true that descriptive statistics describe the characteristics of a numerical dataset, but that doesn't really tell you much about why you should care about that data. In fact, most data scientists are only interested in descriptive statistics because of what they reveal about the real-world measures they describe. For example, a descriptive statistic is often associated with a *degree of accuracy,* indicating the statistic's value as an estimate of the real-world measure.

To better understand this concept, imagine that a business owner wants to estimate his upcoming quarter's profits. He might take an average of his last few quarters' profits to use as an estimate of how much he will make during the next quarter. But if the previous quarters' profits varied widely, a descriptive statistic that estimated the *variation* of this predicted profit value (the amount by which this dollar estimate could differ from the actual profits he will make) would indicate just how far off the predicted value could be from the actual one. (Not bad information to have.)

Like descriptive statistics, *inferential statistics* also reveal something about the real-world measure in which you're interested. In contrast to descriptive statistics, however, inferential statistics provide information about a small data selection, so you can use this information to infer something about the larger dataset from which it was taken. In statistics, this smaller data selection is known as a *sample,* and the larger, complete dataset from which the sample is taken is called the *population.*

If your dataset is too big to analyze in its entirety, then pull a smaller sample of this dataset, analyze that, and then make inferences about the entire dataset based on what you learn from analyzing the sample. You can also use inferential statistics in situations where you simply can't afford to collect data for the entire population. In this case, you'd simply use the data you do have to make inferences about the population at large. Other times, you may find yourself in situations where complete information for the population is simply not available. In these cases, you can use inferential statistics to estimate values for the missing data based on what you learn from analyzing the data that is available.

Descriptive statistics describe the characteristics of your numerical dataset, while inferential statistics are used to make inferences from subsets of data so you can better understand the larger datasets from which the subset is taken. To better understand this distinction, imagine that you have a socio-economic dataset that describes women, from age 18 to 34 that live in Philadelphia, Pennsylvania. Descriptive statistics would allow you to understand the characteristics of the woman population that comprises this subset. Or, you could use inferential statistics with this dataset to make inferences about the larger population of women, who are 18 to 34 years old, but that are living in all cities in the state of Pennsylvania (and not just in Philadelphia).

For an inference to be valid, you must select your sample carefully so that you get a true representation of the population. Even if your sample is representative, the numbers in the sample dataset will always exhibit some *noise* — random variation, in other words — that guarantees the sample statistic is not exactly identical to its corresponding population statistic.

Understanding random variables, probability distributions, and expectations

Imagine you've just rolled into Las Vegas and settled into your favorite roulette table over at the Bellagio. When you turn the roulette wheel, you intuitively understand that there is an equal chance that the ball will fall into any of the slots of the cylinder on the wheel. The slot where the ball will land is totally random, and the *probability*, or likelihood, of the ball landing in any one slot over another is going to be the same. Since the ball could land in any slot, with equal probability, there is an equal probability distribution — or, *uniform probability distribution*, meaning that the ball has an equal probability of landing in any of the slots in the cylinder.

But, the slots of roulette wheel are not all the same — there are 18 black slots and 20 slots that are either red or green. Because of this, there is

18/38 probability that your ball will land on a black slot. You plan to make successive bets that the ball will land on a black slot.

Your net winnings can be considered a *random variable* here. A *random variable* is a measure of a trait or value associated with an object, a person, or a place — something in the real world — that is unpredictable. Because this trait or value is unpredictable, however, doesn't mean you know nothing about it. What's more, you can use what you do know about this thing to help you in your decision making. Here's how . . .

A *weighted average* is an average value of a measure over a very large number of data points. If you take a *weighted average* of your winnings (your random variable) across the probability distribution, this would yield an *expectation value* — or an expected value for your net winnings over a successive number of bets. (An expectation can also be thought of as the best guess, if you had to guess.) To describe it more formally, an *expectation* is a weighted average of some measure associated with a random variable. If your goal is to model an unpredictable variable so that you can make data-informed decisions based on what you know about its probability in a population, you can use random variables and probability distributions to do this.

To further illustrate these concepts, imagine yourself walking down the sidewalk along Rodeo Drive in Hollywood, California, and observing the eye color of people you see. You notice that some people have brown eyes, some green, and so forth. In all honesty, you have no idea what the eye color will be of the next person you see, but you do know that blue and brown seem to be the most common. And, because you've observed this, you can make a somewhat educated guess about the eye color of the next person you see. In this scenario, the random variable you're considering is eye color, and your guess as to what the next person's eye color will be is based on what you've gleaned of the probability distribution of people's eye colors on Rodeo Drive.

Ready to dig down deeper into the Hollywood Eye Color scenario? Time to get a bit more quantitative. Imagine that you actually sat down and recorded counts on what you've observed of people's eye colors. Your observation counts show you that 35 percent of the population has brown eyes, 30 percent blue, 10 percent amber, 10 percent green, 5 percent violet, and 10 percent gray. (Figure 4-1 shows how these observation counts stack up.) These percentiles, in fact, tell you the exact probability of eye color distributed across the population. These percentiles represent a probability distribution. And, the expectation in this example would be the average number of people having any one eye color.

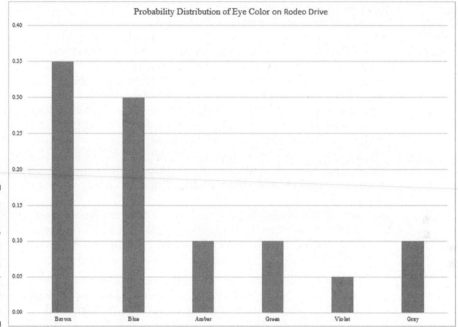

Figure 4-1:
The prob-
ability
distribution
of people's
eye color
on Rodeo
Drive.

Keep in mind the following characteristics of probability. When considering the probability of some event, you must know what other events are possible. Always define the set of events as *mutually exclusive* — only one can occur at a time (think of the six possible results of rolling a die). There are two important characteristics of probability:

✔ The probability of any single event never goes below 0.0 or exceeds 1.0.

✔ The probability of all events always sums to exactly 1.0.

Getting hip to some popular probability distributions

Probability distributions are classified according to the two following types:

✔ **Discrete distribution:** A random variable of which values can be counted (eye color, for example)

✔ **Continuous:** A random variable that assigns probabilities to ranges of values.

To understand discrete and continuous distribution, consider the weight of fashion models. A *discrete variable* would be the weight of one model, whereas a *continuous variable* would be a weight range that is acceptable for models in the fashion industry at large. A *discrete probability distribution* would be a count of the number of models with approximately the same weight (of 40 fashion models, imagine there are 20 models that weigh ~105 lbs., 15 that weigh ~110 lbs., and 5 that weigh ~115 lbs.). A continuous probability distribution would be a distribution of probability density that shows the greater and lesser probabilities for a model's weight, based on the weight values for each of the 40 different models.

If you want to model and describe real-world phenomenon, these eight distinct classes of probability distributions can really come in handy:

- **Uniform distributions:** Used to distribute probability equally over all possible outcomes (discrete) or equal ranges of outcomes (continuous), this distribution is especially useful in virtual experiments or simulations to explore real-world phenomena.

- **Binomial distributions:** Model the number of successes that can occur in a certain number of attempts when only two outcomes are possible (the old heads-or-tails coin-flip scenario, for example).

- **Geometric distributions:** Use these distributions to give the probability of such-and-such number of attempts occurring before you're blessed with your first success. So for example, if you are considering having a baby and want to have a boy . . . a geometric distribution could tell you how many children you'd need to have a high probability of having a male child.

- **Hypergeometric distributions:** A variant on the geometric distribution model, hypergeometric distributions give the probability that some number from a sample will be of a particular value — the probability of drawing a female from a set of males and females, for example. In hypergeometric distributions, there are no replacements when samples are taken from a finite population. As samples are drawn, the size of the remaining population decreases and the probability of drawing a male or a female sample changes based on the net decrease in the population size.

- **Poisson and exponential distributions:** The Poisson (discrete) and exponential (continuous) distributions complement one another. Say that there is an intersection in your town that has a lot of accidents. A Poisson distribution answers the question, "What is the probability that such-and-such number of accidents will occur there within a week?" And an exponential distribution answers the question, "What is the probability that the time until the next accident is such-and-such length of time?"

- **Normal distributions (continuous):** Represented graphically by the (relatively familiar) symmetric bell-shaped curve you see in Figure 4-2.

These distributions model phenomena that tend toward some most-likely value (the top of the bell in the bell curve) with values at the two extremes becoming less likely.

✔ **Gamma distributions:** You have to plan for all possibilities — even the possibility that no pattern exists. Gamma distributions do precisely that by allowing for non-symmetric distributions. The gamma (continuous) distribution assigns probabilities to random variables. In Gamma distribution plots, probabilities never have negative values and they fall within a range of values between 0 and 1. The gamma distribution is useful in modeling *time-to-failure* — a method that's useful for predicting when a device is most likely to fail, based on observational data and probability distributions.

✔ **Beta distributions (continuous):** The most versatile player on the distributions team, beta distributions are structured so that they can be made to fit almost any pattern, as needed.

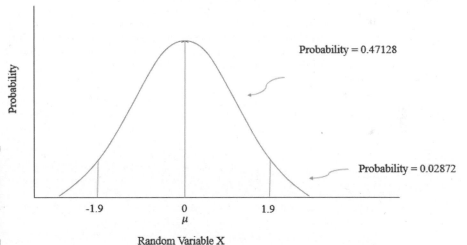

Figure 4-2: An example of a normal probability distribution.

Introducing Linear Regression

Linear regression is a method for modeling the relationships between a dependent variable and one or several independent variables, in order to discover, and quantify the strength of, important correlations between them. I walk you through several stages and types of linear regression in this chapter, but I want to start out in the following sections by first introducing simple linear regression modeling, then showing how to fit a linear regression model, and finally demonstrating a few Ordinary Least Squares (OLS) regression techniques.

Getting a handle on simple linear regression models

Simple linear regression is a mathematical modeling tool that you can use to predict the value of a dependent variable (DV) based on a single independent variable (IV) and the linear relationship you've established between the two. Linear relationships are represented mathematically by a straight line, as shown Figure 4-3, and described by an equation having the following form:

$$y = ax + b$$

In this equation, the elements are as follows:

- ✔ y is the dependent variable.
- ✔ x is the independent variable.
- ✔ a represents the slope of the regression line.
- ✔ b describes the y-intercept — the point on a plot where the graph of a function intersects with the y-axis and x is equal to zero. This value tells you the value of the dependent variable (y) when the value of the independent variable (x) is zero.

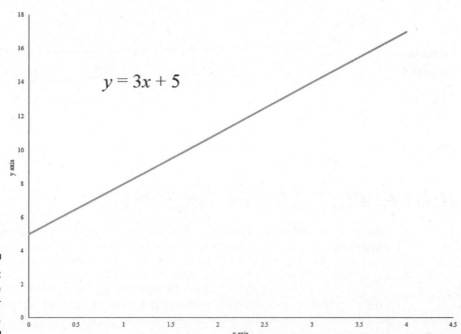

$$y = 3x + 5$$

Figure 4-3: An example of a linear relationship.

If you have some data on a real-world phenomenon and you pair this data as two variables in a linear relationship, you're not saying that one variable necessarily *causes* the other. You're simply using a linear relationship to show that, while one value goes up, the other also increases or decreases proportionally. To illustrate this concept, imagine that you hypothesize that people earn greater salaries the older they get. When evaluating, you pair the wage variable with the age variable in order to discover and quantify the relationship between them. You discover that older people do generally earn higher wages than younger people. But is this relationship correlative or causative? If you consider the possibility that new graduates could start coming out of universities with technical skills that command much higher wages, and that older employees often may not have such skills, then you could understand that it would be possible for younger people to begin earning greater wages than older staff members. This means that age is not causing or driving wages. There is simply a correlation between age and wage, but this correlation is subject to change depending on circumstance.

To further illustrate the concept, imagine two variables: Income ($) and Amount Overweight (lbs). You might imagine that as income rises, people eat more and consequently tend to be overweight. In this case, you're imagining that the relationship between the IV ($) and the DV (lbs) is positive. But maybe higher income people tend to have better nutrition information and can afford to purchase more healthy food, thus cultivating better health by maintaining a healthy weight. Then the relationship between the IV and DV would be negative — while income increases, weight decreases. In this equation, x = Amount of Pounds Overweight and y = Income in Dollars.

As shown in this example, to test evidence for guesses you form about the world, you can use linear regression. If you establish a *statistically significant* relationship between the IV and DV — meaning that you've established and quantified an assuredness that there is a real and significant relationship between the variables — then you have evidence that your guess is correct. Failure to find a statistically significant relationship provides evidence that your guess is wrong.

Learning to create a fitted regression line

Although getting a pair of shoes that fit perfectly is never easy, you *can* generate a fitted linear regression model tailored to your data. So why would you want to do this? Imagine that a researcher has a dataset on a group of human subjects. This dataset contains values for protein concentrations and for the number of cell mutations observed among the human subjects. Each person's record, in statistical terms, is an *observation,* and each observation has a measure for the protein concentration and for the number of cell mutations. The researcher might select the level of protein concentration as her independent variable (IV) and the number of mutations as her DV, and then fit a regression line to this data, meaning she would try to find values of a and b in the equation $y = ax + b$ that would come the closest to generating the observed DVs given the IVs in her dataset.

a and b in this context are called *parameters*, and a is the most important because it defines the relationship between x and y.

The regression line will not fit the data exactly because each observation is assumed to contain another random noise variable, ε. Thus, rather than $y = ax + b$, the equation for any one observation is always going to be $y = ax + b + \varepsilon$, where ε represents this new random variable. In Figure 4-4, actual observations for values of x are shown in black and values predicted by the regression model are shown in light grey. The regression model is represented by the line and can be specified as $y = 3.479x + 17.531$.

A regression equation's value of a, also known as the *slope,* is the most important element in establishing how x and y are related. In this example, the slope — the *rise,* or change in y (going up or down), divided by the *run,* or change in x (going from left to the right) — is 3.479.

Figure 4-4:
An example
of a fitted
regression
line.

How is the line fitted to the data? The answer is in the random variable ε contained in the data. At $x = 9$, the actual value is 56, but the regression line predicted a value of 48.8. (Refer to Figure 4-4.) The difference between the two, $56 - 48.8 = 7.2$, is an instance of ε. Fitting the regression line to the data involves finding the values of a and b such that the sum of ε for all observations in the dataset is minimized.

Regression is a simple yet powerful tool. If you find evidence of a relationship, either positive or negative, between the IV and the DV, then you can use the IV to predict the value of the DV.

You can use statistics to make inferences or test hypotheses. *Hypothesis testing* is the process of using statistics to determine the probability of whether the hypothesis you propose is true. *Noise*, or random noise, is unexplainable variation that is present in almost all datasets. A major assumption in performing hypothesis testing is that *noise* terms are symmetrically distributed. If they're not, then a linear model is not appropriate for your data. Try a curved line instead.

Ordinary Least Squares regression methods

Ordinary Least Squares (OLS) is a statistical method that fits a linear regression line to an observational dataset. With OLS, you do this by squaring the vertical distance values that describe the distances between the observational data points and the best-fit line, adding up those squared distances, and then adjusting the placement of the best-fit line so that this summed squared distance value is minimized. Use OLS if your goal is to construct a function that's a close approximation of observational data.

As always, don't expect the actual value to be identical to the value predicted by the regression. Values predicted by the regression are simply estimates that are most similar to the actual values in the model.

OLS is particularly useful for fitting a regression line to models containing more than one independent variable (IV). As with the fitted regression line (discussed in the preceding section), one obvious purpose is to estimate the value of the dependent variable (DV) given the values of the independent variables (IVs).

When using Ordinary Least Squares regression methods to fit a regression line that has more than one independent variable, two or more of the IVs may be interrelated. When two or more IVs are strongly correlated with each other, this is called *multicollinearity*. Multicollinearity tends to adversely affect the reliability of the IVs as predictors when they're examined apart from one another. Luckily, however, multicollinearity doesn't decrease the overall predictive reliability of the model when it's considered as a whole.

In addition to using OLS to perform fitted linear regressions on models that contain more than one IV, you can also use it to perform statistical tests. Imagine that you're the manager of a major chain store trying to decide where to locate a new store. You're pretty sure that the following location characteristics strongly affect store profitability:

- Mean income of the local population (x_1)
- Distance to the nearest store belonging to your primary competitor (x_2)

You create a regression model by using data from all your other stores to see if these variables are statistically significant predictors of profitability.

You formalize your guesses as hypotheses, like the following:

- H_{A1}: A store's profitability increases as the local population's mean income rises.
- H_{A2}: A store's profitability increases as the distance to the nearest competitor's store increases.

Matching these two alternative hypotheses are corresponding *null* hypotheses, which postulate the exact opposite results:

- H_{O1}: The local population's mean income has no effect on store profitability.
- H_{O2}: Distance to the nearest competitor's store has no effect on store profitability.

You fit the regression model with the data from your other stores and perform statistical tests to determine if statistically significant evidence contradicts these null hypotheses. If you get a positive statistical test result, this doesn't mean that you should accept an alternative hypothesis as true. Rather, as in a jury trial, it just means you haven't . . . yet . . . found any evidence to disprove the alternative hypotheses.

To get meaningful results from your analysis, you need to make certain assumptions about your data. The ε's regression errors for each of the observations should be normally distributed, the regression errors should average out to zero, and the regression errors should have approximately the same amount of variability. If your data does not meet these specification, then a linear model might not be appropriate.

Simulations

The Monte Carlo method is a simulation technique that randomly generates values for independent variables, and then simulates a range of potential process outcomes based on this set of randomly generated IVs. You can use Monte Carlo methods to test hypotheses, to generate parameter estimates, to predict scenario outcomes, and to validate models. The method is powerful because it can be used to very quickly simulate anywhere from 1 to 10,000 (or more) simulation samples for any processes you are trying to evaluate. Interestingly, this method was named after the infamous Casino de Monte Carlo, in Monaco.

The purpose of using Monte Carlo methods is to sample values randomly from a probability distribution and then use those values to make a prediction or validate a hypothesis. You want to sample values randomly so that you can then use those values when you're performing *simulations* — virtual experiments that allow you to play out a certain scenario to its conclusion. If you want to save money that you'd otherwise need to spend on real-world experimentations, then you can use computational simulations to model a natural process mathematically instead.

Simulations aren't very interesting unless you incorporate the natural variability that's part of any real-world phenomenon, which Monte Carlo methods allow you to do.

In the section "Understanding random variables, probability distributions, and expectations," earlier in this chapter, I have you imagine yourself walking down Rodeo Drive, trying to guess the eye color of the next person you meet. You may have neither the time nor the money to jet off to Hollywood to carry out your field work, so instead of actually testing your guess in real life, you may decide you want to perform a simulation of this process. First, create a *cumulative probability distribution* — a distribution function that uses a cumulative probability to estimate the probability of a random variable falling within a particular range of numbers. Start off by listing the eye colors of people on Rodeo Drive with their associated probabilities, as shown in Table 4-1.

The cumulative probability distribution simply adds up, or *cumulates,* these individual probabilities, as shown in Table 4-2.

This cumulative distribution is shown graphically in Figure 4-5.

How would you go about predicting the eye color of the next random person you meet? Doing so involves still another probability distribution, the *continuous uniform distribution* ranging from 0.0 to 1.0, which distributes probability uniformly across all ranges of values of equal size between 0.0 and 1.0. The darker area in Figure 4-6 represents this distribution.

To simulate eye color, you first need to use a uniform probability distribution to generate a set of random variables that ranges between the values of 0.0 and 1.0. This would be an almost impossible task to accomplish without computational simulation software. Fortunately, statistics-capable software like R, Python, and Microsoft Excel have random number generators that you can use to generate this set. So for this example, imagine that you use one of these programs to generate a set of uniformly distributed random variables, and from among that set you select the random number 0.5073.

Table 4-1   Eye Color Probability of People on Rodeo Drive

Eye Color	Probability
Brown	0.35
Blue	0.30
Amber	0.10
Green	0.10
Violet	0.05
Gray	0.10

Table 4-2   Cumulative Rodeo Drive Eye Color Probability

Eye Color	Probability	Cumulative Probability
Brown	0.35	0.35
Blue	0.30	0.65
Amber	0.10	0.75
Green	0.10	0.85
Violet	0.05	0.90
Gray	0.10	1.00

How do you translate this random number into eye color? Looking at Figure 4-5 — showing the cumulative probability distribution — perform the following steps:

1. **Locate 0.5073 on the vertical *y*-axis.**

2. **From that point, look directly across the chart, to the right, until you see the point where *y* = 0.5073 intersects with the probability line.**

3. **When you find that intersection point, follow an imaginary vertical line straight down from that point to the *x*-axis.**

   The labels on the *x*-axis indicate the eye color at that probability.

For this example, the eye color is blue at a probability of 0.5073. Blue is one of the more common, higher probability colors. Consequently, guessing blue as the next eye color might be a pretty good guess, considering all of your options.

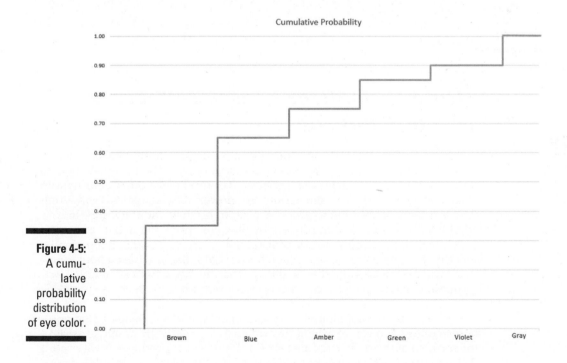

Figure 4-5:
A cumulative probability distribution of eye color.

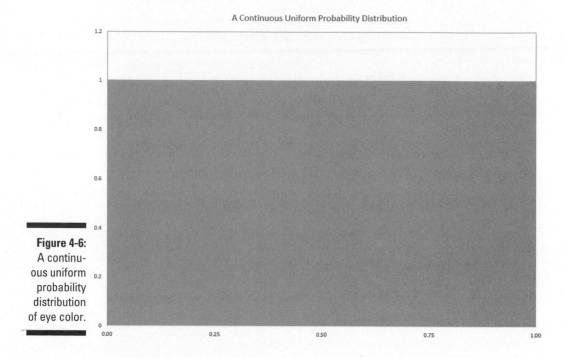

Figure 4-6:
A continuous uniform probability distribution of eye color.

Using simulations to assess properties of a test statistic

In Monte Carlo methods, you generally construct a hypothetical equation or process to describe a real-world phenomenon, and then simulate tens to thousands of outcomes for that process to determine whether your hypothesis is valid. Monte Carlo simulations are powered by statistical computing. Use a statistical program to generate a set of random variables and then simulate the results of that process by plugging those simulated random variables back into the equation or process you've hypothesized. If the results of that simulation are a close match for the data that you have about your real-world phenomenon, then you know that the hypothetical equation or process you've constructed is a good representation.

To get a better idea of Monte Carlo sampling in practice, imagine that you're a researcher and you're attempting to create a genetically modified strain of corn, called Corn X. Your goal for Corn X is that it produces greater corn-kernel weight per ear of corn than is produced by regular, unmodified corn. In other words, you're hoping the Corn X will generate more food mass per ear of corn grown.

You have grown your first crop and measured the weight of kernels per ear of corn. You've generated a set of data that represents the real-world Corn X crop. Now, you want to test this data to see if statistical evidence suggests that Corn X produces more weight than regular corn. Therefore, your hypotheses are as follows:

- ✔ H_0: There is no difference between the average weight of kernels on a Corn X ear and a regular ear of corn.

- ✔ H_A: The weight of the kernels on a Corn X ear of corn is greater than the kernels of a regular ear of corn.

With Monte Carlo sampling, you assume that the null hypothesis is correct and then determine how probable your real-world observations are, given its assumptions. In the example, you assume that there is no difference between the weight of Corn X and regular corn. In other words, you assume that your null hypothesis (H_0) is true. More specifically, on average, you assume that the following statement is true:

$$(\Sigma \text{ Kernel Mass }_{\text{Corn X Ear}}) - (\Sigma \text{ Kernel Mass }_{\text{Regular Corn Ear}}) = 0$$

Set up a simulation to produce per-ear corn weights in such a way that they're *normally* distributed — as shown earlier (see Figure 4-2), *normal* distribution is represented as a symmetric bell-shaped curve that tends toward some most-likely value (the top of the bell in the bell curve) and values at the two extremes being less likely (the tapered ends of the bell). This simulation would involve you repeating the following steps 2,000 times:

1. **Generate per-ear kernel weight for a simulated ear of Corn X and of regular corn.**

2. **Calculate the difference.**

After you have your results from these 2,000 simulations, you want to calculate the mean weight difference and variability from the 2,000 results you've generated. Just to give you an idea of what to expect, repeating the steps above 1,000 times yields the results plotted in Figure 4-7.

Because you've calculated the mean weight difference from a set of 2,000 random variables, this simulation sample size is large enough that the sampling distribution can be considered normal. Consequently, 95 percent of the weight differences you observe should fall below 2.08 ounces, if your null hypothesis is in fact true.

However, you obtain the following values for the real-world weight differences between Corn X and regular corn: 2.91, 2.75, 3.99, 2.73, 1.99, 2.98, and 2.83. All but one exceed 2.08, and so you reject the null hypothesis.

Using Monte Carlo simulations to assess properties of an estimator

An *estimator* is an educated guess about some measure associated with a real-world process. *Point estimators* are used to generate population measures — measures like the mean, standard deviation, and quartiles of a dataset. Estimators form a solid foundation on which you can base conclusions about the population mean. To generate estimators on complex phenomenon or where the underlying probability distribution is unknown or unknowable, use simulations.

Assume that you're the quality assurance manager at a company that manufactures an important piece of medical equipment. These pieces of equipment are manufactured to order, and you estimate that, on average, 1 in 1,000 is defective. If a defective part is found, the manufacturing equipment must be taken offline, checked, and reset. You want to determine how often this must be done. In this situation, the random variable is the number of parts inspected till a defective part is found, and its probability distribution is *geometric* — meaning that the distribution tells you the number of non-defective equipment pieces you will test before you have a high probability of discovering a defective piece of equipment. You decide to set your simulation up to repeat the following steps 52 times:

1. **Use Monte Carlo sampling to generate 400 values of a geometric random variable with probability of a defective piece of equipment being 1 in 1,000.**

   400 simulations is just an example here. You could have generated 4,000 values of 10,000 values — that part is up to you.

2. **For each of the 400 values, average the number manufactured till a defect occurs.**

The results of this simulation are shown in Figure 4-8. You can see that there are 52 simulated outcomes and that they result in average outcomes ranging between 945 and 1058 — meaning that it's likely to test anywhere from 945 pieces of equipment to 1058 pieces of equipment before discovering a defective piece and then having to take the manufacturing equipment offline to reset it.

A point estimator is considered a random variable. It has its very own probability distribution, known as its *sampling distribution*. If the simulation is repeated enough times (usually 30 or more), you can assume that the sampling distribution is normal and that you can estimate its mean and variability, which allows you to conclude some things about the population values you're estimating.

Figure 4-8: Numerical results from a Monte Carlo simulation of medical equipment defectiveness.

Simulation	Average	Simulation	Average	Simulation	Average	Simulation	Average
1	1055	14	1011	27	945	40	1055
2	1058	15	986	28	1012	41	1058
3	970	16	945	29	1055	42	970
4	986	17	1012	30	1058	43	986
5	1009	18	1055	31	970	44	1009
6	998	19	1058	32	986	45	998
7	987	20	970	33	1009	46	987
8	1043	21	986	34	998	47	1043
9	964	22	1009	35	987	48	964
10	1039	23	998	36	1043	49	1039
11	1004	24	987	37	964	50	1004
12	961	25	1043	38	1039	51	961
13	1007	26	964	39	1004	52	1007
Average of Sample Averages = 996; Sample Standard Deviation = 41							

For instance, based on the simulation described above, you guess that the process produces a defective part about every 996th part produced. Employing confidence intervals using the estimators derived from these simulations, you can state the following:

- ✔ The probability that the true mean lies between 983 and 1009 is 0.25.
- ✔ The probability that the true mean lies between 968 and 1024 is 0.50.
- ✔ The probability that the true mean lies between 949 and 1043 is 0.75.

A *confidence interval* is an interval that's calculated from observation data. The values that comprise a confidence interval are good estimators of an unknown population parameter. The level of confidence for a confidence interval is a measure of the likelihood that the unknown parameter is represented within the interval.

Introducing Time Series Analysis

A *time series* is just a collection of data on attribute values over time. Time series analysis is performed in order to predict future instances of the measure based on the past observational data. If you want to forecast or predict future values of the data in your dataset, use time series techniques.

Understanding patterns in time series

Time series exhibit specific patterns. Take a look at Figure 4-9 to get a better understanding of what these patterns are all about. *Constant* time series remain at roughly the same level over time, but are subject to some random error. In contrast, *trended* series show a stable linear movement up or down. Whether constant or trended, time series may also sometimes exhibit *seasonality* — predictable, cyclical fluctuations that reoccur seasonally throughout a year. As an example of seasonal time series, consider how many businesses show increased sales during the holiday season.

If you're including seasonality in your model, incorporate it in the quarter, month, or even six-month period — wherever it's appropriate. Time series may show *non-stationary processes* — or, unpredictable cyclical behavior that's not related to seasonality as a result of economic or industry-wide conditions. Since it's not predictable, non-stationary processes can't be forecasted. You must transform non-stationary data to stationary data before moving forward with an evaluation.

Patterns Exhibited by Time Series

Figure 4-9:
A comparison of patterns exhibited by time series.

The data, which include random error, are in blue and the forecast models fitted to the data are in orange.

Take a look at the solid lines in Figure 4-9. These represent the mathematical models used to forecast points in the time series. The mathematical models shown in Figure 4-9 represent very good, precise forecasts because they're a very close fit to the actual data. The actual data contains some random error, thus making it impossible to forecast perfectly.

Figure 4-10 shows you the different time series types, and the mathematical models that describe them.

Modeling univariate time series data

Similar to how multivariate analysis is the analysis of relationships between multiple variables, *univariate analysis* is a quantitative analysis of only one variable. When you model univariate time series, you are modeling time series changes that represent changes in a single variable over time.

Time Series Type	Mathematical Model
Constant	$y_t = b + random\ error$
Trended	$y_t = at + b + random\ error$
Constant Seasonal	$y_t = b + S^{(1)}I^{(1)} + S^{(2)}I^{(2)} + S^{(3)}I^{(3)} + S^{(4)}I^{(4)} + random\ error$
Trended Seasonal	$y_t = at + b + S^{(1)}I^{(1)} + S^{(2)}I^{(2)} + S^{(3)}I^{(3)} + S^{(4)}I^{(4)} + random\ error$
Cyclical	Here cycles are unpredictable and hence impossible to model

Figure 4-10: Mathematical models for various time series patterns.

Explanation of Notation:

- y_t is the observation at the *t*th time period;
- a, b are constants; $t = 1, 2, 3, \ldots$ is time period;
- $S^{(i)}$ is seasonal constant for season $i = 1,\ 2,\ 3,\ 4^*$ and $\sum_{i=1}^{4} I^{(i)} = 1$ with $I^{(i)} = 0$ or 1

Autoregressive Moving Average (ARMA) is a class of forecasting methods that you can use to predict future values from current and historical data. As its name implies, the family of ARMA models combines *autoregression* techniques (analyses that assume that previous observations are good predictors for future values and perform an autoregression analysis to forecast for those future values) and *moving average* techniques — models that measure the level of the constant time series and then update the forecast model if any changes are detected.

Here is an example of an equation for the ARMA model:

$ARMA(p, q)$

$$y_t = a_1 y_{t-1} + a_2 y_{t-2} + \ldots + a_p y_{t-p} + b_0 + e_t - b_1 e_{t-1} - b_2 e_{t-2} + \ldots - b_q e_{t-q}$$

In this equation

- y_t equals the actual value of the time series at time *t*.

- y_{t-1} equals the actual value of the time series at time *t – 1*.

- $y_t - y_{t-1}$ equals the net change in the value of time series between time *t* and time *t – 1*. — the change in value of the time series over one interval of time, in other words.

- e_{t-1} equals the error term at time *t - 1* (a quantification of the error processes in the model at time *t - 1*).

- a_1 equals the autoregressive parameter for y_{t-1}.

- b_1 equals the moving average parameter for e_{t-1}.

- $e_t, e_{t-1}, e_{t-2}, \ldots$, and e_{t-q} are uncorrelated.

Autoregression assumes that the previous p observations in the time series provide a good estimate of future observations. The moving average part of the model allows the model to update the forecasts if the level of a constant time series changes. If you're looking for a simple model or a model that will work for only a small dataset, then the ARMA model is not a good fit for your needs. An alternative in this case might be to just stick with simple linear regression.

REMEMBER

In order to use the ARMA model for reliable results, you need to have at least 50 observations and a trained analyst who can fit and interpret the model for you.

Figure 4-11 shows a chart of the ARMA model that corresponds to this equation:

$$y_t = 0.91y_{t\text{-}1} + 11.6 - 1.412y_{t\text{-}1} + 0.987y_{t\text{-}2}$$

In Figure 4-11, you can see that the model forecast data and the actual data are a very close fit. This means that the equation that formulated above is a good representation of the time series it models.

Figure 4-11:
An example
of an ARMA
forecast
model.

Chapter 5

Clustering and Classification

· ·

In This Chapter

▶ Understanding the basics of clustering and classification

▶ Clustering your data with the k-means algorithm and kernel density estimation

▶ Getting to know hierarchical and neighborhood clustering algorithms

▶ Checking out decision tree and random forest algorithms

· ·

Data scientists use clustering to help them divide their data into subsets and classification methods to help them build predictive models that they can then use to forecast the classification of future data points. The basics behind clustering and classification are relatively easy to understand, but things get tricky fast when you get into using some of the more advanced algorithms. In this chapter, I introduce the basics behind clustering and classification. I follow that by introducing several nuanced algorithms that offer clustering and classification solutions to meet your requirements, based on the specific characteristics of your feature dataset.

Introducing the Basics of Clustering and Classification

To grasp advanced methods for use in clustering your data, you should first take a few moments to make sure you have a firm understanding of the basics that underlie all forms of clustering and classification.

Clustering is a form of *machine learning* — the machine in this case is your computer, and *learning* refers to an algorithm that's repeated over and over until a certain set of predetermined conditions are met. Learning algorithms are generally run until the point that the final analysis results will not change no matter how many additional times the algorithm is passed over the data.

Clustering is one of the two main types of machine learning — called *unsupervised* machine learning, meaning that the data in the dataset is unlabeled, which means the algorithms must use inferential methods to discover patterns, relationships, and correlations within the raw data set. Classification, the other type of machine learning, is called *supervised machine learning*. Classification involves using machine learning algorithms to learn from labeled data. Data labels make it easier for your models to make decisions based on the logic rules you've defined.

To put clustering and classification through their paces, I want to use a readily available sample dataset from the World Bank's open datasets on country income and education. This data shows the percentage of income earned by the bottom 10 percent of the population in each country and the percentage of children who complete primary school in each country.

For the purpose of this chapter's discussion, I'm going to isolate the median reported statistic from the years 2000 to 2003. (Some countries report on these statistics only every few years, and during 2000 to 2003, this data was fully reported by 81 of 227 countries.)

In datasets about the percentage of children who complete primary school, some are reported at over 100 percent. That's because some countries count this statistic at different ages, but the data was *normalized* so that the percentage distribution is proportionally scaled across the range of countries represented in the dataset. In other words, although the total scale exceeds 100 percent, the values have been normalized so that they're proportional to one another and you're getting an apples-to-apples comparison. As a result, the fact that some countries report completion rates greater than 100 percent doesn't have an adverse effect on the analysis you do in this chapter.

Getting to know clustering algorithms

You use clustering algorithms to subdivide your datasets into clusters of data points that are most similar for a predefined attribute. If you have a dataset that describes multiple attributes about a particular feature and want to group your data points according to their attribute similarities, then use clustering algorithms.

A simple scatter plot of our Country Income and Education datasets yields the chart you see in Figure 5-1.

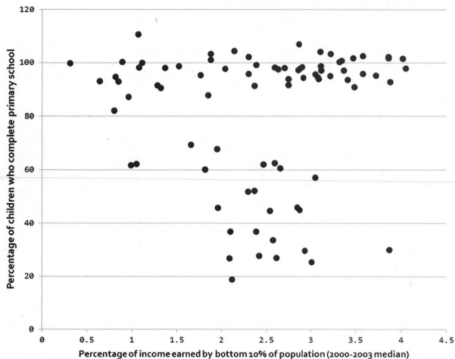

In unsupervised clustering, you start with this data and then proceed to divide it into subsets. These subsets are called *clusters* and are comprised of data points that are most similar to one another. In Figure 5-1, it appears that there are at least two clusters, probably three — one at the bottom with low income and education, and then the high education countries look like they might be split between low and high income.

Figure 5-2 shows the result of *eyeballing* — making a visual estimate of — clusters in this dataset.

Although you can generate visual estimates of clustering, you can achieve much more accurate results when dealing with much larger datasets by using algorithms to generate clusters for you. Visual estimation is a rough method that's only useful on smaller datasets of minimal complexity. Algorithms produce exact, repeatable results, and you can use algorithms to generate clustering for multiple dimensions of data within your dataset.

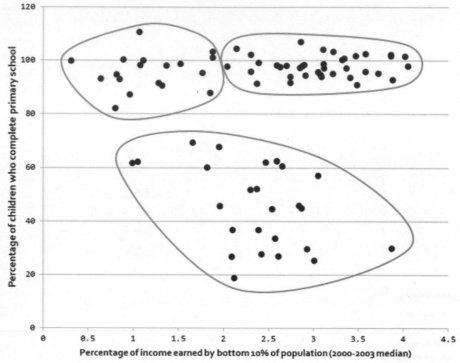

Figure 5-2:
A simple
scatter plot
showing
eyeballed
estimations
of clus-
tering.

Clustering algorithms are one type of approach in unsupervised machine learning — Other approaches include Markov methods (discussed in Chapter 7) and methods for dimension reduction. Clustering algorithms are appropriate in situations where the following characteristics are true:

✔ You know and understand the dataset you're analyzing.

✔ Before running the clustering algorithm, you don't have an exact idea as to the nature of the subsets (clusters). Often, you won't even know how many subsets there are in the dataset before you run the algorithm.

✔ The subsets (clusters) are determined by only the one dataset you're analyzing.

✔ Your goal is to determine a model that describes the subsets in a single dataset and only this dataset.

If you add more data, you should rerun the analysis from scratch to get complete and accurate model results.

Getting to know classification algorithms

With classification algorithms, you take an existing dataset and use what you know about it to generate a predictive model for use in classification of future data points. If your goal is to use your dataset and its known subsets to build a model for predicting the categorization of future data points, you'll want to use classification algorithms.

When implementing supervised classification, you should already know your data's subsets — these subsets are called *categories.* Classification helps you see how well your data fits into the dataset's predefined categories so that you can then build a predictive model for use in classifying future data points.

Figure 5-3 illustrates how it looks to classify the World Bank's Income and Education datasets according to the Continent category.

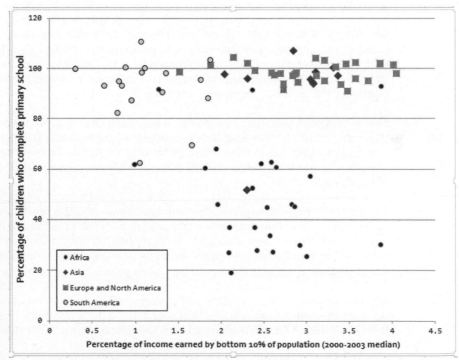

Figure 5-3:
A classification of the World Bank data according to the Continent category.

In Figure 5-3, you can see that, in some cases, the subsets you might identify with a clustering technique do correspond to the continents category, but in other cases, they don't. For example, look at the one Asian country in the middle of the African data points. That's Bhutan. You could use the data in this dataset to build a model that would predict a continent category for incoming data points. But if you introduced a data point for a new country that showed statistics similar to those of Bhutan, then the new country could be categorized as being part of either the Asian continent or the African continent, depending on how you define your model.

Now imagine a situation in which your original data doesn't include Bhutan, and you use the model to predict Bhutan's continent as a new data point. In this scenario, the model would wrongly predict that Bhutan is part of the African continent. This is an example of *model overfitting* — situations in which a model is so tightly fit to its underlying dataset, as well as the noise or random error inherent in that dataset, that the model performs poorly as a predictor for new data points.

To avoid overfitting your models, divide your data into a training set and a test set. A typical ratio is to assign 80 percent of the data into the training set and the remaining 20 percent into the test set. Build your model with the training set, and then use the test set to evaluate the model by pretending that the test-set data points are unknown. You can evaluate the accuracy of your model by comparing the categories assigned to these test-set data points by the model to the true categories.

Model overgeneralization can also be a problem. *Overgeneralization* is the opposite of overfitting: It happens when a data scientist tries to avoid misclassification due to overfitting by making a model extremely general. Models that are too general end up assigning every category a low degree of confidence.

To illustrate model overgeneralization, consider again the World Bank Income and Education datasets. If the model used the presence of Bhutan to cast doubt on every new data point in its nearby vicinity, then you end up with a wishy-washy model that treats all nearby points as African but with a low probability. This model would be a poor predictive performer.

A good metaphor for overfitting and overgeneralization can be illustrated through the well-known phrase, "If it walks like a duck and talks like a duck, then it's a duck." Overfitting would turn this phrase into, "It's a duck if, and only if, it walks and quacks exactly in the ways that I have personally observed a duck to walk and quack. Since I've never observed the way an Australian spotted duck walks and quacks, an Australian spotted duck must not really be a duck at all." In contrast, overgeneralization would say, "If it moves around on two legs and emits any high-pitched, nasal sound, it's a duck. Therefore, Fran Fine, Fran Drescher's character in the '90s American sitcom *The Nanny* must be a duck."

Supervised machine learning — the fancy term for classification — is appropriate in situations where the following characteristics are true:

- ✔ You know and understand the dataset you're analyzing.

- ✔ The subsets (categories) of your dataset are defined ahead of time and aren't determined by the data.

- ✔ You want to build a model that correlates the data within its predefined categories so that the model can help predict the categorization of future data points.

When performing classification, keep the following points in mind:

- ✔ **Model predictions are only as good as the model's underlying data.** In the World Bank data example, it could be the case that, if other factors such as life expectancy or energy use per capita were added to the model, its predictive strength might increase.

- ✔ **Model predictions are only as good as the categorization of the underlying dataset.** For example, what do you do with countries like Russia that span two continents? Do you distinguish North Africa from sub-Saharan Africa? Do you lump North America in with Europe because they tend to share similar attributes? Do you consider Central America to be part of North America or South America?

There is a constant danger of overfitting and overgeneralization. A happy medium must be found between the two.

Getting to know similarity metrics

Both clustering and classification are based on calculating the similarity or difference between two data points. If your dataset is *numeric* — comprised of only number fields and values — and can be portrayed on an *n*-dimensional plot, then there are various geometric metrics you can use to scale your multidimensional data.

An *n-dimensional plot* is a multidimensional scatter plot chart that you can use to plot *n* number of dimensions of data.

Some popular geometric metrics used for calculating distances between data points include Euclidean, Manhattan, or Minkowski distance metrics. These metrics are just different geometric functions that are useful for modeling distances between points. The Euclidean metric is a measure of the distance between points plotted on a Euclidean plane. The *Manhattan metric* is a measure of the distance between points where distance is calculated as the sum of the absolute value of the differences between two point's Cartesian coordinates. The Minkowski distance metric is a generalization of the Euclidean and Manhattan distance metrics. Quite often, these metrics can be used interchangeably.

If your data is numeric but non-plottable (such as curves instead of points), you can generate similarity scores based on *differences* between data, instead of the actual values of the data itself.

Lastly, for non-numeric data, you can use metrics like the Jaccard distance metric, which is an index that compares the number of features that two data points have in common. For example, to illustrate a Jaccard distance, think about the two following text strings: `Saint Louis de Ha-ha, Quebec` and `St-Louis de Ha!Ha!, QC`. What features do these text strings have in common? And what features are different between them? The Jaccard metric generates a numerical index value that quantifies the similarity between text strings.

Identifying Clusters in Your Data

You can use many different algorithms for clustering, but the speed and robustness of the k-means algorithm makes it a very popular choice among experienced data scientists. As alternatives, Kernel Density Estimation methods, hierarchical algorithms, and neighborhood algorithms are also available to help you identify clusters in your dataset.

Clustering with the k-means algorithm

You generally deploy k-means algorithms to subdivide data points of a dataset into clusters based on nearest mean values. To determine the optimal division of your data points into clusters, such that the distance between points in each cluster is minimized, you can use k-means clustering.

In the term *k-means,* k denotes the number of clusters in the data. Since the k-means algorithm doesn't determine this, you're required to specify this quantity. The quality of the clusters is heavily dependent on the correctness of the k value specified. If your data is two- or three-dimensional, a plausible range of k values may be visually determinable. In the eyeballed approximation of clustering from the World Bank Income and Education data scatter plot (look back to Figure 5-2), a visual estimation of the k value would equate to 3 clusters, or $k = 3$.

If your dataset has more than three dimensions, however, you can use computational methods to generate a good value for k. One such method is the *silhouette coefficient* — a method that calculates the average distance of each point from all other points in a cluster, and then compares that value with the average distance to every point in every other cluster. Luckily, since the k-means algorithm is so efficient, it does not require much computer processing power, and you can easily calculate this coefficient for a wide range of k values.

The k-means algorithm works by placing sample cluster centers on an n-dimensional plot and then evaluating whether moving them in any one direction would result in a new center with higher *density* — with more data points closer to it, in other words. The centers are moved from regions of lower density to regions of higher density until all centers are within a region of *local maximum density* — a true center of the cluster, where each cluster gets a maximum number of points closest to its cluster center. Whenever possible, you should try to place the centers yourself, manually. If that's not possible, then simply place the centers randomly and run the algorithm several times to see how often you end up with the same clusters.

One weakness of the k-means algorithm is that it may produce incorrect results by placing cluster centers in areas of *local minimum density*. This happens when centers get lost in *low-density regions* — in other words, regions of the plot that have relatively few points plotted in them — and the algorithm-driven directional movement — the movement that's meant to increase point density — starts to bounce and oscillate between faraway clusters. In these cases, the center gets caught in a low-density space that's located between two high-point density zones.This results in erroneous clusters based around centers that converge in areas of low, local minimum density. Ironically, this happens most often when the underlying data is very well-clustered, with tight, dense regions that are separated by wide, sparse areas.

To try things out for yourself, you can get started clustering your data with the k-means methods by using either R's `cluster` package or Python's `SciPy` library. (For more on R's `cluster` package, check out `http://cran.r-project.org/web/packages/cluster/cluster.pdf`; for more on `Scipy`, check out `http://docs.scipy.org/doc/`.)

Estimating clusters with Kernel Density Estimation

If the k-means algorithm doesn't appeal to you, one alternative way to identify clusters in your data is to use a density smoothing function instead. *Kernel density estimation* (KDE) is just such a smoothing method; it works by placing a *kernel* — a weighting function that is useful for quantifying density — on each data point in the data set and then summing the kernels to generate a kernel density estimate for the overall region. Areas of greater point density will sum out with greater kernel density, while areas of lower point density will sum out with less kernel density.

Because kernel smoothing methods don't rely on cluster center placement and clustering techniques to estimate clusters, they don't exhibit a risk of generating erroneous clusters by placing centers in areas of local minimum density. Where k-means algorithms generate hard-lined definitions between points in different clusters, KDE generates a plot of gradual density change between data points. For this reason, it's a helpful aid when eyeballing clusters. Figure 5-4 shows what the World Bank Income and Education scatter plot looks like after a KDE has been applied.

Figure 5-4: A KDE smoothing of the World Bank's Income and Education data scatter plot.

Percentage of children who complete primary school

Percentage of income earned by bottom 10% of population (2000-2003 median)

In Figure 5-4, you can see that the white spaces between clusters have been reduced. Looking at the figure, it's fairly obvious that there are at least three clusters, and possibly more, if you want to allow for small clusters.

Clustering with hierarchical and neighborhood algorithms

A hierarchical clustering algorithm — yet another alternative to k-means algorithms — results in a dataset that's called a *dendrogram* — the top, or *root,* of a dendrogram is the entire dataset, each level down is a node where the data is split into two sets (usually of unequal size), and finally at the bottom are leaves that each correspond to a single data point. You can use a number of different algorithms to build a dendrogram, and the algorithm you choose dictates where and how branching occurs within the clusters.

If you want to get started working with hierarchical clustering algorithms, check out R's hclust package or (yet again) Python's SciPy library. (If you're curious about hclust, check out https://stat.ethz.ch/R-manual/R-patched/library/stats/html/hclust.html.

In the example dendrogram that's shown in Figure 5-5, it appears that the underlying dataset has either three or four clusters. Dendrograms can be built either *bottom-up* (by assembling pairs of points together and then agglomerating them into larger and larger groups) or *top-down* (by starting with the full dataset and splitting into smaller and smaller groups).

Hierarchical clustering algorithms are more computationally expensive than k-means algorithms because with each iteration of hierarchical clustering, many points must be compared to many other points. The benefit, however, is that hierarchical clustering algorithms are not subject to errors caused by center convergence at areas of local minimum density (as exhibited with the k-means clustering algorithms).

Neither k-means nor hierarchical clustering algorithms perform well when clusters are *non-globular* — a configuration where some points in a cluster are closer to points in a different cluster than they are to points in the center of their own cluster.

If your dataset shows non-globular clustering, then you can use neighborhood clustering algorithms, like DBSCAN, to determine whether each point is closer to its neighbors in the same cluster, or whether it is closer to its neighboring data points in other clusters. (Figure 5-6 shows an example of neighborhood clustering.)

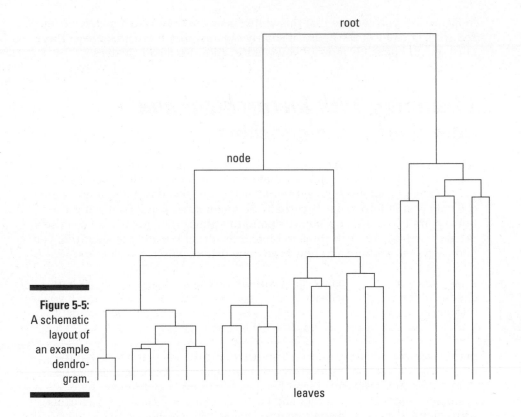

Figure 5-5:
A schematic
layout of
an example
dendro-
gram.

If you can't wait to get started worked with hierarchical clustering algorithms, check out R's `fpc` package or Python's `SciKit` library. (For more on R's `fpc` package, check out `http://cran.r-project.org/web/packages/fpc/fpc.pdf`; for more on Python's `SciKit` library, check out `http://scikit-learn.org/stable/modules/clustering.html`.)

Neighborhood clustering algorithms are very effective, but they are subject to the two following weaknesses:

- ✔ Neighborhood clustering can be very computationally expensive because, at every iteration of this method, every data point might have to be compared to every other data point in the dataset.

- ✔ With neighborhood clustering, you might have to provide the model with empirical parameter values for expected cluster size and cluster density. If you guess either of these parameters incorrectly, the algorithm misidentifies clusters, and you have to start the whole long process over again to fix the problem. If you choose to use the DBSCAN method, then you're required to specify these parameters. (As an alternative, you could try the average nearest neighbor and k-nearest neighbor algorithms that are discussed in Chapter 6.)

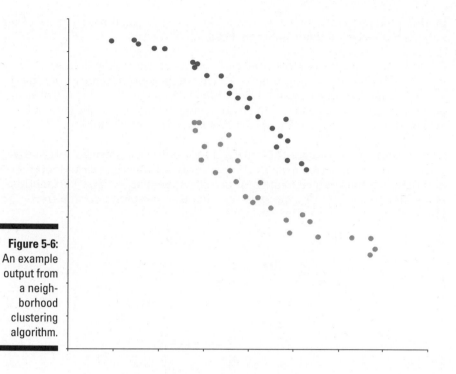

Figure 5-6:
An example
output from
a neigh-
borhood
clustering
algorithm.

To avoid making poor guesses for the cluster size and cluster density parameters, you can use a quick k-means algorithm to first determine plausible values.

Categorizing data with decision tree and random forest algorithms

In cases where other clustering algorithms fail, decision tree and random forest algorithms might just offer you a perfect solution.

At certain times, you can get stuck trying to cluster and classify data from a non-numerical dataset. It's times like these that you can use a decision tree model to help you cluster and classify your data correctly. A decision tree algorithm works by developing a set of yes or no rules that you can follow for new data in order to see exactly how it will be characterized by the model. But you must be careful when using decision tree models, because they run a high risk of what is referred to as *error propagation*. This occurs when one of the model rules is incorrect. Errors are generated in the results of decisions made based on that incorrect rule, and then propagated through every other subsequent decision made along that branch of the tree.

To illustrate this type of algorithm, consider a dataset that's often used in machine learning demonstrations — the list of passenger names from the *Titanic*. Using a simple decision tree model, you can predict that if a passenger was female or was a male child with a large family, he or she probably survived the catastrophe. Figure 5-7 illustrates this determination.

Lastly, random forest algorithms are a slower but more powerful alternative. Instead of building a tree from the data, the algorithm creates random trees and then determines which one best classifies the testing data. This method eliminates the risk of error propagation that is inherent in decision tree models.

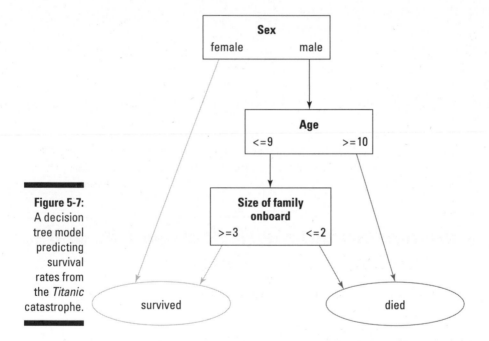

Figure 5-7:
A decision tree model predicting survival rates from the *Titanic* catastrophe.

Chapter 6

Clustering and Classification with Nearest Neighbor Algorithms

In This Chapter

▶ Seeing the benefits of nearest neighbor analysis

▶ Tackling clustering

▶ Working through average nearest neighbor algorithms

▶ Mastering the core features and characteristics of k-nearest neighbor algorithms

▶ Seeing how nearest neighbor algorithms can be used in the retail sector

*Y*our plain-vanilla clustering and classification algorithms can help you subdivide your datasets so that you can build predictive models that you can then use to classify future data points. But there's more to life than plain vanilla. I think it's about time we take things one step further by exploring the more subtle nuances of clustering and classification algorithms. More specifically, this chapter introduces some deeper classification concepts as they relate to the average nearest neighbor and k-nearest neighbor algorithms.

Making Sense of Data with Nearest Neighbor Analysis

At its core, the purpose of a nearest neighbor analysis is to search for and locate either a nearest point in space or nearest numerical value, depending on the attribute you use for the basis of comparison. Since the nearest neighbor technique is a classification method, you can use it to do things as scientific as deducing the molecular structure of a vital human protein or uncovering key biological evolutionary relationships, and as business-driven as designing recommendation engines for e-commerce sites or building predictive models for consumer transactions. The applications are limitless.

A good analogy for the nearest neighbor analysis concept is illustrated in GPS technology. Imagine you're in desperate need of a Starbucks iced latte, but you have no idea where the nearest Starbucks is located. What do you do? One easy solution is simply to ask your smartphone where the nearest Starbucks is located.

When you do that, the system looks for businesses named Starbucks within a reasonable proximity of your current location. After generating a results listing, the system reports back to you with the address of the Starbucks coffeehouse closest to your current location — the Starbucks that is your nearest neighbor, in other words.

As the term *nearest neighbor* implies, the primary purpose of a nearest neighbor analysis is to examine your dataset and find the data point that's quantitatively most similar to your observation data point. Note that similarity comparisons can be based on any quantitative attribute, whether that be distance, age, income, weight, or anything else that can describe the data point you're investigating. The simplest comparative attribute is distance.

In the above Starbucks analogy, the *x, y, z* coordinates of the Starbucks reported to you by your smartphone are the most similar to the *x, y, z* coordinates of your current location. In other words, its location is closest in actual physical distance. The quantitative *attribute* being compared is distance, your current location is the *observation data point,* and the reported Starbucks coffeehouse is the *most similar feature*.

Modern nearest neighbor analyses are almost always performed using computational algorithms. The nearest neighbor algorithm is known as a *single-link algorithm* — an algorithm that merges clusters if the clusters share at least one *connective edge* (a shared boundary line, in other words) between them. In the following sections, you can learn the basics of the average nearest neighbor algorithm and the k-nearest neighbor algorithm.

Seeing the Importance of Clustering and Classification

The purpose of clustering and classification algorithms is to make sense of and extract value from large sets of structured and unstructured data. If you're working with huge volumes of unstructured data, it only makes sense to try to partition the data into some sort of logical groupings before attempting to analyze it. Clustering and classification allows you to take a sweeping glance of your data en masse, and then form some logical structures based on what you find there before going deeper into the nuts-and-bolts analysis.

In their simplest form, *clusters* are sets of data points that share similar attributes, and *clustering algorithms* are the methods that group these data points into different clusters based on their similarities. You'll see clustering algorithms used for disease classification in medical science, but you'll also see them used for customer classification in marketing research and for environmental health risk assessment in environmental engineering.

There are different clustering methods, depending on how you want your dataset to be divided. The two main types of clustering algorithms are

- ✔ **Hierarchical:** Algorithms create separate sets of nested clusters, each in their own hierarchal level.
- ✔ **Partitional:** Algorithms create just a single set of clusters.

You can use hierarchical clustering algorithms only if you already know the separation distance between the data points in your dataset. The k-nearest neighbor algorithm that's described in this chapter belongs to the hierarchical class of clustering algorithms.

You might have heard of classification and thought that classification is the same thing as clustering. Many people do, but this is not the case. In classification, before you start, you already know the number of classes into which your data should be grouped and you already know what class you want each data point to be assigned. In classification, the data in the dataset being learned from is labeled. When you use clustering algorithms, on the other hand, you have no predefined concept for how many clusters are appropriate for your data, and you rely upon the clustering algorithms to sort and cluster the data in the most appropriate way. With clustering techniques, you're learning from unlabeled data.

To better illustrate the nature of classification, though, I'm going to make an example that's closer to home — I mean, of course, Twitter. Twitter and its hash-tagging system is a terrific analogy for classification. Say you just got ahold of your favorite drink in the entire world; an iced caramel latte from Starbucks. You're so happy to have your drink that you decide to tweet about it with a photo and the phrase "This is the best latte EVER! #StarbucksRocks." Well, of course you include "#StarbucksRocks" in your tweet so that the tweet goes into the #StarbucksRocks stream and is classified together with all the other tweets that have been labeled as #StarbucksRocks. Your use of the hashtag label in your tweet told Twitter how to classify your data into a recognizable and accessible group, or *cluster*.

Classifying Data with Average Nearest Neighbor Algorithms

Average nearest neighbor algorithms are basic, yet powerful, classification algorithms, useful for finding and classifying data points that are most similar on average. Average nearest neighbor algorithms are used in pattern recognition, in chemical and biological structural analysis, and in spatial data modeling. They're most often used in biology, chemistry, engineering, and geosciences.

In the following sections, you can find out how to use average nearest neighbor algorithms to compare multiple attributes between data points and, subsequently, identify which of your dataset's data points are most similar. You can also find out how to use average nearest neighbor algorithms to identify significant patterns in your dataset.

Understanding how the average nearest neighbor algorithm works

The purpose of using an average nearest neighbor algorithm is to determine average similarities between data points in your dataset, based on a similarity comparison of attributes shared between them. If your goal is to identify and group data points according to average similarity, then the average nearest neighbor algorithm is a great way to do that.

Exploring the basic concepts in average nearest neighbor algorithms

You can use average nearest neighbor algorithms to compare the qualitative or quantitative data points of your choosing. With respect to nearest neighbor classifiers, a dataset is comprised of data points and each data point is comprised of an x- and y-variable. The x-variable represents the input value and the y-variable represents the data label.

To keep all these terms straight, consider a few concrete examples: If you're looking at an organizational management dataset, then the data points might represent employee identification numbers, while your *labels* — the comparative attributes, in other words — could be wage rate, productivity, and seniority. If you're doing market research, then the data points could represent the customer identification number, while your labels could be average dollars spent, age, and family size. Or, if you're an immunologist, your data points could represent a type of viral strain, and your labels could be length, virility, and viability.

An advantage of classifying with average similarity values is that the clusters usually come out pretty well-formed and easily accessible, compared to the chained clusters that are formed using a nearest neighbor chaining algorithm.

The attributes you use as a basis to compare your data points must be quantitative, but the data points you choose to compare can represent either a quantitative or qualitative category.

To bring all this technical jargon to life, the following section looks at a simple example of using average nearest neighbor algorithms in data science for business applications.

Comparing average similarities with Business Analyst Stu

Your friendly neighborhood business analyst, Business Analyst Stu by name, is using average nearest neighbor algorithms to perform a classification analysis of datasets in his organization's database. In particular, he's comparing employees based on their age, number of children, annual income, and seniority. Here, each employee in Stu's organization is a four-dimensional *tuple* — or, data points — in the sample dataset, and each attribute corresponds to a dimension.

As you can see from Table 6-1, Employee Mike can be represented with the tuple (34, 1, 120000, 9), Employee Liz can be represented with the tuple (42, 0, 90000, 5), Employee Jin can be represented with the tuple (22, 0, 60000, 2), and Employee Mary can be represented with the tuple (53, 3, 180000, 30). Using these four tuples for Employee Mike, Employee Liz, Employee Jin, and Employee Mary, Business Analyst Stu can generate values to represent the distance between each of the employees, based on the differences in their attributes. Table 6-1 shows the Employee dataset with which Stu is working and Figure 6-1 shows the calculated distances between the employees in that dataset.

Table 6-1	Business Analyst Stu's Employee Data			
Employee Name	**Age**	**Number of Children**	**Annual Income**	**Seniority**
Mike	34	1	$120,000	9
Liz	42	0	$90,000	5
Jin	22	0	$60,000	2
Mary	53	3	$180,000	30

Mike	34	1	120000	9
Liz	42	0	90000	5
Distance	**8**	**1**	**30000**	**4**
Mike	34	1	120000	9
Jin	22	0	60000	2
Distance	**12**	**1**	**60000**	**7**
Mike	34	1	120000	9
Mary	53	3	180000	30
Distance	**19**	**2**	**60000**	**21**
Liz	42	0	90000	5
Jin	22	0	60000	2
Distance	**20**	**0**	**30000**	**3**
Liz	42	0	90000	5
Mary	53	3	180000	30
Distance	**11**	**3**	**90000**	**25**
Jin	22	0	60000	2
Mary	53	3	180000	30
Distance	**31**	**3**	**120000**	**28**

Figure 6-1: The distances between the employees' tuples.

After Business Analyst Stu has this measure of distance between the employees based on similarities between their attributes, he continues clustering the data using the same steps as before. But now, rather than using the nearest neighbor similarity measure, he takes an average of the separation distances between the attributes being compared and uses that averaged value as a measure of the average similarity between the employees. Figure 6-2 shows that average similarity.

Finding Average Similarities	
Average Distance (Mike - Liz)	
Average Distance Value - (Average of 8, 1, 30000, 4)	7503.25
Average Distance (Mike - Jin)	
Average Distance Value - (Average of 12, 1, 60000, 7)	15005
Average Distance (Mike - Mary)	
Average Distance Value - (Average of 19, 2, 60000, 21)	15010.5
Average Distance (Liz - Jin)	
Average Distance Value - (Average of 20, 0, 30000, 3)	7505.75
Average Distance (Liz - Mary)	
Average Distance Value - (Average of 11, 3, 90000, 25)	22509.75
Average Distance (Jin - Mary)	
Average Distance Value - (Average of)	30015.5

Figure 6-2: Finding the average similarity between the employees.

He then groups the employees according to the average similarity values between them. Because the average distance value between Mike, Liz, and Jin is the smallest, this means that Mike, Liz, and Jin have the most average similarity. Business Analyst Stu goes ahead and groups Mike, Liz, and Jin in Cluster A, while he classifies Mary into Cluster B.

Classifying with K-Nearest Neighbor Algorithms

Machine learning — all the rage these days — is the class of artificial intelligence that's dedicated to developing and applying algorithms to data so that the algorithms can automatically learn and detect patterns in large datasets. In the larger context of machine learning, K-nearest neighbor is what's known as a *lazy* machine learning algorithm — in other words, it has little to no training phase. It simply memorizes training data and then uses that information as the basis on which to classify new data points. The goal of the k-nearest neighbor is to estimate the class of the query point P based on the classes of its k-nearest neighbors. In this way, the k-nearest neighbor works in ways quite similar to how the human brain works.

Think of how you treat a stove burner. You generally avoid touching or placing objects on top of a burner, right? Well, that's because your brain has observed that burners are hot and that they burn things. Instead of investigating whether a burner is on or is warm, most people take the lazy approach, classify it as dangerous (based on previous experience), and avoid contact.

The k-nearest neighbor (known affectionately as kNN) algorithm is just a generalization of the nearest neighbor algorithm. Instead of considering the nearest neighbor, you consider k-nearest neighbors from a dataset containing *n* data points — *k* defines how many nearest neighbors will have an influence on the classification process. In kNN, the classifier classifies the query point P according to the classification labels found in a majority of k-nearest points surrounding the query point.

kNN is a good classification method for you to use if you know very little about the distribution of your dataset. What's more, if you do have a solid idea about your dataset's distribution and feature selection criteria — or algorithm criteria to identify and remove noise in the dataset — then you can leverage this information to create significant enhancements in the algorithm's performance.

kNN is among the simplest and most easy-to-implement classification methods, yet it yields competitive results when compared to some of the most sophisticated machine-learning methods. Probably because of its simplicity and because of the competitive results it provides, the kNN algorithm has been ranked among the top ten most influential data mining algorithms in the research community.

Understanding how the k-nearest neighbor algorithm works

To use k-nearest neighbor (kNN), you simply need to pick a query point — usually called *P* — in the sample dataset and then compute the k-nearest neighbors to this point. The query point P is classified with a label that's the same as the label of the majority of k-nearest points that surround it. (Figure 6-3 gives a bird's eye view of the process.)

K-nearest neighbors are quantified by either distance or similarity based on some other quantitative attribute.

Consider the following example: A dataset is given by [1, 1, 4, 3, 5, 2, 6, 2, 4] and point *P* is equal to 5. Figure 6-3 shows how kNN would be applied to this dataset.

Now, if you were to specify that *k* is equal to 3, then based on distance, there are three nearest neighbors to the point 5. Those neighbors are 4, 4, and 6. So based on the k-nearest neighbor (kNN) algorithm, query point *P* will be classified as 4 because 4 is the majority number in the *k* number of points nearest to it. Similarly, the kNN goes on defining other query points using the same majority principle.

When using kNN, it's crucial that you choose a *k* value that minimizes *noise* — unexplainable random variation, in other words. At the same time, it's vital that you choose a *k* value that includes sufficient data points in the selection process. If your data points aren't uniformly distributed, then it's generally harder to predetermine a good *k* value. You'll need to be careful to select an optimum *k* value for each dataset you're analyzing.

Large *k* values tend to produce less noise and more *boundary smoothing* — clearer definition and less overlap — between classes than small *k* values do.

Figure 6-3:
How kNN
works.

Knowing when to use the k-nearest neighbor algorithm

kNN is particularly useful for *multi-label learning* — supervised learning where the algorithm is applied so that it automatically *learns from* — detects patterns in — multiple sets of instances, each potentially with several classes of their own, so that the algorithm learns how to predict class labels for each new instance it encounters.

The problem with kNN is that it takes a lot longer than other classification methods to classify a sample. Because nearest neighbor classifier performance depends on the distance function and the value of the neighborhood parameter k, you can get around this slow performance time by specifying optimal values for k and n. As with other hierarchical algorithms, you want to use kNN only on datasets that have a few thousand data points or less.

Exploring common applications of k-nearest neighbor algorithms

kNN is often used for Internet database management purposes. In this capacity, kNN is useful for website categorization, web-page ranking, and other user dynamics across the web.

kNN classification techniques are also quite beneficial in customer relationship management (CRM). CRM is a set of processes that ensures a business sustains improved relationships with its clients, while simultaneously experiencing increased business revenues. Most CRMs get tremendous benefit from using kNN to data-mine customer information to find patterns that are useful in boosting customer retention.

The method is so versatile that, even if you're a small business owner or a marketing department manager, you can easily use kNN to boost your own marketing return on investment. Simply use kNN to analyze your customer data for purchasing patterns, and then use those findings to customize marketing initiatives so they're more exactly targeted for your customer base.

Using Nearest Neighbor Distances to Infer Meaning from Point Patterns

Distance-based point pattern measurement, as in nearest neighbor algorithms, is useful for describing the *second order effects* inherent within a dataset — those effects caused by interactions between data points in a dataset. Most of the time, you probably wouldn't know that your data points are influencing one another, but you can test for this kind of influence by using nearest neighbor distances to draw inferences from point patterns.

To illustrate the idea of second order effects within a dataset, consider a dataset that describes the spread of Ebola in Sierra Leone populations. Population density is definitely a risk factor for the spread of Ebola within the community, due to the fact that the disease is more likely to spread when infected people are in close proximity to non-infected people. The spread of Ebola is an effect that's directly caused by interactions between "data points" — the individuals in an Ebola-affected population.

Average nearest neighbor algorithms calculate a descriptive index value that represents the average distance between a data point and its nearest neighbor. If the calculated index value is less than 1, then the data is said to show *clustered patterning.* If the index value is greater than 1, then the data is said to show *dispersion patterning.*

So how can you detect interactions between data points? You have to look at the patterns within the data. Clustered patterning indicates that there is some sort of interaction going on between the data points and that this interaction is causing an increase in average similarity values. The easiest way to understand this concept is to think of two oppositely charged magnets in close, proximate distance of one another. If you look at the descriptive index value for the magnets and see that it is less than 1, then you can even assume that the magnets are of the opposite charge — and thus attracting one another — just based on this index value alone.

In dispersion patterning, on the other hand, interaction between the data points causes a decrease in average similarity values. Going back to the magnets analogy, this time the two magnets repel one another. If you look at the descriptive index value for the magnets and see that it is greater than 1, then you can assume that the magnets are of like charge — and thus repelling one another.

Solving Real-World Problems with Nearest Neighbor Algorithms

Hierarchical clustering algorithms — and nearest neighbor methods, in particular — are used extensively to understand and create value from patterns in retail business data. In the following sections, I present two powerful cases where these simple algorithms are being used to simplify management and security in daily retail operations.

Seeing k-nearest neighbor algorithms in action

K-nearest neighbor techniques for pattern recognition are often used for theft prevention in the modern retail business. Of course, you're accustomed to seeing CCTV cameras around almost every store you visit, but most people have no idea how the data gathered from these devices is being used.

You might imagine that there is someone in the back room monitoring these cameras for suspicious activity, and perhaps that is how things were done in the past. But today, a modern surveillance system is intelligent enough to analyze and interpret video data on its own, without a need for human assistance. The modern systems are now able to use k-nearest neighbor for visual pattern recognition to scan and detect hidden packages in the bottom bin of a shopping cart at check-out. If an object is detected that's an exact match for an object listed in the database, then the price of the spotted product could even automatically be added to the customer's bill. While this automated billing practice is not used extensively at this time, the technology has been developed and is available for use.

K-nearest neighbor is also used in retail to detect patterns in credit card usage. Many new transaction-scrutinizing software applications use kNN algorithms to analyze register data and spot unusual patterns that indicate suspicious activity. For example, if register data indicates that a lot of customer information is being entered manually rather than through automated scanning and swiping, this could indicate that the employee who's using that register is in fact stealing customer's personal information. Or if register data indicates that a particular good is being returned or exchanged multiple times, this could indicate that employees are misusing the return policy or trying to make money from doing fake returns.

Seeing average nearest neighbor algorithms in action

Average nearest neighbor algorithm classification and point pattern detection can be used in grocery retail to identify key patterns in customer purchasing behavior, and subsequently increase sales and customer satisfaction by anticipating customer behavior. Consider the following story:

> As with other grocery stores, buyer behavior at (the fictional) Waldorf Food Co-op tends to follow very fixed patterns. Managers have even commented on the odd fact that members of a particular age group tend to visit the store during the same particular time window, and they even tend to buy the same types of products.

> One day, Manager Mike got extremely proactive and decided to hire a data scientist to analyze his customer data and provide exact details about these odd trends he'd been noticing. When Data Scientist Dan got in there, he quickly uncovered a pattern among working middle-aged male adults — they tended to visit the grocery store only during the weekends or at the end of the day on weekdays, and if they came into the store on a Thursday, they almost always bought beer.

> Well, when Manager Mike was armed with these facts, he quickly used this information to maximize beer sales on Thursday evenings by offering discounts, bundles, and specials. Not only was the store owner happy with the increased revenues, but Waldorf Food Co-op's male customers were happy because they got more of what they wanted, when they wanted it.

Chapter 7

Mathematical Modeling in Data Science

A lot gets said about using statistics to solve problems in data science, but the data science community rarely mentions mathematical methods. Despite their less-than-superstar status, however, mathematical methods can be extremely helpful, especially if you're interested in building concise decision models. You can also use them to make fast approximations and to predict future values based on what you know of your present data. In this chapter, I discuss how you can use multi-criteria decision making and numerical methods, as well as Markov chains, to do all of the above.

Introducing Multi-Criteria Decision Making (MCDM)

Life is complicated. We're often forced to make decisions where several different criteria come into play, and it often seems unclear what criterion should have priority. Mathematicians, being mathematicians, have come up with a mathematical approach that you can use for decision support when you have several criteria or alternatives on which to base your decision. This mathematical technique is called *multi-criteria decision making* (MCDM, for short), and it's useful in a multitude of domains. You can use this analysis methodology in anything from stock-portfolio management to fashion-trend evaluation, from disease-outbreak control to land development decision making. Anywhere you have several criteria on which you need to base your decision, you can use MCDM methods to help you evaluate alternatives.

Understanding multi-criteria analysis by looking at it in action

The best way to get a solid grasp on MCDM is to see how it's used to solve real-world problems. Imagine a scenario where you're analyzing spatial data to evaluate potential sites for a land development project. Say you've been tasked with selecting an ideal site for the XYZ Power Company to develop their next data center. The land developers who represent XYZ Power Company have told you that you must consider the following criteria when evaluating potential development sites:

- ✔ **Proximity to major roads:** Ease of access is important, so a site will get a score of 0 or 1 based on whether it's within a 2-mile radius of a major road.

- ✔ **Proximity to water and electric utilities:** The closer the better when it comes to water and utilities, so a site will get a score of 0 or 1 based on whether it is within a 2-mile radius of major utilities.

- ✔ **Future land use (FLU) designation:** Knowing what the future brings is also important, so a site will get a 1 if it has a favorable FLU designation and a 0 if it's not quite so favorable.

- ✔ **Zoning designation:** Future use is important, but you also need favorable zoning designations in the here-and-now. A favorable zoning-class designation gets a site a 1; an unfavorable designation lands it a 0.

So, in this evaluation, each potential site is designated with an *x, y* position at the site center — this represents the geographical location of the site on a map. If you imagine that you're evaluating 20 different potential sites in your city, you'd assign each of those sites a score for each of the four criteria, and then sum those scores to generate a score for each of the sites you're evaluating. To develop a data center on a site, the site must satisfy each of the four criteria; therefore, you would dismiss any sites that do not score a 4 out of 4 in this part of the evaluation.

Let me stop here and underscore a concept that's central to the MCDM approach. That is, selection preferences are a core requisite in MCDM. You need selection preferences to distinguish between the suitability of different possible solutions on the efficient frontier. Selection preferences are not objective. In the preceding example, the site selection criteria discussed are examples of selection preferences.

In mathematics, a *set* is a group of numbers that shares some similar characteristic. In traditional set theory, membership is *binary* — in other words, an individual is either a member of a set or it's not. If the individual is a member, then it is represented with the number 1. If it is not a member, then it is represented by the number 0. MCDM is characterized by its binary membership.

As another example, MCDM is also commonly used in investment-portfolio theory. Pricing of individual financial instruments typically reflects the level of risk you incur, but an entire portfolio can be a mixture of virtually riskless investments (U.S. Government bonds, for example) and minimum-, moderate-, and high-risk investments. Your level of risk aversion will dictate the general character of your investment portfolio. Highly risk-averse investors seek safer and less lucrative investments, and less risk-averse investors choose riskier investments. In the process of evaluating the risk of a potential investment, you'd likely consider the following criteria:

- **Earnings growth potential:** Here, an investment that falls under a particular earnings growth potential threshold gets scored as a 0; anything above that threshold gets a 1.

- **Earnings quality rating:** If an investment falls within a particular ratings class for earnings quality, it gets scored as a 0; otherwise, it gets scored as a 1. (For you non–Wall Street types out there, *earnings quality* refers to various measures used to determine how kosher a company's reported earnings actually are; such measures attempt to answer the question, "Do these reported figures pass the smell test?")

- **Dividend performance:** When an investment doesn't reach a particular dividend performance threshold, it gets a 0; if it reaches or surpasses that threshold, it gets a 1.

Imagine that you're evaluating 20 different potential investments. In this evaluation, you'd score each criteria for each of the investments. To eliminate poor investment choices, simply sum the criteria scores for each of the alternatives and then dismiss any investments that do not get a total score of 3 — leaving you with the investments that fall within a certain threshold of earning growth potential, that have good earnings quality, and whose dividends perform at a level that's acceptable to you.

MCDM techniques are in no way limited to just land use issues or investment-portfolio theory. Some other real-world applications where MCDM is useful include sustainable energy development, resource management, scheduling, nuclear medicine, and oilfield development. Since MCDM is now a mature field of decision science, it's been applied to almost every area of human endeavor.

Factoring in fuzzy multi-criteria programming

You can use fuzzy multi-criteria decision making (FMCDM) to evaluate all the same types of problems as you would with MCDM. With respect to MCDM, the term *fuzzy* refers to the fact that the criteria being used to evaluate alternatives offer a range of acceptability— instead of the binary, crisp set criteria associated with traditional MCDM earlier. Evaluations based on fuzzy criteria lead to a range of potential outcomes, each with its own level of suitability as a solution. Possible solutions comprise a spectrum of suitability that's plotted on a chart as something called an *efficient frontier*.

Fuzzy-set membership is expressed as some gradation of membership. Although fuzzy-set membership can be represented by the numbers 0 and 1, it can also be represented by any number that lies between 0 and 1. The closer an individual gets to 1, the closer it is to being a full member of the fuzzy set. In fuzzy MCDM, you'd assign individuals a membership score based on your certainty or uncertainty about the state of that individual's being a member of the set. Encoding and decoding fuzzy-set membership allows a decision model to prioritize or rank individual items within that model.

The purpose of incorporating the fuzzy element into the MCDM approach is simply to build in a little more flexibility in how the decision model works when evaluating alternatives. If you want to include decision nuances and even some "gut-feel" into your decision model, you can use FMCDM. To illustrate the FMCDM concept, in the following sections, consider how you'd use this approach in the land development example discussed in the preceding section.

Understanding fuzzy multi-criteria analysis by looking at it in action

In the land development evaluation example from the section "Understanding multi-criteria analysis by looking at it in action," earlier in this chapter, you started with 20 sites, but after doing the MCDM evaluation, you're left with only 11 sites that scored a perfect 4. Now you need to evaluate which of these 11 are the most suitable for developing a large data center, so it's back to the MCDM drawing board. This time, you're going to use FMCDM to make a comparative analysis of the remaining sites based on the same class of criteria used for the MCDM evaluation:

✔ **Proximity to major roads:** With FMCDM, a site is now scored a number between or including 0 and 1, based on how close it is to a major road. The closer a site is to a major road, the closer the site scores to a perfect 1 for this criteria.

✔ **Proximity to water and electric utilities:** Again, a site is scored a number between or including 0 and 1, based on how close it is to major utilities. The closer a site is to major utilities, the closer the site scores to a perfect 1 for this criteria.

✔ **Future land use (FLU) designation:** You get the drill. Sites are scored between 0 and 1, based on the favorability of their FLU designation — ranked in order from most favorable to least favorable, or highest score to lowest.

✔ **Zoning designation:** To close things off, sites are scored between 0 and 1, based on the favorability of their zoning designation — ranked in order from most favorable to least favorable, or highest score to lowest

After evaluating each of the remaining 11 sites and scoring them based on each of the criteria, you simply need to sum the scores for each of the sites. The sites whose total scores are closest to 4 will be the most favorable sites, and the sites with lower scores will be less favorable for use as a data center development site.

Using weighting factors in FMCDM

One last point to mention about FMCDM: You're likely to have a list of several fuzzy criteria, but these criteria might not all hold the same significance in your evaluation. For example, in the site-development scenario, the developers may have told you that it's more important to them that the site be closer to major utilities than to major roads. In this situation, you'd want to make sure that the utilities-proximity criterion is weighted more heavily than the roads-proximity criterion in your evaluation. You can use weighting factors to quantify the relative significance of criteria in your decision model. The relative importance of utilities proximity and roads proximity might look something like the following:

1.0 × Fuzzy score for proximity to major utilities = Site score for utility-proximity criteria

0.5 × Fuzzy score for proximity to major roads = Site score for roads-proximity criteria

The weighting factors are represented by the multipliers at the start of each of the equations shown above.

Knowing when and how to use MCDM

You can use MCDM whenever you have two or more criteria you need to evaluate to make a sound decision based on underlying datasets. In practice, MCDM and FMCDM are usually integrated into one well-rounded decision model. For the rest of this section, when I refer to MCDM, I'm referring to decision models that utilize both binary and fuzzy sets. You can use the

MCDM method to help you derive an efficient solution in the face of several competing alternatives.

To use multi-criteria decision making (MCDM), the following two criteria must be met:

✔ **Multi-criteria evaluation:** You must have more than one criterion that you need to optimize.

✔ **Zero-sum system:** Optimizing with respect to one criterion must come at the sacrifice of at least one other criterion. This means that there must be tradeoffs between criteria — to gain with respect to one means losing with respect to at least one other.

The best way to explain how MCDM works in the real world is through a simple illustration. Figure 7-1 is a graphical representation of a multiple-criteria problem that includes a simple linear criteria and two decision variables, *x* and *y*. Imagine that the *x*-variable and *y*-variable here represent quantity values for two manufactured products and that the manufacturer is trying to decide on the optimal quantities for each of the products. In this example, the manufacturer's criteria would be

Optimal Quantity: Product 1 — shown on the *x*-axis

Optimal Quantity: Product 2 — shown on the *y*-axis

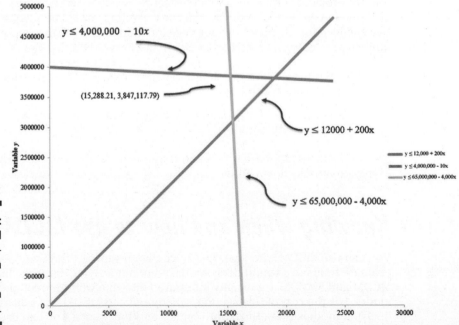

Figure 7-1:
A graphical representation of a multiple-criteria problem.

To understand what's happening in this problem, take note of the following features. First off, each line in Figure 7-1 actually represents an *inequality* — the solution includes all points on the lines, as well as any points within graphical regions that also satisfy the inequality. As an example of this concept, check out where exactly — on what side of the lines — you can find the origin $(x, y) = (0, 0)$. The *solution space* contains all points that satisfy the inequalities, plus it also includes the places where $x \geq 0$ and $y \geq 0$. This final solution space is shown as the shaded region in Figure 7-2.

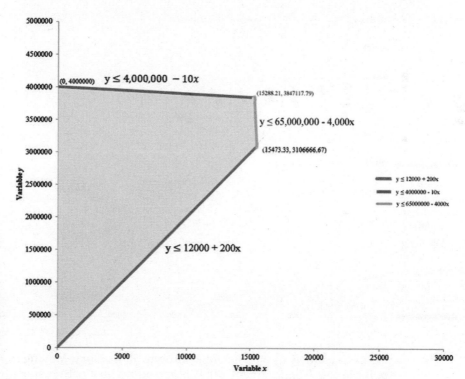

Figure 7-2: The solution space (shaded) that satisfies the inequality.

As you can see in this example, A MCDM evaluation doesn't have just one optimal solution. Instead, you end up with many efficient solutions all caught up in a zero-sum system — in other words, for each solution where you improve with respect to one criterion, you must always give up or lose something with respect to another criterion. This is the *efficient frontier*.

Figure 7-3 shows how you would find the efficient frontier in the manufacturing optimization MCDM analysis.

The (x, y) solutions that are not on the efficient frontier are said to be *dominated* by those that are. Although the equation $y \le 12{,}000 + 200x$ appears to be one of the criteria, a quick gander at every point on this line quickly shows that you can get a better result by going with one of the other lines.

Figure 7-3:
Finding the efficient frontier in the manufacturing optimization MCDM analysis.

Figure 7-4 shows us an efficient frontier in all its glory. Moving from any point in this frontier to any other represents a gain with respect to one criterion and a loss with respect to the other. So in the manufacturing example, if you choose to manufacture less of product y, then the optimized solution along the efficient frontier will suggest that you should manufacture more of product x. Which point you choose depends on the subjective valuations of the decision model. The efficient frontier is the central concept of MCDM.

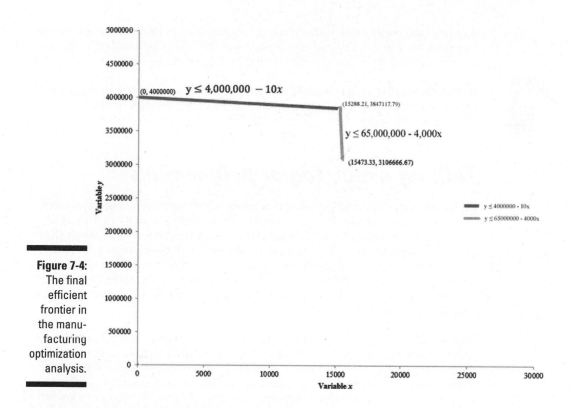

Figure 7-4:
The final efficient frontier in the manufacturing optimization analysis.

Using Numerical Methods in Data Science

In data science, numerical approximation methods provide a standardized approach that you can use to quickly find simplified solutions to complex mathematical problems.

The term *numerical methods* is often used in the literature. This generally refers to numerical approximation and related techniques.

With *approximations,* you generate approximate solutions that are "close enough." Because these near-optimal solutions usually function just as well as an optimal solution would, you don't need to use more elaborate and complicated methods to find a more exact solution. In the following sections, I discuss how to use Taylor polynomials and the bisection method to generate time-saving approximations that are useful in data science.

In this discussion about numerical methods for data science, I've made the assumption that you have a basic grasp of concepts that are central to algebra and calculus.

Talking about Taylor polynomials

Taylor polynomials and Taylor series are a fundamental concept in modern calculus. A *Taylor series* is a power series representation of a function that serves as an approximation method for finding a function's value when that value is generated by summing its derivatives at any given degree, *n*. The *Taylor polynomial* is the polynomial function that forms the basis of a Taylor series, and it's expanded when you take *n* number of derivatives to solve a Taylor series problem. Use a Taylor series to approximate the value of a function simply by looking at its first few terms.

Taylor polynomials are useful in science because you can use them to form quick estimates for the value of a function in any given region of interest. In data science, it's common for a practitioner to have some rough knowledge about what part of the solution space holds the optimal solution. Taylor polynomials offer a standardized method by which you can use your knowledge of the solution space to generate a quick approximation for the value of the function in that region.

To illustrate the Taylor series and Taylor polynomial concept, imagine you've got a really complicated function *f(x)* (see Figure 7-5) and you want to find the value of this function near the number *a*. You can use a Taylor polynomial to do that.

Figure 7-5:
The standard form of a Taylor polynomial.

$$P_n(x) = f(a) + \frac{f'(a)}{1!}(x-a) + \frac{f''(a)}{2!}(x-a)^2 + \cdots + \frac{f^{(n)}}{n!}(x-a)^n$$

In the standard form of a Taylor polynomial, *f'(a), f"(a), and f"⁽ⁿ⁾(a)* are the first, second, and *n*th derivatives of the function *f(x)*, respectively, and *n!* is *n factorial* — meaning $n \cdot n{-}1 \cdot n{-}2 \cdot \ldots \cdot 2 \cdot$.

Use Taylor's polynomial to see how *f(x)* behaves near *x* = 0. You can make the *degree* — that is the power, *n* — of the Taylor polynomial as high as you want. The higher you go, the more accurate your approximation value will be. Just keep in mind that higher *n* values do incur greater computational costs, and if the approximated value doesn't change significantly with increases in *n*, then you don't need to continue taking further derivations.

Imagine now that you select a polynomial of degree 3 — *n* = 3. To approximate *f(x)*, just follow these steps:

1. **Let *p(a)* = *f(a)*, *p'(a)* = *f'(a)*, and *p"(a)* = *f"(a)*.**
2. **Expand the Taylor polynomial.**

   The expanded equation is shown in Figure 7-6.
3. **Simplify the equation.**

   The equation here simplifies to $p(x) = 1 + x + x^2 + x^3$.
4. **Graph the Taylor polynomial and the function.**

Figure 7-6:
A Taylor polynomial expanded to the third derivative — *n* = 3.

$$p(x) = f(0) + (x - 0)f'(0) + (x - 0)^2 \frac{f''(0)}{2} + (x - 0)^3 \frac{f'''(0)}{3 \cdot 2}$$

When you graph both *p(x)* and *f(x)* near *x* = 0, it yields the chart shown in Figure 7-7. Notice how close the value for the Taylor polynomial, *p(x)*, is to the value of *f(x)* at the point where *x* = 0. This closeness indicates that the Taylor polynomial generates a good approximation of the function at this point.

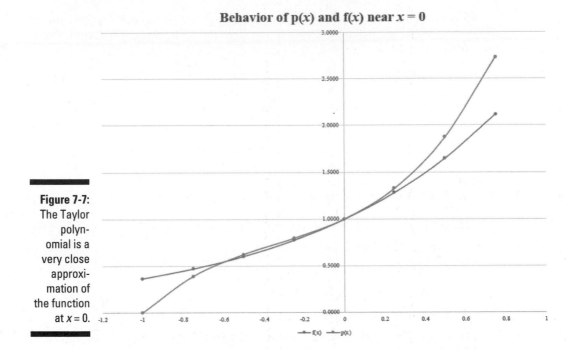

Figure 7-7:
The Taylor polynomial is a very close approximation of the function at *x* = 0.

Bisecting functions with the bisection search algorithm

A bisecting search algorithm is a method for bisecting intervals and searching for input values of a continuous function. Data scientists use a bisection search algorithm as a numerical approach to find a quick approximation of a solution. (See Figure 7-8.) The algorithm does this by searching and finding the roots of any continuous mathematical function — it's the simplest root finding method that's available. This algorithm also functions as an ideal way to quickly find the midpoint in a dataset.

The bisection search algorithm is particularly relevant in cases in which you're seeking to generate an approximation for a root of an *irrational number* — a number that has no finite root. In these situations, the algorithm will compute the minimum degree of accuracy that the root approximation needs in order to be valid.

To illustrate how the bisection method could be used in the real world, imagine the physics that cause a hot air balloon to rise. With a hot air balloon, the balloon's burner heats the air inside the balloon, resulting in a decrease in air density. Since the air inside the balloon is less dense than the atmospheric air, the less dense air (plus the balloon and its passengers) rises. Using the bisection method to bisect a function describing balloon altitude as a function of mass lifted, it's possible for you to predict an approximate balloon altitude based on what you know about the mass of the balloon and its passengers.

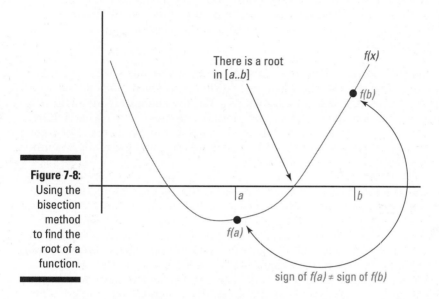

Figure 7-8:
Using the
bisection
method
to find the
root of a
function.

To get started using bisection search in R, you'd simply define your function and variables. R's base package can handle bisection procedures just fine. If you prefer working in Python, you can use the `bisect` method of the `SciPy` library to get the job done. (For more on the SciPy library, check out `http://docs.scipy.org/doc/`.)

Mathematical Modeling with Markov Chains and Stochastic Methods

Imagine that you love to travel but that you travel only to places that are a) a tropical paradise, b) ultramodern cities, or c) mountainous in their majesty. When choosing where to travel next, you always make your decisions according to the following rules:

- You travel exactly once every two months.

- If you travel somewhere tropical today, next you will travel to an ultramodern city (with a probability of 7/10) or to a place in the mountains (with a probability of 3/10), but you will not travel to another tropical paradise next.

✔ If you travel to an ultramodern city today, you will travel next to a tropical paradise or a mountainous region with equal probability, but definitely not to another ultramodern city.

✔ If you travel to the mountains today, you will travel next to a tropical paradise (with probability of 7/10) or an ultramodern city (with a probability of 2/10) or a different mountainous region (with a probability of 1/10).

Because your choice on where to travel tomorrow depends solely on where you travel today and not where you've traveled in the past, you can use a special kind of statistical model known as a Markov chain to model your destination decision making. (More on Markov chains in a bit.) What's more, you could use this model to generate statistics to predict how many of your future vacation days you will spend traveling to a tropical paradise, a mountainous majesty, or an ultramodern city.

Looking a little closer at what's going on here, the above-described scenario represents both a stochastic model and a Markov chain method. A *stochastic model* is a tool that you can use to estimate probable outcomes when one or more model variables is changed randomly. The model includes one or more random variables and shows how changes in these variables affect the predicted outcomes. A Markov chain — also called a *discreet time Markov chain* — is a stochastic process that acts as a mathematical method to chain together a series of randomly generated variables representing the present state in order to model how changes in those present state variables affect future states. In Markov methods, future states must depend on the value of the present state and be conditionally independent from all past states.

You can use Markov chains as a data science tool by building a model that generates predictive estimates for the value of future data points based on what you know about the value of the current data points in a dataset. To predict future states based solely on what's happening in the current state of a system, use Markov chains. Markov chains are extremely useful in modeling a variety of real-world processes. They're commonly used in stock-market exchange models, in financial asset-pricing models, in speech-to-text recognition systems, in webpage search and rank systems, in thermodynamic systems, in gene-regulation systems, in state-estimation models, for pattern recognition, and for population modeling.

An important method in Markov chains is in Markov chain Monte Carlo (MCMC) processes. A Markov chain will eventually reach a *steady state* — a long-term set of probabilities for the chain's states. You can use this characteristic to derive probability distributions and then sample from those distributions by using Monte Carlo sampling to generate long-term estimates of future states. (Chapter 4 includes an in-depth discussion of Monte Carlo methods.)

Chapter 8

Modeling Spatial Data with Statistics

T he average person's experience with spatial data goes no further than querying locations on Google Maps or checking in on Facebook from cool places around town. People with expertise in computer science, geo sciences, environmental engineering, criminal science, or epidemiology are likely to have experience using spatial data for basic quantitative analysis and visualization, but that is generally done using GIS software. (For more on GIS and mapmaking, check out Chapter 13 of this book.) This chapter goes above and beyond the offerings of Google Maps or Facebook. Get ready to find out how you can use advanced statistics to make models that can help you predict spatial dataset attribute values based on a feature's location coordinates.

Generating Predictive Surfaces from Spatial Point Data

Most spatial data analyses don't involve predictive modeling and can therefore be carried out in a standard Geographic Information Systems (GIS) software application. But in some instances, you may need to do more advanced analyses to predict values at particular locations based on known values of points that are in close proximity. In these situations, you can get truly accurate results only by implementing statistical modeling to generate predictive, raster surfaces across the area of interest.

A *raster surface* is a continuous surface that visually represents the x-, y-, and z- values of a spatial dataset by distributing those values across a grid of equally-sized squares. With spatial data, the x- and y- coordinates represent a feature's location on Earth, and the z-coordinate represents an attribute of the data — this could be altitude, or any other numerical attribute that belongs to the dataset being mapped.

Learning how to use statistics to generate predictive spatial data surfaces is not easy, but this skill can be very valuable — particularly if you're using data science in the context of the earth sciences. You can use these techniques to do anything from predicting an area from which uranium can be mined to predicting the spatial spread of incurable TB in India.

It's powerful stuff and, after you get a handle on it, it's not really *that* hard. To get started, you need to grasp the basic concepts involved in modeling x-, y-, and z-parameters in spatial data, and you need to develop a firm understanding of various kriging methods and variograms. Other topics such as krige and trend surface analysis are useful also, although they aren't likely to provide you the sort of accuracy you need to strike gold.

The terms "Kriging" and "krige" are here used to denote different things. *Kriging* methods are a set of statistical estimation algorithms that curve-fit known point data and produce a predictive surface for an entire study area. *Krige* represents an automatic implementation of kriging algorithms, where you use simple default parameters to help you generate predictive surfaces. Etymologically, the term "kriging" was adopted in the 60's to celebrate the contribution of a South African mining engineer, Danie G. Krige, to the development of this technique.

Understanding the (x, y, z) of spatial data modeling

The purpose of taking the time required to understand the x-, y-, and z-parameters in spatial data modeling is so that you can use this knowledge to help you model changes in your chosen parameter across space. With a solid understanding of spatial data and x-, y-, and z- parameter modeling, you can do things like model land surface elevations (such as on a topographic map) or changes in disease incidence across an area of land.

Spatial data modeling is unique because it requires you to simultaneously model at least three spatially-dependent parameters. The x- and y-parameters are used to model the physical location of the data being analyzed. Sometimes you'll be working with x- and y-parameters that are in units of latitude and longitude, other times they'll be expressed as decimal degrees. Since kriging is based on the concept of distance, it is useful to project first your x- and y-parameters so that distances are expressed in meaningful units, such as feet or meters instead of decimal degrees. Whatever the case, you use x- and y-parameters to describe the position of your z-parameter on the surface of the Earth.

As for the z-parameter, you use it to model any attribute that belongs to your spatial dataset. Your spatial dataset might have data for many different types of attributes; therefore, you could potentially model each of these attributes separately as its own z-parameter.

Z-parameters represent attributes or characteristics of your spatial data. Because they're part of a spatial dataset, these attributes or characteristics are typically autocorrelated and spatially dependent. As an example, imagine you're an epidemiologist studying a measles outbreak in an isolated village. Since you know of a few inhabitants who are infected with measles, you know that other people living in this village have a chance of having and catching measles also. In your analysis, when you compare this village to a far-away city with no known measles outbreaks, you find that the village people have a much greater likelihood of being infected with measles than do the city people. This increased likelihood of infection is due to the phenomenon of spatial dependency and autocorrelation. Simply put, objects that are more proximate in space tend to be more similar than objects that are distant.

In other instances, you may want to model elevation data with the z-parameter, as is the case with 3D and topographic modeling. Even when you use the z-parameter to represent land elevation data, it's a spatially dependent parameter. That makes sense when you consider that places on Earth that are closer to one another are naturally more likely to share similar elevations. Likewise, places that are far away from each other are likely to have more dissimilar elevations. This is another example of spatial autocorrelation; it's a unique characteristic of spatial datasets, and it's important!

Spatial data is not random. It's spatially dependent and autocorrelated. If you're modeling spatial data, avoid statistical methods that assume your data is random.

Introducing kriging

Before getting into the nuts and bolts of kriging, I want to provide you an example of how kriging techniques are used to solve real-world problems. Imagine that you've collected hydrologic rainfall data from rainfall gauges that are stationed at various points across your county. With kriging techniques, you can take the rainfall depth data from the gauge stations and interpolate from those depths to produce an entire coverage area that predicts rainfall depths across the entire county. That would allow you to get a reliable idea about rainfall depths, even in areas where rain gauge stations aren't located. This is just one basic and easy-to-understand example of where and how kriging methods are being used, but the potential applications are innumerable.

With that out of the way, it's time to give you a more detailed and technical explanation of what kriging actually is. *Kriging* methods are a set of statistical estimation algorithms that curve-fit known point data and produce a predictive surface for an entire study area. They are used to predict for unknown values from sparse spatial datasets. Kriging methods are more commonly used for data interpolation, though they have been used for extrapolation also (with generally less accurate results). You can use predictive surfaces produced from kriging methods to predict values for points that lie anywhere within your surface area boundaries. Your predictions will be more or less accurate depending on the kriging method you choose for your particular analysis. (Note that there are two main ways to conduct spatial interpolation — krige and explicitly-defined kriging, both of which will be discussed in the following sections.)

The purpose behind using kriging methods is to produce a predictive surface for an entire study area based on a set of known points in geographic space. If your goal is to predict for an unknown z-value and you have a set of known z-values in the same proximate area, then you can use kriging algorithms to make the prediction. Using kriging methods, you can predict for things like elevation, disease risk, environmental contamination, or even mineral content of the earth at a particular location.

Krige for automated kriging interpolations

When you krige, you use variogram models with internally-defined parameters to generate interpolative, predictive surfaces. Consequently, you can generate a roughly accurate predictive surface without having to spend extra time messing with parameter selections during the estimation process. The trade-off cost is that you ignore the characteristics of your z-parameter, such as its spatial pattern.

Choosing and using models for explicitly-defined kriging interpolations

By using explicitly-defined variogram models, you can produce more accurate predictive kriging surfaces than you would through krige. Using explicitly-defined variograms provides you choices with respect to variogram models and parameters, thereby facilitating more accurate results. If your goal is to produce an interpolative, predictive surface using kriging algorithms and custom-defined variogram models, then kriging with explicitly-defined variograms is the only way to go.

Interpolating with explicitly-defined variogram models

So far I have used the term "variogram" several times and you might start wondering what it is. Remember that a key property of spatial data is that they tend to be more similar when they are located in close proximity instead of far away. This characteristic of spatial data can be illustrated using a statistical tool, called a *variogram*, which measures how different spatial data becomes as the distance between data points increases. In other words, the variogram is a measure of "spatial dissimilarity". The computation of the variogram is based on the assumption that the difference between two spatial data points is only a function of their separation distance, not their exact location. In statistical jargon, this is called *intrinsic stationarity* and it corresponds to the concept that your study area is spatially homogeneous; the amount of spatial variability is more or less the same wherever you are in your county.

Estimating your variogram

To estimate your variogram, you first need to pair each of your z-values with all the other z-values. This will generate a large set of data pairs, including pairs of data that are very close geographically to data that are very far away. You then assign each data pair to a class based on their separation distance, say the first class is 0 to 1 km, then 1 to 2 km, and so on. The last step is to compute the average squared difference between data pairs in each class of distance, which gives you an experimental variogram such as the one displayed in Figure 8-1 (dots).

You can compute a variogram for each z-parameter and they will all be different because each z-parameter has its own spatial pattern. However, when you krige, you always use the same internally-defined parameters and thus ignore the spatial pattern specific to each z-parameter. This is why you should not expect to get results as accurate as when you go through the pain of actually estimating the variogram.

Due to the autocorrelative nature of spatial data, the data should show less variance at smaller distances and greater variance at larger distances. The value of the variogram is thus expected to increase as the separation distance increases.

Once you have estimated the experimental variogram for specific classes of distance, you need to fit a model so that the variogram is known for all possible distances. Only specific functions can be used to model a variogram (e.g. spherical, exponential) and Figure 8-1 shows some of them. You need to make sure to evaluate the appropriateness of your variogram model selection. You can do this quite simply by looking at how well each variogram model fits your experimental values. Figure 8-1 shows some common variogram models, and the next few sections take a closer look at each one.

Figure 8-1:
Linear, exponential, Gaussian, power, and spherical variogram curves. Black dots represent the experimental variogram values.

Going deeper down the kriging rabbit hole

When you use kriging algorithms, the value of the z-parameter for each raster cell or square is computed as a weighted average of the data located in the vicinity of that cell. The weight allocated to each data is based on the variogram model and decreases as the distance between the raster cell and the data increases. Intuitively it makes sense because (remember that) spatial data points tend to be more similar when they are located in close proximity instead of far away. These weights are a solution of a system of linear equations, but you don't have to worry about all that because it's all done internally. Your only responsibility is to come up with the variogram model.

You can choose from many, many different types of kriging algorithms, but the most common include ordinary kriging, block kriging, regression kriging, and cokriging. You can see some example outputs from these methods in the following sections.

Exploring ordinary kriging surface estimators

Ordinary kriging is the most common type of kriging used to produce predictive spatial surfaces because it's the most flexible method and because it's a commonly offered feature of standard geospatial analysis software. You might use ordinary kriging if you're, for example, an environmental engineer who needs to use known water table elevations from local wells to predict the groundwater level at a nearby location.

Ordinary kriging assumes that the z-value of your data exhibits a constant, local mean. Your z-values should be a close fit to the average value trend line for the entire set of z-value data. You could check this by generating a trendline on a simple scatter plot of z-values and then visually inspecting it to see that there is not much variance between the trendline and the z-value data points.

Exploring regression kriging surface estimators

If your z-values display a spatial trend that can be explained by another variable that is known everywhere, look no further than regression kriging as a prediction algorithm. Regression kriging (also called *residual kriging*) is a commonly offered feature of most geospatial analysis software programs. This method assumes that the local mean of your z-values show a trend or change across the entire study area which is related to another parameter. Regression kriging would be appropriate, for example, if you're a soil scientist studying an area of land that has rather sharp fluctuations in elevation over a small area and you incorporate this information to form an accurate prediction of related soil properties, such as pH or organic carbon content.

This kriging technique deploys — you guessed it — multiple linear regressions to describe the relationship between the trend in your dataset and a contextually relevant, yet independent dataset. Regression kriging provides estimates that help users understand a trend that their z-values exhibit across space.

Figure 8-2 highlights the differences between ordinary and regression kriging.

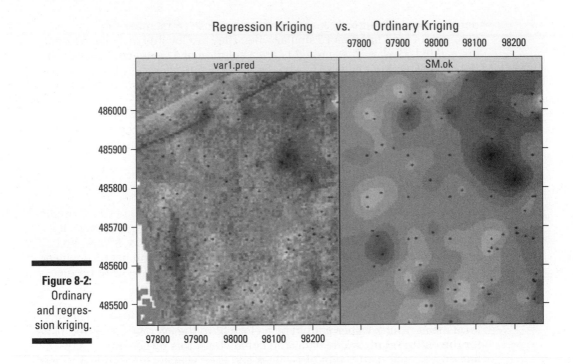

Regression Kriging   vs.   Ordinary Kriging

Figure 8-2:
Ordinary
and regres-
sion kriging.

Exploring block kriging surface estimators

If your goal is to predict average values of the z-parameter for *block areas* — geographical units of any size or shape (not necessarily a square or a rectangle) — based on measurements recorded at discrete locations, then block kriging offers you a great solution. This is a form of "spatial upscaling" since you go from point data to block predictions. (See Figure 8-3.) Block kriging would be appropriate, for example, if you're a soil scientist and you want to create a map of soil fertility for management purposes. You are not interested in a detailed mapping of this soil property since you cannot manage efficiently at such a small scale. Another application is if you are a mining engineer and want to map the gold concentration in a mining deposit. Then you want to get predictions for the size of blocks that will be sent to the mill, not for the size of cores used for data collection.

Figure 8-4 compares ordinary and block kriging.

Compared to point kriging methods that predict at the same scale as your data, block kriging generates smooth interpolated surfaces and smaller prediction variances. In general, one must keep in mind why we are creating a map and what type of spatial resolution is needed for the application at hand. One should also avoid having a false sense of confidence about how accurate a map can be based on the data available. For example, if you've collected

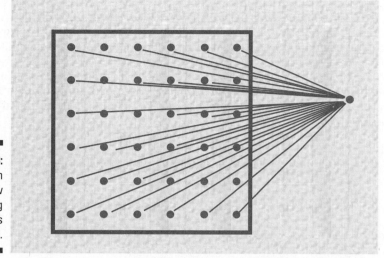

Figure 8-3:
A diagram
of how
block kriging
algorithms
work.

Ordinary Kriging   vs.   Block Kriging

Figure 8-4:
Ordinary
and block
kriging.

data every 100 meters, you should not expect to be able to make accurate predictions every one meter.

Exploring cokriging surface estimators

Cokriging is a multivariate extension of kriging that uses interpolation to predict for one variable based on a set of variables that are correlated to it.

If you have data for multiple variables in the same study area, and your goal is to use the information from these variables to better predict a primary variable, then you should use cokriging. (See Figure 8-5.) For cokriging to provide useful results, all the variables considered must be correlated.

Cokriging would be appropriate, for example, if you're a hydrologist who needs to model and predict the spatial distribution of rainfall quantities in a watershed based on a few rainfall gauges supplemented by a digital elevation model.

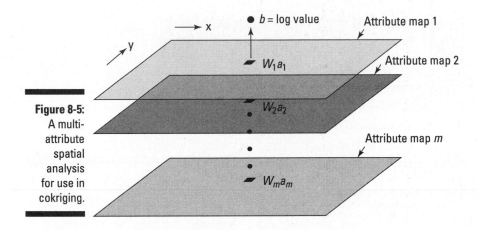

Figure 8-5:
A multi-attribute spatial analysis for use in cokriging.

Choosing the best-estimation method in kriging

To generate the most accurate predictive surface, you need to ensure that you've chosen the best estimation that's available. Test several different kriging methods before deciding what method to use in generating your final predictive surface. Also, evaluate several different types of variogram models to decide which is the most appropriate for your dataset. The best-fit kriging method and variogram model will be the one that produces best goodness-of-fit statistics and the smallest error estimates. More about this will be discussed later in this chapter.

Isotropic spatial data is spatial data that display the same level of spatial autocorrelation in different directions; there is no directional bias in either the decreases or increases in spatial autocorrelation. In *anisotropic* spatial data, the level of autocorrelation is direction-dependent. In other words, the average difference between two data is not only a function of their separation distance, but also the azimuth of their alignment. Many datasets are isotropic. For example, data on air pollution are often anisotropic because variability will be the largest in the direction of prevailing winds. When investigating kriging methods, you should test for both isotropic and anisotropic variation in the underlying dataset, to see which produces the most accurate predictive surface.

Figure 8-6 illustrates the conceptual difference between isotropy and anisotropy.

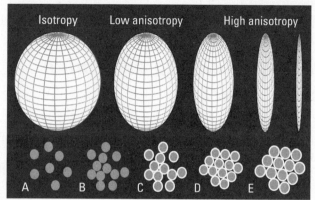

Figure 8-6:
Isotropy vs.
anisotropy.

To save time and computing power when working with large datasets, consider testing best-estimation methods on only a small, randomly selected subset of your data. To select the best-estimation method, you should always examine the *residuals* (the error estimations, in other words) that are assigned to the trend surface area that's produced from your observational dataset.

If your dataset has sharp outliers in its z-values, then kriging should be approached with caution because these extreme highs or lows will strongly influence the estimation of the variogram and the predictions. A common approach is to first transform the data, for example by taking the logarithm of the z-values.

Keep in mind that in spatial statistics, *residuals* refers to the net difference between actual z-values and the model-predicted z-values, per any given unit of space. Figure 8-7 compares a residuals surface with a standard kriging surface.

Figure 8-7:
A kriging
surface and
a residuals
surface.

Analyzing residuals to determine the best-fit model

To ensure that your kriging model is a good fit for your data, you should conduct some validation; for example, you can set aside a subset of your data that will be used only to validate the accuracy of the surface created using the other data. The test data can then be compared to their predicted values. First, you could quantify the relationship between observations and predictions using a regression line and compute the R-squared value. (An *R-squared value* is a measure that represents closeness-of-fit of a regression model between your data values and predicted values. When you get higher R-squared values, this generally means that your model is better fit to your data than models that produce lower R-squared values.)

You might assume that if you have a high R-squared value, then your model must be a good fit for your data, but this isn't necessarily true. You can't reliably validate a model's fitness by looking only at high R-squared values. For example, you might have a high R-squared value while systematically underestimating or overestimating z-values. Such prediction bias can be detected by analyzing your kriging residuals. *Residuals* represent the difference between the values of your observational data and the values that are predicted as a model output.

A bias in the prediction is detected by computing the mean of the residuals, known as *mean error of prediction* (ME). A ME value close to zero indicates unbiased prediction. Even if there is no bias, the prediction could still be inaccurate if large overestimations are balanced by large underestimations — large positive residuals canceling out large negative residuals, in other words. Another useful statistic is thus the mean of the absolute value of residuals, known as *mean absolute error of prediction* (MAE). This quantity is easily inter-pretable and will tell the user on average how different the predictions are from the observations. For example, a mean absolute value of prediction of 5 ppm for arsenic concentration in groundwater indicates that, on average, the predicted concentration will be 5 ppm below or above the actual concentra-tion. This type of error might not be acceptable if the objective is to detect any exceedance of the Environmental Protection Agency's threshold of 10 ppm.

To evaluate the best-fit model for your data, follow these steps:

1. **Look at your goodness-of-fit statistics.**

   The summary statistics for your model should show a high R-squared value.

2. **Evaluate your residuals.**

   Look at the distribution of your residuals. Create a histogram plot from your residuals data. For the model to be well-fit, your residuals should show random errors and be normally distributed, as shown in Figure 8-8. If the residuals distribution is skewed, your residual errors are not random, and you shouldn't use this model.

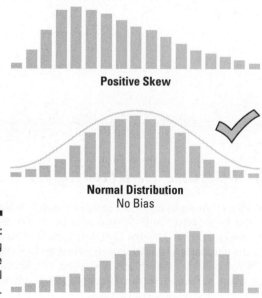

Positive Skew

Normal Distribution
No Bias

Figure 8-8: Evaluating variance of residual errors.

Negative Skew

If there are extreme outliers in the z-values of your dataset (see Figure 8-9), make sure to either a) transform your data first or b) exclude that spatial area from your interpolative kriging analysis. Never remove outliers not caused by measurement errors because these are typically the most interesting observations; for example, they might indicate a hotspot of contamination or the location of mineral deposits,

Figure 8-9:
Evaluating
outliers.

Knowing your options in kriging

To know where to look when you want answers fast, you need to be aware of what software packages and applications offer kriging analysis capabilities. If you're lucky enough to own Esri's proprietary ArcGIS, then you can go ahead and use its Spatial Analyst toolbox to help you with kriging your data. If you're using SAS/STAT software, the KRIGED2D procedure offers kriging capabilities. (For more on KRIGED2D, check out `http://support.sas.com/documentation/cdl/en/statug/63033/HTML/default/viewer.htm#krige2d_toc.htm`.)

Another option is the SpaceStat software developed by BioMedware, Inc., which includes an automatic kriging procedure.

But, if you're not privy to all that fancy stuff, fear not — you can do open-source kriging using R's 'geoR' and 'gstat' packages or Python's 'scipy' library. These packages and this library have been used to carry out all sorts of kriging-based analyses, including analyses that are critical to studies in hydrology, land cover, urban air pollution, mining/resource evaluation, weather prediction, and soil science. (For more on R packages, check out Chapter 15; for more on Python libraries, check out Chapter 14.)

Using Trend Surface Analysis on Spatial Data

Trend Surface Analysis is a useful method for exploratory data analysis. If you simply want to visualize the spatial distribution of your data values over a given unit area, and you're not overly concerned about the accuracy of your output raster surface, then you can use trend surface analysis as a quick fix. Trend surface analysis is a mathematical interpolation method that uses least-squares regression on spatial data to produce a fitted surface that represents the overall trend exhibited by the data. This method produces a good overall surface to represent your spatial data, but it's not an accurate method for predictive spatial data modeling.

To understand trend surface analysis, think back once more to the earlier scenario about hydrologic rainfall data from rainfall gauges that are stationed at various points across your county. I mentioned that you can use kriging techniques to interpolate from those depths and produce an entire coverage area that predicts rainfall depths across the entire county. You can also use trend surface analysis to get this same type of result. The difference is that trend surface analysis generates a surface based on least-squares regression, and kriging methods deploy variogram models to do the trick.

Whether you're working in soil science, archeology, geology, or environmental science, you can use trend surface analysis methods to generate surfaces that will quickly show you the overall trends in your spatial datasets. Trend surface analysis can easily be carried out using Ersi's ArcGIS, R's 'spatial' package, and Python's 'pysal' library.

Part III

Creating Data Visualizations that Clearly Communicate Meaning

To find out more about matching audiences to the right data visualization type, check out www.dummies.com/extras/datascience.

In this part . . .

- ✔ Explore the principles of data visualization design.
- ✔ Use D3.js resources to create dynamic data visualizations.
- ✔ Work with web-based data visualization applications.
- ✔ Create maps using spatial data.

Chapter 9

Following the Principles of Data Visualization Design

. . . .

In This Chapter

▶ Choosing the perfect type of data visualization for your audience's needs

▶ Picking the right design style for your audience

▶ Leveraging good design style to influence your audience

▶ Crafting clear and powerful visual messages with the right data graphic

. . . .

Any standard definition of data science will tell you that it's there to help you extract meaning and value from your raw data. While finding and deriving insights from raw data is at the crux of data science, these insights mean nothing if you don't know how to communicate your findings to others. Data visualization is an excellent means by which you can visually communicate your data's meaning. To design your visualizations well, however, you must know and truly understand your target audience and the core purpose for which you're designing. You must also understand the main types of data graphics that are available to you, as well as the significant benefits and drawbacks of each. In this chapter, I present you with the core principles in data visualization design.

Understanding the Types of Visualizations

A *data visualization* is a visual representation that's designed for the purpose of conveying the meaning and significance of data and data insights. Since data visualizations are designed for a whole spectrum of different audiences, different purposes, and different skill levels, the first step to designing a great data visualization is to *know your audience*. Audiences come in all shapes, forms, and sizes. You could be designing something for the young and edgy readers of *Rolling Stone* magazine, or perhaps you need to design a visualization to convey scientific findings to a research group. It's possible that your audience is comprised of board members and organizational decision makers, or perhaps you're designing a piece that's meant to stir up a ruckus with members of a local grassroots organization.

Since each audience will be comprised of a unique class of consumers, each with their unique data visualization needs, it's essential to clarify exactly for whom you're designing. In the following sections, you get to know the three main types of data visualizations and how to pick the one that best meets your audience's needs.

Data storytelling for organizational decision makers

Sometimes you have to design data visualizations for a less-technical audience, perhaps in order to help members of this audience make better-informed business decisions. The purpose of this type of visualization is to tell your audience the story behind the data. In data storytelling, the audience depends on you to make sense of the data behind the visualization and then turn useful insights into visual stories that they can understand.

With *data storytelling,* your goal should be to create a clutter-free, highly focused visualization so that members of your audience can quickly extract meaning without much effort. These visualizations are best delivered in the form of static images, but more adept decision makers may prefer to have an interactive dashboard that they can use to do a bit of exploration and what-if modeling.

Data showcasing for analysts

If you're designing for a crowd of logical, calculating analysts, you can create data visualizations that are rather open-ended. The purpose of this type of visualization is to help audience members visually explore the data and draw their own conclusions.

When using *data showcasing* techniques, your goal should be to display a lot of contextual information that supports your audience members in making their own interpretations. These visualizations should include more contextual data and less conclusive focus, so people can get in there, analyze the data for themselves, and draw their own conclusions. These visualizations are best delivered as static images or dynamic, interactive dashboards.

Designing data art for activists

You could be designing for an audience of idealists, dreamers, and change-makers. When designing for this audience, you want your data visualization to make a point! You can assume that your typical audience member isn't that analytical. What these people lack in math skills, however, they more than compensate for in solid convictions.

These people look to your data visualization as a vehicle by which to make a statement. When designing for this audience, *data art* is the way to go. The main goal in data art is to entertain, to provoke, to annoy, or to do whatever it takes to make a loud, clear, attention-demanding statement. Data art has little to no narrative and doesn't offer room for viewers to form their own interpretations.

 It's important to emphasize here that data scientists have an ethical responsibility to always represent data accurately. A data scientist should never distort the message of the data to fit what the audience wants to hear — not even for data art! Non-technical audiences won't even know what the possible issues are, let alone be able to see them. They rely on the data scientist to provide honest and accurate representations, thus amplifying the level of ethical responsibility that the data scientist must assume.

Focusing on Your Audience

To make a functional data visualization, you must get to know your target audience and then design precisely for their needs. But to make every design decision with your target audience in mind, you need to take a few steps to make sure you really understand your data visualization's target consumers.

To gain the insights you need about your audience and purpose, follow this process:

✔ **Brainstorm.** Think about a specific member of your visualization's audience and make as many educated guesses as you can about that person's motivations.

It helps to give this (imaginary) audience member a name and a few other identifying characteristics. I always imagine a 45-year-old divorced mother of two named Brenda.

✔ **Define the purpose of your visualization.** Narrow the purpose of your visualization by deciding exactly what action or outcome you want your audience members to make as a result of your visualization.

✔ **Choose a functional design.** Review the three main data visualization types (which I discuss in the preceding sections) and decide which type can best help you achieve your desired outcome.

The following sections delve into these processes in more detail.

Step one: Brainstorming about Brenda

To do a proper brainstorming, start by getting out a sheet of paper and really thinking about your imaginary audience member, Brenda. Answer the following questions to help you better understand her, and thus better understand and design for your target audience.

Form a picture of what Brenda's average day looks like — what she does when she gets out of bed in the morning, what she does over her lunch hour, and what her workplace is like. Also consider how Brenda will use your visualization.

To form a comprehensive view of who Brenda is and how you can best meet her needs, consider the following questions:

✔ Where does Brenda work? What does Brenda do for a living?

✔ What kind of technical education or experience, if any, does she have?

✔ How old is Brenda? Is she married? Does she have children? What does Brenda look like? Where does she live?

✔ What social, political, caused-based, or professional issues are important to Brenda? What does Brenda think of herself?

✔ What problems and issues does Brenda have to deal with on a daily basis?

✔ How does your data visualization help solve Brenda's work problems or her family problems, or improve her self-esteem?

✔ Through what avenue will you present the visualization to Brenda — for example, through the Internet or in a staff meeting?

✔ What does Brenda need to be able to do with your data visualization?

Spend some time thinking about Brenda (your target audience) and answering these questions. These answers can help you create a more functional and effective data visualization.

So, say that Brenda is the manager of the Zoning department in Irvine County. She is 45 years old and a single divorcee with two children who are about to start college. She is really interested in local politics and would eventually like to be on the county's Board of Commissioners. But to achieve that position, she has to get some major wins on her county management resume. Brenda derives most of her feelings of self-worth from her job and her keen ability to make good management decisions for her department.

Up until now, Brenda's been forced to manage her department according to her gut-feel intuition backed by a few disparate business-systems reports. She is not extraordinarily analytical, but she knows enough to understand what she sees. The problem is that Brenda hasn't had the visualization tools required to show her all the relevant data she should be considering. Because she has neither time nor skill to code something up herself, she's been waiting in the lurch. Brenda is very excited that you'll be attending next Monday's staff meeting to present the data visualization alternatives available to help her get underway in making data-driven management decisions.

Step two: Defining your purpose

After you brainstorm about your typical audience member (see the preceding section), you can much more easily pinpoint exactly what you're trying to achieve with this data visualization. Are you attempting to get your consumer to feel a certain way about themselves or the world around them? Are you trying to make a statement? Are you seeking to influence organizational decision makers to make good business decisions? Or do you simply want to lay all the data out there, for all viewers to make sense of and deduce from what they will?

Returning now to our hypothetical Brenda . . . What decisions or processes are you trying to help her achieve? Well, you need to make sense of her data, and then you need to present it to her in a way that she can clearly understand. What's happening within the inner mechanics of her department? Through your visualization, you seek to guide Brenda into making the most prudent and effective management choices.

Step three: Choosing the most functional visualization type for your purpose

Keep in in mind that you have three main types of visualization from which to choose: data storytelling, data art, and data showcasing. If you're designing for organizational decision makers, then you're most likely going to want to use data storytelling to directly tell your audience what their data means with respect to their line of business. If you're designing for a social justice organization or a political campaign, then data art can best make a dramatic and impactful statement with your data. Lastly, if you're designing for engineers, scientists, or statisticians, then stick with data showcasing so that these analytical types have plenty of room to figure things out on their own.

Referring back to Brenda, because she's not extraordinarily analytical and because she's depending on you to help her make excellent data-driven decisions, you need to employ *data storytelling* techniques. Create either a static or interactive data visualization with some, but not too much, context. The visual elements of the design should tell a clear story so that Brenda doesn't have to work through tons of complexities to get the point of what you're trying to tell her about her data and her line of business.

Picking the Most Appropriate Design Style

Analytical types might say that the only purpose for a data visualization is to convey numbers and facts through charts and graphs — no beauty or design is needed. But more artistic folks may insist that they have to feel something in order to really understand it. Truth be told, a good data visualization is neither artless and dry nor completely abstract in its artistry. Rather, its beauty and design lie somewhere on the spectrum between these two extremes.

To choose the most appropriate design style, you must first consider your audience (which I discuss in the preceding sections) and then decide how you want them to respond to your visualization. If you're looking to entice your audience into taking a deeper, more analytical dive into the visualization, employ a design style that induces a calculating and exacting response in its viewers. But if you want your data visualization to fuel your audience's passion, use an emotionally compelling design style instead.

Using design to induce a calculating, exacting response

If you're designing a data visualization for corporate types, engineers, scientists, or organizational decision makers, then keep your design simple and sleek, using the data showcasing or data storytelling visualization. To induce a logical, calculating feel in your audience, include a lot of bar charts, scatter plots, and line charts. Color choices here should be rather traditional and conservative. The look and feel should scream "corporate chic." (See Figure 9-1.) Visualizations of this style are meant to quickly and clearly communicate what's happening in the data — direct, concise, and to the point. The best data visualizations of this style convey an elegant look and feel.

Figure 9-1: A design style that conveys a calculating and exacting feel.

Using design to elicit a strong emotional response

If you're designing a data visualization to influence or persuade people, then incorporate design artistry that invokes an emotional response in your target audience. These visualizations usually fall under the data art category, but an extremely creative data storytelling piece could also inspire this sort of strong emotional response. Emotionally provocative data visualizations often support the stance of one side of a social, political, or environmental issue.

These data visualizations include fluid, artistic design elements that flow and meander, as shown in Figure 9-2. Additionally, rich, dramatic color choices can influence the emotions of the viewer. This style of data visualization leaves a lot of room for artistic creativity and experimentation.

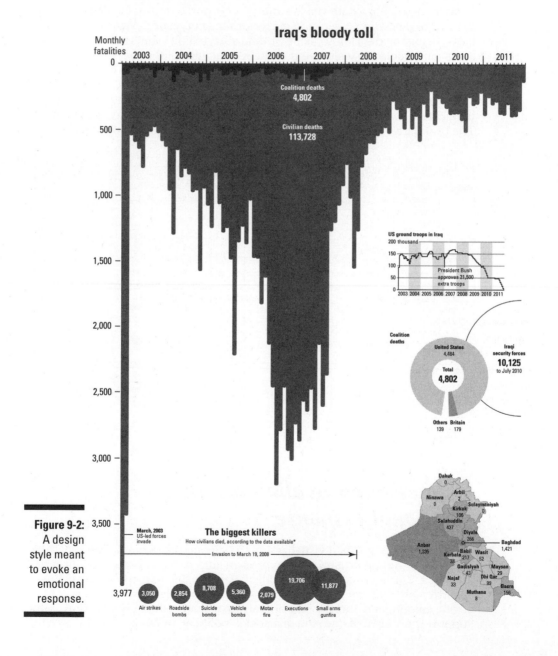

Figure 9-2: A design style meant to evoke an emotional response.

It's important to keep artistic elements relevant — and to know when they're likely to detract from the impression you want to make. This is particularly true when you're designing for analytical types.

Knowing When to Add Context

Adding context helps people understand the value and relative significance of the information your data visualization conveys. Adding context to calculating, exacting data visualization styles helps to create a sense of relative perspective. In pure data art you should omit context because, with data art, you're only trying to make a single point and don't want to add information that would distract from that point.

Using data to create context

In data showcasing, you should include relevant contextual data for the key metrics shown in your data visualization. An example of this would be a situation where you're creating a data visualization that describes conversion rates for e-commerce sales. The key metric would be represented by the percentage of users that convert to customers by making a purchase. Contextual data that's relevant to this metric could include shopping cart abandonment rates, average number of sessions a user has before making a purchase, average number of pages visited before making a purchase, or what pages are visited before a customer decides to convert. This sort of contextual information will help viewers understand the why and how behind sales conversions.

Adding contextual data tends to decentralize the focus of a data visualization, so add this data only in visualizations that are intended for an analytical audience. Those are the ones in a better position to assimilate the extra information and use it to draw their own conclusions — with other types of audiences, context will only be a distraction.

Creating context with annotations

Sometimes you can more appropriately create context by including annotations that provide a header and small description of the context of the data shown. (See Figure 9-3.) This method of creating context is most appropriate for data storytelling or data showcasing. Good annotation is helpful to both analytical and non-analytical audiences alike.

Using graphic elements to create context

Another awesome way to create context in a data visualization is to include graphical elements that convey the relative significance of your data. Such graphical elements include moving average trend lines, single-value alerts, target trend lines (as shown in Figure 9-4), or predictive benchmarks.

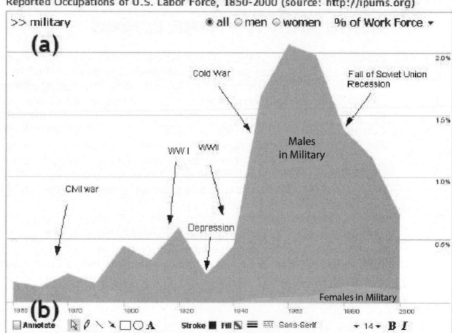

Reported Occupations of U.S. Labor Force, 1850-2000 (source: http://ipums.org)

Figure 9-3: Using annotation to create context.

Figure 9-4:
Using graphical elements to create context.

Knowing When to Get Persuasive

Persuasive design needs to confirm or refute a point. It doesn't leave room for audience interpretation. Persuasive data visualizations generally invoke a strong emotional response. Persuasive design is appropriate for both data art and data storytelling, but since it does not leave much room for audience interpretation, this type of design is not very good for use in data showcasing. Use persuasive design when you're making data visualizations on behalf of social, political, or cause-based organizations.

Choosing the Most Appropriate Data Graphic Type

Your choice in data graphic type can make or break a data visualization. Because you probably need to represent many different facets of your data, you can mix and match among the different graphical classes and types. Even among the same class, certain graphic types perform better than others; therefore, create test representations to see which graphic type conveys the clearest and most obvious message.

This book introduces only the most commonly used graphic types among hundreds. You really don't want to wander too far off the beaten path. The further you stray from familiar graphics, the harder it becomes for people to understand the information you're trying to convey.

Pick the graphic type that most dramatically displays the data trends you're seeking to reveal. You can display the same data trend in many ways, but some methods deliver a visual message more effectively than others. The point is to deliver a clear, comprehensive visual message to your audience so that people can use the visualization to help them make sense of the data presented.

Among the most useful types of data graphics are standard chart graphics, comparative graphics, statistical plots, topology structures, and spatial plots and maps. The next few sections take a look at each type in turn.

Exploring the standard chart graphics

When making data visualizations for an audience of non-analytical people, then, stick to standard chart graphics. The more foreign and complex your graphics are, the harder it is for non-analytical people to understand them. And not all standard charts are boring — you actually have quite a variety to choose from, as the following list makes clear:

- **Area charts:** Area charts (see Figure 9-5) are a fun yet simple way to visually compare and contrast attribute values. You can use them to effectively tell your visual story when data storytelling and data show-casing.

- **Bar charts:** Bar charts (see Figure 9-6) are a very simple way to visually compare and contrast values of parameters in the same category. Bar charts are best for data storytelling and data showcasing.

- **Line charts:** Line charts (see Figure 9-7) most commonly show changes in time-series data, but they can also plot relationships between two or even three parameters. Line charts are so versatile that you can use them in all data visualization design types.

- **Pie charts:** Pie chart graphics (see Figure 9-8) are among the most commonly used. They provide a simple way to compare values of parameters in the same category. Their simplicity, however, can be a double-edged sword; deeply analytical people tend to scoff at them precisely because they seem so simple, so you may want to consider omitting them from data-showcasing visualizations.

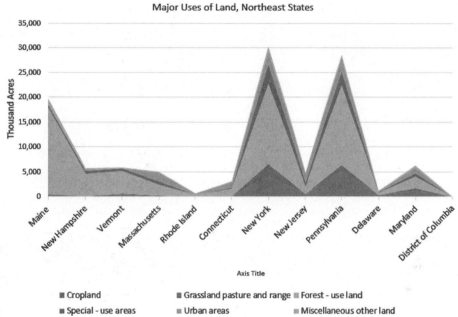

Figure 9-5:
An area
chart.

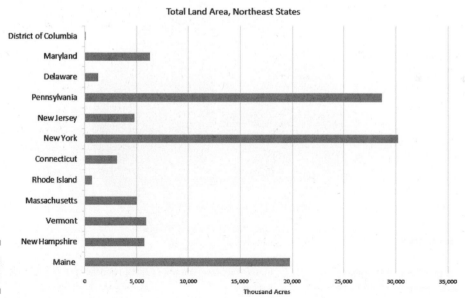

Figure 9-6:
A bar chart.

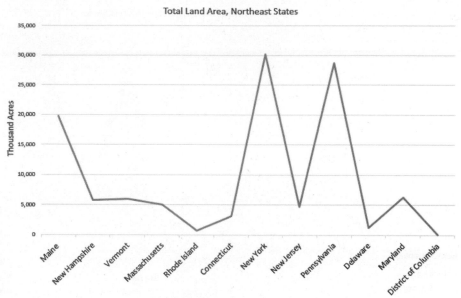

Total Land Area, Northeast States

Figure 9-7:
A line chart.

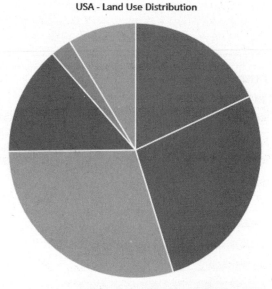

USA - Land Use Distribution

Figure 9-8:
A pie chart.

■ Cropland ■ Grassland pasture and range ■ Forest - use land
■ Special - use areas ■ Urban areas ■ Miscellaneous other land

Exploring comparative graphics

A *comparative graphic* is a graphic that displays the relative value of multiple parameters in a shared category or the relatedness of parameters within multiple shared categories. The core difference between comparative graphics and standard graphics is that comparative graphics offer you a way to simultaneously compare more than one parameter and category. Standard graphics, on the other hand, provide you a way to view and compare only the difference between one parameter of any single category. Comparative graphics are geared for an audience that's at least slightly analytical, so you can easily use these graphics in either data storytelling or data showcasing. Visually speaking, comparative graphics are more complex than standard graphics. The list below shows a few different types of popular comparative graphics:

- **Bubble plots:** *Bubble plots* (see Figure 9-9) use bubble size and color to demonstrate the relationship between three parameters of the same category.

- **Packed circle diagrams:** *Packed circle diagrams* (see Figure 9-10) use both circle size and clustering to visualize the relationships between categories, parameters, and relative parameter values.

- **Gantt charts:** A *Gantt chart* (see Figure 9-11) is a bar chart that uses horizontal bars to visualize scheduling requirements for project management purposes. This type of chart is useful when you're developing a plan for project delivery. It's also helpful when working to determine the sequence in which tasks must be completed in order to meet delivery timelines.

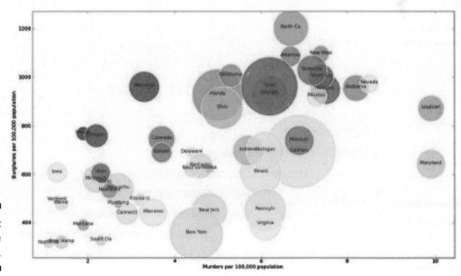

Figure 9-9:
A bubble chart.

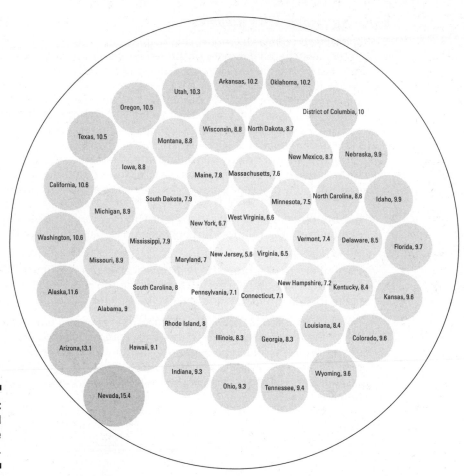

Figure 9-10:
A packed
circle
diagram.

Figure 9-11:
A Gantt
chart.

Gantt charts are great for project management and scheduling.

✔ **Stacked charts:** *Stacked charts* (see Figure 9-12) are used to compare multiple attributes of parameters in the same category. To ensure that it doesn't become difficult to make a visual comparison, don't include too many parameters.

✔ **Tree maps:** *Tree maps* aggregate parameters of like categories and then use area to show the relative size of each category compared to the whole, as shown in Figure 9-13.

✔ **Word clouds:** *Word clouds* use size and color to show the relative difference in frequency of words used in a body of text, as shown in Figure 9-14. Colors are generally employed to indicate classifications of words by usage type.

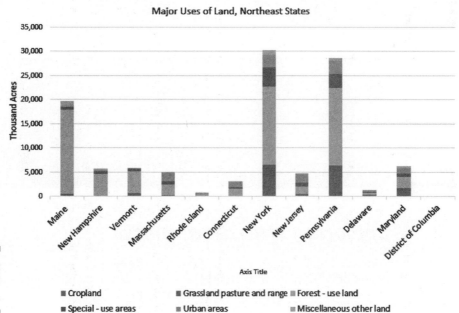

Figure 9-12:
A stacked chart.

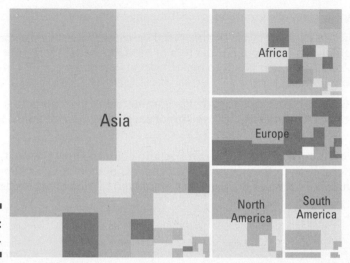

Figure 9-13:
A tree map.

Figure 9-14:
A simple
word cloud.

Exploring statistical plots

Statistical plots, which show the results of statistical analyses, are usually useful only to a deeply analytical audience (so not useful for making data art). Your statistical-plot choices are as follows:

✔ **Histograms:** Diagrams that plot a variable's frequency and distribution as rectangles on a chart, histograms (see Figure 9-15) can help you get a quick handle on the distribution and frequency of data in your dataset.

Get comfortable with histograms; you're going to see a lot of them in the course of statistical analyses.

Figure 9-15:
A histogram.

✔ **Scatter plots:** A terrific way to quickly uncover significant trends and outliers in your dataset, scatter plots plot data points according to their x- and y- values in order to visually reveal any significant patterns. (See Figure 9-16.) If you use data storytelling or data showcasing, start off by generating a quick scatter plot to get a basic idea for areas in the dataset that you could likely find interesting — areas that could potentially uncover significant relationships or yield persuasive stories.

✔ **Scatter plot matrixes:** A good choice when you want to explore the relationships between several variables, scatter plot matrixes place their scatter plots in a visual series that shows coorelations between multiple variables, as shown in Figure 9-17. Discovering and verifying relationships between variables can help you to identify clusters amoung your variables and to identify odd-ball outliers in your dataset.

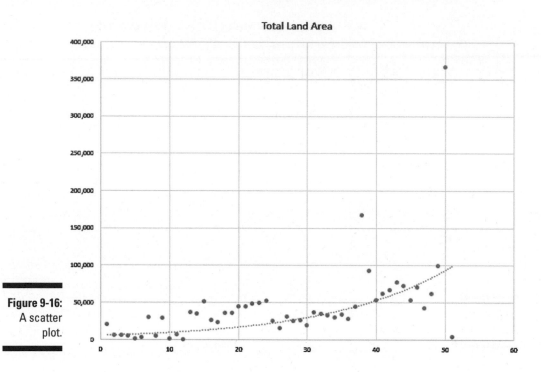

Figure 9-16:
A scatter
plot.

Figure 9-17:
A scatter
plot matrix.

Exploring topology structures

Topology is the practice of using geometric structures to describe and model the relationships and connectedness between entities and variables in a dataset. You need to understand basic topology structures so that you can accurately structure your visual display to match the fundamental underlying structure of the concepts you're representing. The following list shows a series of topological structures that are popular in data science:

✔ **Linear topological structures:** Representing a pure one-to-one relationship, linear topological structures are often used in data visualizations that depict time-series flow patterns. Any process that can only occur through a sequential series of dependent events is linear (see Figure 9-18), and you can effectively represent it by using this underlying topological structure.

✔ **Graph models:** These kinds of models underlie group communication networks and traffic flow patterns. You can use graph topology to represent many-to-many relationships (see Figure 9-19), like those that form the basis of social media platforms.

A *many-to-many* relationship is a relationship structure where each variable or entity has more than one link to the other variables or entities in that same dataset.

✔ **Tree network topology:** This topology represents a *hierarchical* classification, where a network is distributed in a top-down order — nodes act as receivers and distributors of connections and lines represent the connections between nodes. End nodes act only as receivers and not as distributors. (See Figure 9-20.) Hierarchical classification underlies clustering and machine learning methodologies in data science. Tree network structures can represent one-to-many relationships, such as the ones that underlie a family tree or a taxonomy structure.

Figure 9-18:
A linear topology.

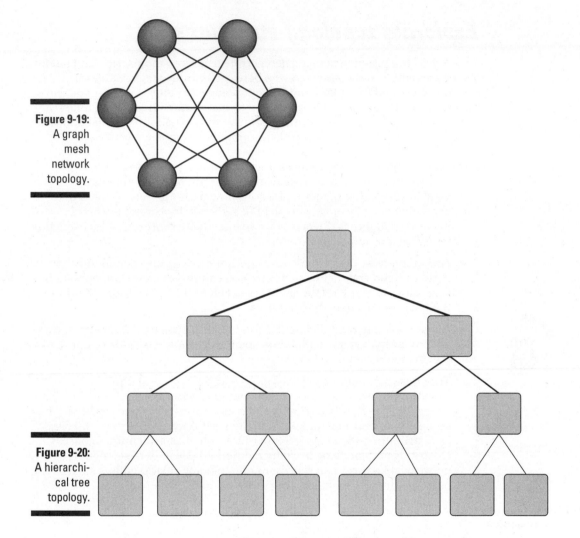

Figure 9-19:
A graph
mesh
network
topology.

Figure 9-20:
A hierarchi-
cal tree
topology.

Exploring spatial plots and maps

Spatial plots and maps are two different ways of visualizing spatial data. A *map* is just a plain figure that represents the location, shape, and size of features on the face of the Earth. *Spatial plots* are, visually, more complex than maps. They show the values for, and location distribution of, a spatial feature's attributes. Listed below are a few types of spatial plots and maps that are commonly used in data visualization:

- **Cloropleth maps:** Despite the fancy name, a Cloropleth map is really just spatial data plotted out according to area boundary polygons rather than by point, line, or raster coverage. To get a better understanding of what I mean, look at Figure 9-21. In this map, each state boundary represents an *area boundary* polygon. The color and shade of the area within each boundary represents the relative value of the attribute for that state — where red areas have a higher attribute value and blue areas have a smaller attribute value.

- **Point maps:** Comprised of spatial data plotted out according to specific point locations, point maps present data in a graphical point form (see Figure 9-22), rather than in polygon, line, or raster surface formats.

- **Raster surface maps:** These spatial maps can be anything from a satellite image map to a surface coverage with values that have been interpolated from underlying spatial data points (see Figure 9-23).

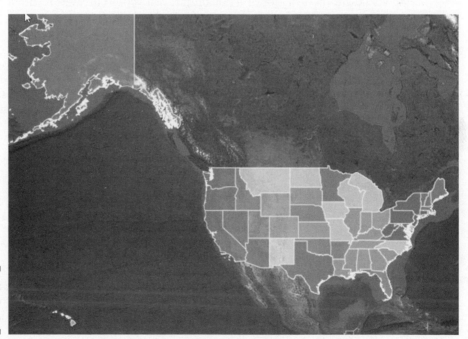

Figure 9-21:
A Cloropleth
map.

Figure 9-22:
A point map.

In data visualization, there are some common pitfalls of which you should be aware. Simply put, data visualizations can be misleading if they're not constructed correctly. Common problems include pie-charts that don't add up to 100%, bar-charts with a scale that starts in a strange place, or multi-column bar charts with incommensurate vertical axes. Whether you're a data visualization designer or a consumer, you should be alert to these kinds of issues.

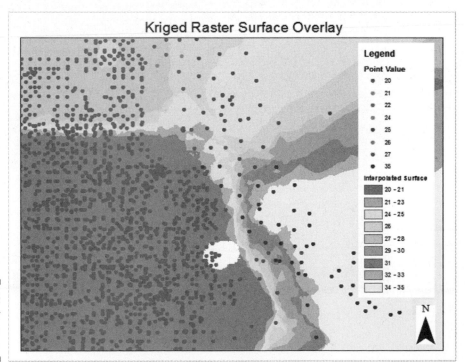

Figure 9-23:
A raster
surface
map.

Choosing Your Data Graphic

Follow these three steps to test and determine whether the data graphics you choose can effectively communicate your data's meaning:

1. **Scope out the questions.**

   Ask yourself the questions that your data visualization should answer, then look at your visualization and determine whether the answers to those questions jump right out at you.

2. **Take users and media into account.**

   Consider who will consume your data visualization, using which medium. Do your data graphics make sense in that context?

3. **Take a final step back.**

   Look over your data visualization to ensure its message is clearly conveyed through the data graphic alone.

The following sections take a look at each step in a bit more detail.

Scoping out the questions

Before thinking about what graphics to use, first consider the questions you want to answer for your audience. In a marketing setting, your audience may want to know why their overall conversion rates are low. Or, if you're designing for business managers, they may want to know why service times are slower in certain customer service areas than in others. Many graphic types can fulfill the same purpose, but whatever you choose, step back and check that your choices clearly answer the exact and intended questions.

Taking users and media into account

Consider where your data visualization will be used. Will an audience of scientists consume it, or will you use it for content marketing to generate Internet traffic? Do you want to use it to prove a point in a board room? Or do you want to support a story in an upcoming newspaper publication? Pick graphic types that are appropriate for the intended consumers and for the medium through which they'll consume the visualization.

Taking a final step back

Finally, to ensure that you've chosen the best graphic form, take a step back from your data visualization and evaluate whether the graphics you've used make sense. If viewers have to stretch their minds to make a visual comparison of data trends, you probably need to use a different graphic type. If viewers have to read numbers or annotations to get the gist of what's happening, it's not good enough. Test other graphic forms to see whether you can convey the visual message more effectively.

Close your eyes and ask yourself the questions that you seek to answer through your data visualization. Now, open them and look at your visualization. Do the answers jump out at you? If not, try another graphic type.

Chapter 10

Using D3.js for Data Visualization

The truth of the matter is, you can come up with the perfect data visualization you need to meet the exact needs of your target audience gathered in that meeting room down the hall, but what works in the physical meeting room may not work in that virtual meeting room out on the World Wide Web. In this chapter, I show you how you can use D3.js technology to build custom web-based visualizations — the type of visualizations you need if you're showcasing your work online. The power of programming in D3.js is that it enables you to create absolutely stunning, dynamic data visualizations with which your audience can interact and explore, straight from their browsers, with no add-ons required.

D3.js is not the only option available for constructing dynamic, web-based data visualizations, it's just an excellent one. Other options include jQuery Javascript library (http://jquery.com/), JpGraph PHP library (http://jpgraph.net/), HighCharts (www.highcharts.com/), and iCharts (http://icharts.net/).

Introducing the D3.js Library

D3.js is an open-source JavaScript library that's taken the data visualization world by storm since its first release in 2011. It was created (and is maintained) by Mike Bostock — famous data visualization guru and Graphics Editor for the *New York Times*. You can use this library to create high-quality Data-Driven Documents (D3) in a fraction of the time and with a fraction of the effort required to code in plain (aka vanilla) JavaScript.

In its essence, D3.js is a collection of classes and functions that, with just a little coding, you can use to execute much longer strings of lower-level JavaScript. D3.js calls on only a special class of commands in the JavaScript library — the ones that are typically used in data visualization. You use these commands to do things like draw axes, plot elements, and recalculate positions when resizing graphs.

If your goal is to create *dynamic* web-based data visualizations — visualizations that change in response to user interactions — D3.js is the perfect JavaScript library to use.

If you want users to be able to interact with your data visualization and choose what data to display, then you need to create a dynamic visualization.

With dynamic data visualizations, your users can

- ✔ Interact with the visualization to choose what data to display.
- ✔ See additional data when they hover over or click parts of the visualization.
- ✔ Drill down into deeper levels of related data, to get more detailed views on the parts of the data that are of most interest.
- ✔ Bring up animated visualizations that show changes over time.
- ✔ Choose from a variety of different transitions between views.

The D3.js library is still being developed. With Mike Bostock and countless other users contributing new types of visualizations, the library's capabilities are expanding on a daily basis. The D3.js design philosophy is rather open-ended. It doesn't limit you to using predefined, cookie-cutter data visualizations. Rather, this library can accommodate the individual creativity and imagination of each unique user.

Knowing When to Use D3.js (and When Not To)

The main purpose of D3.js in the data visualization world is to make creative, interactive, web-based visualizations with only a small bit of code. Because D3.js is so powerful and open-ended, it's also more complex than some other JavaScript libraries, web applications, or software packages. D3.js has the same basic syntax as JavaScript, so you need a basic working knowledge of JavaScript in order to code in D3.js. Beyond a bit of JavaScript, you need to know a whole vocabulary and programming style before getting started. This chapter covers the basics of getting started in D3.js, but if you wish for more extensive training then you can get that by working through the tutorials that Mike Bostock has developed and hosted at his GitHub repository at `https://github.com/mbostock/d3/wiki/Tutorials`.

With the help of a few D3.js learning resources, you might be able to learn both JavaScript and D3.js at the same time. But many online tutorials presuppose a level of programming experience that you might not have.

Because you have to face a significant learning curve in mastering even the basic concepts of D3.js, use this library only if you want to create unique, interactive, scalable web-based visualizations. Otherwise, just stick with static data visualizations. In this case, the simpler, less open-ended frameworks available for creating static data visualizations are easier and can provide everything you might need.

If you choose to go with D3.js, however, you can find thousands of online open-source examples from which to learn and create. In addition to Mike Bostock's tutorials, another good place to start is with the Dashing D3.js Tutorials at `www.dashingd3js.com/table-of-contents`.

These tutorials will get you started knowing how to build visualizations with data. From there, you can get into more advanced stuff like building drillable sunburst diagrams, to building adjustable force-directed network graphs. You can even use D3.js to make a heat-map calendar, to visualize time-series trends in your data. The options and alternatives expand on a near-daily basis.

Getting Started in D3.js

I want to introduce you to the underlying concepts you need to master to create dynamic web-based data visualizations using D3.js. In the following sections, I cover the basics of JavaScript, HTML, CSS, and PHP as they pertain to creating visualizations using D3.js. Also, I tell you how you can maximize the portion of client-side work that's done by the JavaScript language. (*Client-side work* is the portion of work that's done on your computer, rather than on the network server.) If you're not content with stopping there, you can find out about JavaScript's Document Object Model (DOM) and how it interacts with HyperText Markup Language (HTML) to produce dynamic changes in a web page's HTML.

In the section "Bringing in the JavaScript and SVG," later in this chapter, I talk about how you can use D3.js to efficiently display and change *Scalable Vector Graphics (SVG)* — an XML-based image format that's useful for serving images to interactive visualization designs and animation applications — in your data visualization. You can find out how to make sweeping style changes across a web page by using *C*ascading *S*tyle *S*heets (CSS) in the section "Bringing in the Cascading Style Sheets (CSS)," later in this chapter. And lastly, this chapter's section on "Bringing in the web servers and PHP" explains how to minimize the amount of client-side work that's required by deploying PHP programs across a web server.

Bringing in the HTML and DOM

*H*yper*T*ext *M*arkup *L*anguage (HTML) is the backbone of a web page. It delivers the static content you see on many websites, especially the older ones. HTML is recognizable by its plain text and limited interactivity. The only interactive features you get with plain HTML websites are perhaps some hyperlinks that lead you to other boring static pages throughout the site.

You can use HTML to display plain text with a series of tags that give instructions to the client's browser. The following HTML code is pretty basic, but at least it gives you an idea of what's involved:

```
<html>
    <head>
        <title>This is a simple HTML page</title>
    </head>
    <body>
    <p>This is a paragraph.</p>
    </body>
</html>
```

Just in case you're not aware, HTML relies on start tags and end tags. The above sample has a couple nice examples, like <p> </p> and <body> </body>

JavaScript uses the HTML *D*ocument *O*bject *M*odel (DOM). Through the HTML DOM, JavaScript can interact with HTML tags and their content. DOM treats tags as hierarchical layers, just like objects in an object-oriented programming language (like JavaScript). For example, the <body> tag in the preceding HTML is a child of the top-level <html> tag; it has one sibling, <head>, and one child, <p>. In the DOM, that <p> tag is fully defined by its path while you traverse from the top of the model (html > body > p, for example). DOM allows you to control object selections based on object attribute properties.

In D3.js, the purpose of HTML is to provide a bare scaffold of static tags and web page content that can be interacted with via JavaScript's DOM to produce dynamic, changeable HTML pages. D3.js is built on top of a bare backbone of HTML. Although HTML is static, it becomes dynamic in D3.js if a programmer or user interaction causes predetermined scripts to make on-the-fly changes to the underlying HTML code. This means that the HTML that is displayed is often dynamic and different from that which was originally sent to the browser.

Bringing in the JavaScript and SVG

Using the JavaScript language gives you a simple way to get work done *client-side* (on the user's machine). The slowest part of any interaction between a user and a website is in sending data from the server to the client's computer over the Internet. That interaction can be vastly accelerated if, instead of sending all of the information needed for a browser display, you send a much shorter, simpler chain of instructions that the client's web browser can use to re-create that information and then create the web page using the client computer's own processing speed. This is how client-side work is carried out.

If your goal is to retain a decent level of security, without needing plugins or special permissions to run code on your browser, then JavaScript offers you a terrific solution. What's more, JavaScript is very fast! Because it's a programming language intended for browsers, JavaScript is unencumbered by the advanced features that make other languages more versatile but less speedy.

A note about Microsoft Internet Explorer: Different versions of Internet Explorer are compatible with different versions of JavaScript. It's a complex problem that can sometimes cause even an experienced JavaScript programmer to pull his or her hair out. As a general rule of thumb, JavaScript doesn't run on IE versions that are older than IE8.

In JavaScript, graphics rendering is based on Scalable Vector Graphics (SVG) — a vector image format that delivers images to interactive visualizations and web-based animations. In D3.js, SVG functions as a file format that stores vector graphics for use in two-dimensional, interactive web-based data visualizations. Vector graphics require a lot less bandwidth than images because vector graphics contain only instructions for how to draw them, as opposed to the final pixel-by-pixel raster renderings of images. If your goal is to rapidly deploy web-based graphics that also provide you lossless scaling capabilities, then SVG is a perfect solution. SVG is optimal for use in creating graphical elements such as bars, lines, and markers.

You can use D3.js to select, add, modify, or remove SVG elements on a page, in just the same way you do with HTML elements. Since D3.js is most useful for working with web-based graphic elements, most of your D3.js scripting will interact with SVG elements.

Bringing in the Cascading Style Sheets (CSS)

The purpose of using *Cascading Style Sheets* (CSS) is to define the look of repeated visual elements, such as fonts, line widths, and colors. You can use CSS to specify the visual characteristics of your page elements all at one time, and then efficiently apply these characteristics to an entire HTML document (or to only the parts of the document defined in the DOM, if you wish). If you want to make sweeping, all-at-once changes to the look and feel of your web page elements, then use CSS.

As an example, the basic CSS for a simple web page might include the following:

```
<style type="text/css">
    p {
    font-family: arial, verdana, sans-serif;
font-size: 12 pt;
color: black;
    }
.highlighted {
    color: red;
}
</style>
```

The preceding example would render the text in this HTML example:

```
<p>This text is black and <span class="highlighted">this
        text is red.</span></p>
```

The preceding CSS and HTML code generates text in the `<p>` tag that has a default value of black, while the inner object is designated as a `highlighted` class and generates a red-colored text.

D3.js leverages CSS for drawing and styling text elements and drawn elements so that you can define and change the overall look of your visualization in one compact, easy-to-read block of code.

Bringing in the web servers and PHP

While one of the main purposes behind using JavaScript and D3.js is to maximize the portion of work that's carried out on the client's machine, some work is just better carried out on the web server. (In case you aren't familiar with the term, a *web server* can be thought of as a server-based computer that sends information over the Internet to users when they visit a website.)

In web programming, the words *client* and *user* can be used interchangeably. Both words refer to either the end user or the end user's computer.

As an example of how web servers work, think of a sales site that has millions of products available for purchase. When you go to search for a type of product, of course the website doesn't send the company's entire product catalog to your computer and expect your PC to do the work of paring down the product information. Instead the site's web server processes the search parameters you've defined and then sends only the information that's relevant to answer your particular search questions.

In web programming, you commonly have a SQL database set up as a main information source and also a PHP program that defines the HTML code to be sent to the client's computer. You use PHP programs to query the SQL database and determine what information to send over to the client. PHP is a scripting language that's run on a server and produces on-the-fly HTML code in response to user interactions.

In pre-D3.js days, you'd have had to use a lot more time and bandwidth constructing web-based, interactive data visualizations. Due to the effectiveness of the PHP/D3.js combination, things are simpler now. In response to a request from the user, PHP selects information from the server and sends it to the client's computer in the form of HTML with embedded CSS, JavaScript, and D3.js code. At this point, the D3.js can take over and expand the HTML. If necessary, D3.js can even make on-the-fly HTML expansions in response to additional user interactions. This process uses only a fraction of the bandwidth and time that would have been required in a PHP-only or JavaScript-only setup.

Understanding More Advanced Concepts and Practices in D3.js

In this section, you can see the ways more advanced D3.js features can help you become more efficient in using the library to create dynamic data visualizations. In the following section, I explain how to use so-called *chain syntax* — syntax that chains together functions and methods into a single line of code — to minimize your coding requirements. You can also find out how to use the scale and axis functions to automatically define or change the proportions and elements for graphic outputs in the section "Getting to know scales and axes," later in this chapter. In the section "Getting to know transitions and interactions," later in this chapter, you see how to use transitions and interactions to maximize audience exploration, analysis, and learning from your end-product data visualization.

For the rest of this chapter, refer to Listing 10-1 (a complete HTML file that contains CSS, JavaScript, and D3.js elements) when working through the examples. Don't get too stressed out by the listing itself. I know it's lengthy, but simply take a look through it, and then focus on the snippets I pull from it for later discussion.

Listing 10-1: An HTML File with CSS, JavaScript, and D3.js Elements

```html
<!DOCTYPE html>
<html>
<head>
  <meta http-equiv="content-type" content="text/html;
        charset=UTF-8">
  <title>D3.js example</title>
    <script type='text/javascript'
          src="http://d3js.org/d3.v3.min.js"></script>
  <style type='text/css'>
    rect:hover {
    fill: brown;
}
  </style>

<script type='text/javascript'>//<![CDATA[
window.onload=function(){
var column_data = [{
    position: 0,
    quantity: 5
}, {
    position: 1,
    quantity: 20
}, {
    position: 2,
    quantity: 15
}, {
    position: 3,
    quantity: 25
}, {
    position: 4,
    quantity: 10
}];

var total_width = 400;
var total_height = 200;

var scale_y = d3.scale.linear()
    .domain([0, d3.max(column_data, function (d) {
    return d.quantity;
})])
    .range([0, total_height]);
```

```
var scale_x = d3.scale.ordinal()
    .domain(d3.range(column_data.length))
    .rangeRoundBands([0, total_width], 0.05);

var position = function (d) {
    return d.position;
};

var svg_container = d3.select("body")
    .append("svg")
    .attr("width", total_width)
    .attr("height", total_height);

svg_container.selectAll("rect")
    .data(column_data, position)
    .enter()
    .append("rect")
    .attr("x", function (d, i) {
    return scale_x(i);
})
    .attr("y", function (d) {
    return total_height - scale_y(d.quantity);
})
    .attr("width", scale_x.rangeBand())
    .attr("height", function (d) {
    return scale_y(d.quantity);
})
    .attr("fill", "teal");

var sort = function () {
    bars_to_sort = function (a, b) {
        return b.quantity - a.quantity;
    };

    svg_container.selectAll("rect")
        .sort(bars_to_sort)
        .transition()
        .delay(0)
        .duration(300)
        .attr("x", function (d, n) {
        return scale_x(n);
    });
};

d3.select("#sort").on("click", sort);
d3.select("#unsort").on("click", unsort);
```

(continued)

Listing 10-1 *(continued)*

```
function unsort() {
    svg_container.selectAll("rect")
        .sort(function (a, b) {
        return a.position - b.position;
    })
        .transition()
        .delay(0)
        .duration(1200)
        .attr("x", function (d, i) {
        return scale_x(i);
    });

};
}//]]>

</script>

</head>

<body>
    <button id="sort" onclick="sortBars()">Sort</button>
    <button id="unsort" onclick="unsort()">Unsort</button>
    <p>
</body>

</html>
```

And for future reference, the preceding code produces the interactive bar chart shown in Figure 10-1.

Figure 10-1:
An inter-
active,
web-based
bar chart
made in
D3.js.

Getting to know chain syntax

As mentioned in the section "Bringing in the HTML and DOM," earlier in this chapter, you can use D3.js to take a bare scaffold of HTML and turn it into a complex visualization by modifying page elements. The D3.js library uses a very efficient operator syntax called *chain syntax.* The purpose of chain syntax is to chain together several methods, thereby allowing you to perform multiple actions using only a single line of code. Instead of name-value pair syntax (like what you would see in CSS), D3.js chains multiple expressions together, each one creating a new object and selection for the next.

The fundamental concept behind D3.js is the Append, Enter, and Exit selections. These methods select, add, or remove HTML tags that are *bound*, or assigned, to your data. The Append selection refers to existing data elements that are paired with existing HTML tags. When there are more data elements than tags, the Enter selection adds tags paired with the surplus data elements. When there are more tags than data elements, you can use the Exit selection to remove those tags.

Taking another look at a section of Listing 10-1, notice the code block that draws the bars of the graph:

```
svg_container.selectAll("rect")
    .data(column_data, position)
    .enter()
    .append("rect")
    .attr("x", function (d, i) {
    return scale_x(i);
```

This D3.js script defines an object `svg_container`. The first element, `selectAll("rect")`, defines the container to be all the `"rect"` elements in the document. To this container, the script then goes through the data in `column_data` and `position`, and binds each data item to one of the `rects` in the container. To handle data items that don't (yet) have a `rect` in the container, the `enter` expression creates new placeholder elements that can be turned into real document elements by further expressions. And, in fact, this is just what the next expression — `append("rect")` — does, creating a new `rect` element for each new data item. The key idea is that datasets can be bound to document elements and used to create, destroy, and modify them in a variety of very flexible ways.

Getting to know scales

In D3.js, the `scale` function plots input domains to output ranges so that the output data visualization graphics are drawn at appropriate, to-scale proportions. Looking at the following section of Listing 10-1, notice how `scale` variables are defined using D3.js:

```
var scale_y = d3.scale.linear()
    .domain([0, d3.max(column_data, function (d) {
    return d.quantity;
})])
    .range([0, total_height]);

var scale_x = d3.scale.ordinal()
    .domain(d3.range(column_data.length))
    .rangeRoundBands([0, total_width], 0.05);
```

One of the main features of D3.js is its ability to do difficult and tedious calculations under the hood. A key part of this work is done in scaling plots. If you want to automatically map the range of your data to actual pixel dimensions in your graph, then you can use the `scale` function to change either or both parameters without having to do any manual recalculations.

From the snippet shown above, you can see the total height of the graph has been specified as a `.range`. This means you no longer need to calculate margins, positions, or how your values map to fixed positions. The following section from Listing 10-1 shows that your greatest `quantity` value in the total height range is 25.

```
var column_data = [{
    position: 0,
    quantity: 5
}, {
    position: 1,
    quantity: 20
}, {
    position: 2,
    quantity: 15
}, {
    position: 3,
    quantity: 25
}, {
    position: 4,
    quantity: 10
}];

var total_width = 400;
var total_height = 200;
```

By automatically mapping the range of your data (0–25) to the actual pixel height of your graph, you can change either or both parameters without having to do any manual recalculations.

Although you can use D3.js to automatically handle the placement of axis labels and tick marks, the library can also handle all calculations involved in date ranges. This functionality leaves you free to concentrate on the overall look and feel of the visualization, instead of tinkering with its mechanics.

Getting to know transitions and interactions

The true beauty of D3.js is in how you can use it to easily incorporate dynamic elements into your web-based data visualization. If you want to encourage your users to really explore and analyze the data in your dynamic visualization, then create features that offer a lot of user interactivity. Also, incorporating transitions into your dynamic visualization can help you capture the interest of your audience. Transitions in D3.js build the aesthetic appeal of a data visualization by incorporating elements of motion into the design.

As a prime example of D3.js interactivity, take a look at the following code from Listing 10-1.

```
<style type='text/css'>
    rect:hover {
    fill: brown;
}
  </style>
```

Here, a single piece of CSS code changes the color of the bars when the user hovers the cursor over them.

And, looking at another snippet taken from Listing 10-1 (shown below), you can see code that defines a `sort` function and then creates buttons to transition the bars between sorted and unsorted states. If you tried for the same effect using vanilla JavaScript, it would be more tedious and time-consuming.

```
var sort = function () {
    bars_to_sort = function (a, b) {
        return b.quantity - a.quantity;
    };
```

```
        svg_container.selectAll("rect")
            .sort(bars_to_sort)
            .transition()
            .delay(0)
            .duration(300)
            .attr("x", function (d, n) {
            return scale_x(n);
        });
    };

    d3.select("#sort").on("click", sort);
    d3.select("#unsort").on("click", unsort);

    function unsort() {
        svg_container.selectAll("rect")
            .sort(function (a, b) {
            return a.position - b.position;
        })
            .transition()
            .delay(0)
            .duration(1200)
            .attr("x", function (d, i) {
            return scale_x(i);
        });

    };
    }//]]>

    </script>
    </head>
    <body>
        <button id="sort" onclick="sortBars()">Sort</button>
        <button id="unsort" onclick="unsort()">Unsort</button>
        <p>
    </body>
    </html>
```

The D3.js wiki has a gallery of visualizations that'll give you an idea of this library's enormous potential (https://github.com/mbostock/d3/wiki/Gallery). Across the web, people are finding new ways to use the library or adding to it for improved usability in specialized applications. As a modern interactive data visualization designer, you can use skills in D3.js to create almost anything you can imagine.

Chapter 11

Web-Based Applications for Visualization Design

• •

In This Chapter

▶ Checking out some online collaborative data visualization platforms

▶ Knowing your options for web-based spatial data analysis and mapping

▶ Getting the scoop on some powerful, non-collaborative data visualization platforms

▶ Digging into the best visualization platforms for creative infographic design

• •

*I*n recent years, the World Wide Web has seen an impressive rise in the number of easy-to-use online tools available for data visualization and infographic design. So you no longer need to purchase, download, install, and maintain proprietary software packages to help you do this type of work. Instead, you can choose from a seemingly limitless number of open-source web-based solutions available to help you achieve practically any visualization goal you're after. In this chapter, I bring you up to speed on the best options available to help you reach your specific goals.

Don't worry if you're not overly technical. With many of these web-based applications, you simply need to upload your data (often using a simple copy-and-paste operation), format it, and then quickly experiment with different chart-type offerings. Usually, the hardest part of this work involves finding answers to the following (quite agreeable) questions:

✔ Does my data look better in a bar chart or a line plot?

✔ Does my data look better in a map or a bubble chart?

✔ Should I go with something a bit more creative, like a text cloud or a heat map?

So get ready to be introduced to some of the web's most popular and effective visualization tools. For each service, I give you a description of the platform, some examples of chart types offered by the application, and some links you can use to find and explore visualizations for yourself.

For sample data, I've used a dataset from the U.S. Census Bureau's American Communities Survey (www.census.gov/acs/www/) that shows the number of people per state who, during the year 2011, changed addresses but remained within the same county. (Intriguingly, these nearby moves are three times more common in Nevada than in New Jersey.)

Using Collaborative Data Visualization Platforms

Collaborative data visualization platforms are web-based platforms through which you can design data visualizations and then share those visualizations with other platform users to get their feedback on design or on the data insights conveyed.

Collaborative data visualization platforms have been described as the YouTube of data visualization, but actually, these platforms are far more interactive than YouTube. Collaborative data visualization platforms are like a version of YouTube that lets you instantly copy and edit every video using your own software tools, and then republish the video through your own social channels.

Collaborative platforms are very efficient and effective for working in teams. Instead of having to e-mail versions back and forth, or (heaven forbid) learn a dedicated version-control system like GitHub, you and your teammates can use the platform's sharing features to work on visualizations as a team.

Even if you don't need or want to work with collaborators, collaborative platforms still have much to offer in the way of useful data analysis and visualization tools. These tools are often as powerful as (sometimes even more powerful than) comparable desktop packages — just keep in mind that they often require users to publicly share their data and results so that others can view, modify, or use those results for their specific needs.

Many sites offer _freemium_ plans that allow you to keep your work private if you purchase a paid account.

Working with IBM's Watson Analytics

The brand name "IBM" is synonymous with cutting-edge ingenuity, quality, and stability. IBM Watson Analytics is no exception to this rule. Watson Analytics is the first full-scale data science and analytics solution that's been made available as a 100% cloud-based offering. The application is available in a freemium version, or on a paid-subscription basis, to match all levels of needs and requirements. Although Watson Analytics is a full-scale data science accelerator, it also offers robust collaborative functionality so that users can share, interact, engage, and provide feedback on data insights that are generated.

IBM's purpose for building Watson Analytics was to democratize the power of data science by offering a platform across which users of all skill levels and backgrounds can access, refine, discover, visualize, report, and collaborate upon data-driven insights. No matter whether you're an advanced data scientist that's looking for automation functionality to make your daily work easier, or if you're an entry-level data analyst that's looking for a way to generate deep data insights without learning to code things up yourself, Watson Analytics has something for everyone. The pre-requisite skill level is simply that users know how to use a basic application like Microsoft Excel to do advanced data analysis — such as that which is done through pivot tables and custom VBA scripts.

If you're looking for a cloud-based, mobile-optimized, collaborative platform that you can use to automate your data analysis, visualization, and reporting tasks, then Watson Analytics is the solution for you. To get started, you need to first go over to the Watson Analytics landing page and sign-up for an account (at www.ibm.com/analytics/watson-analytics/). For chart types, Watson Analytics offers everything from simple bar and line charts, scatter plots, and pie charts, to geo-spatial maps, heat maps, decision trees (see Figure 11-1), and bubble plots. The application even offers a unique, patented "bullseye" visualization and analysis tool that you can use to adjust your analysis and discover the predictive strength of insights that you've generated, as shown in Figure 11-2.

Visualizing and collaborating with Plotly

The Plotly collaborative platform aims to accommodate the data collaboration needs of professionals and non-professionals alike. This powerful tool doesn't stop at data visualization; it goes one step further by providing you the tools you need to make sense of your data through advanced statistical analysis. Plotly even offers seamless integration with dedicated programming environments like Python, MATLAB, and R.

Figure 11-1:
A decision tree that was automatically generated by Watson Analytics.

Figure 11-2:
Results of predictive analysis in IBM's Watson Analytics.

If you want a quick and easy way to create interesting and attractive data visualizations, Plotly offers a great solution. Although Plotly focuses on traditional data chart types, you can much more easily portray variables by size or color in Plotly than in most other web applications. If you work in one of the STEM fields, Plotly may be particularly well-suited for your needs. In addition to standard bubble plots, line charts, bar charts, and area graphs, Plotly also offers histograms, two-dimensional histograms, heat maps, scatter charts, box plots, three-dimensional scatter charts, three-dimensional surface charts, and polar plots.

As far as collaborative functionality goes, Plotly provides you features for social-media sharing, user commenting, visualization modification and sharing, data sharing, and using embed codes so that you can embed and display your visualization directly on your website if you wish.

For all you techies out there, a very cool collaborative feature of Plotly is its code-sharing feature. Each visualization hosted on Plotly offers you an option to see and copy the data visualization's source code.

To use Plotly, you need to sign up for an account first. To do that, start by clicking the Sign-Up button in the upper-right hand corner of Plotly's home page (at `https://plot.ly/`). Luckily, the Plotly platform has a large user base and is in active development, with new features being added all the time. If you get stuck, you can find a lot of answers, either in its extensive online documentation (at `https://plot.ly/learn`) or at the Plotly corner of the popular technical Q&A website Stack Overflow (`http://stackoverflow.com/questions/tagged/plotly`).

Figures 11-3 and 11-4 show two visualizations created with Plotly — a simple bar chart of the in-county moving data and a scatter chart of that data compared to the area in square miles of each state. You can also monitor a feed of new visualizations as they're published at Plotly's Graphing News Feed (at `https://plot.ly/feed`).

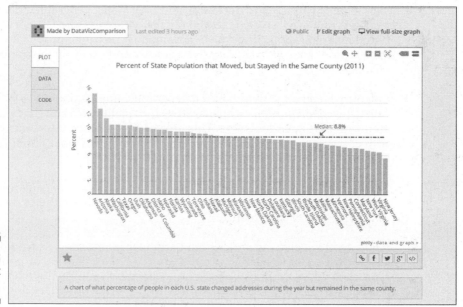

Figure 11-3:
A bar chart on Plotly.

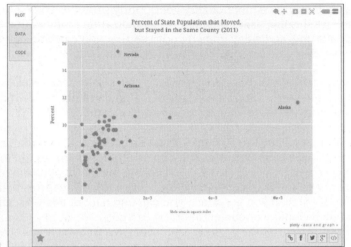

Figure 11-4:
A scatter
chart on
Plotly.

Visualizing Spatial Data with Online Geographic Tools

With the advent of online Geographic Information Systems (GIS, for short) like Google Maps, Open Street Map, and Bing Maps, geographic data visualization is no longer solely reserved for cartographers and GIS gurus. Web-based mapping applications have now made it possible for data enthusiasts from a wide range of backgrounds to quickly and easily analyze and map spatial data.

The purpose behind all web-based geographic applications is to visually present *geographic data* — quantitative and qualitative data that's associated with particular locations. This area of data science intersects heavily with cartography and spatial statistics. You can learn more about GIS in Chapter 13 and about spatial statistics in Chapter 8.

Newbies often get confused about one important aspect of geographic data visualization — geographic data is always presented as either a point, a line, or a polygon area on a map.

If you need to define an area within particular boundaries, as would be the case with a county boundary, country border, sales district, or political focus area, then you want to use a polygon — since polygons include boundary lines as well as the entire area that lies within those boundary lines, they're the best way of representing areas on a map.

In web-based geographic data visualization, you're likely to represent areas using either a categorical fill or a chloropleth map. A *categorical fill* is a way of visually representing qualitative attributes of your spatial dataset. So, for example, when you are looking at a map that shows an election outcome, states with a majority of Democrat votes are colored blue, and states with a majority of Republican votes are colored red. The categorical attribute is "Political Party", and the fill color is determined by whether the value of that categorical attribute is "Republican" or "Democrat". On the other hand, *choropleths* are map representations where spatial areas are filled with a particular hue or intensity of color to represent the comparative distribution of your data quantities across space.

If you want to represent your data as single markers plotted by latitude and longitude, then you plot point data. Google Maps' red, inverted droplet is a prime example of point data on a web-based mapping application. You can represent spatial data with line features as well. A line feature consists of a start node, an end node, and a connective line between them. Lines are commonly used to represent streets, highways, and rivers.

Lastly, you can also create heat maps from point data. To illustrate this concept, imagine that you want to show the density of coffee shops in Seattle. Rather than display thousands (and thousands) of markers on a map, it would be far more effective to aggregate your data into bands of color that correspond to coffee shop density per unit area. So, in this example, if you have 30 coffee shops in a 1-square-mile area, then you cover this area in a hot red color on the map, but if you have only three coffee shops in 1 square mile, you cover that area of the map in a cool blue color.

The area and marker display type can change with the zoom level, depending on what web application you use and how it renders markers. For example, in a view of the entire Earth, New York City may appear as a marker, but if you zoom into the state of New York, the city is represented as an area.

Web-based geographic data visualizations depend heavily on *geocoding* — the automatic association of data points with geographic points, based on the location information that you provide. If you have a column of state names, or even street addresses, web applications generally can auto-map that data for you.

Web-based geographic applications can sometimes be quite finicky with their data standards. For geocoding functions to work effectively, you may need to reformat some of your data so that it better meets those standards. For example, a web-application that recognizes **District of Columbia** might not recognize **Washington, D.C.**. Format your data accordingly. Since each application has its own requirements, you have to check those on an application-by-application basis.

Making pretty maps with OpenHeatMap

OpenHeatMap is a user-friendly service that allows you to upload and geocode spatial data. OpenHeatMap can automatically geocode spatial identifiers, requiring only minimal user oversight. It's not as versatile as Google Fusion Tables or CartoDB, but it's so easy to use that many people consider it their favorite web-based mapping application. A unique feature of OpenHeatMap is that it doesn't offer user accounts. Anyone and everyone can upload data and use the service anonymously. To learn more, just go over and check out the OpenHeatMap homepage (at www.openheatmap.com/).

If your goal is to quickly create a choropleth or marker-based heat map, OpenHeatMap is the easiest solution on the Internet. "How easy?" you ask? Figure 11-5 shows a choropleth of the in-county moving dataset created in OpenHeatMap, which I managed to put together in a matter of seconds. Not bad, right?

People who move but stay in the same county

OPENHEATMAP

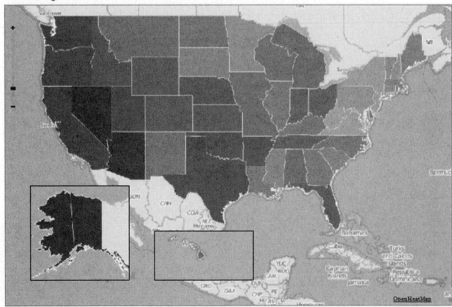

Figure 11-5: A choropleth map in OpenHeat Map.

Percent Moved Within Same County During 2011   6.60   9.10   11.6

Map-making and spatial data analytics with CartoDB

If you're not a professional programmer or cartographer, CartoDB is about the most powerful online mapping solution that's available. People in information services, software engineering, media and entertainment, and urban development industries often use CartoDB for digital visual communications.

By using CartoDB, you can create a heat map simply by uploading or linking to a list of spatial coordinates. Likewise, if you want to create a choropleth map to show values for quantitative attributes, then simply upload or link to a set of spatial coordinates that includes attribute data.

CartoDB allows you to overlay markers and shapes on all sorts of interesting base maps. You can use it to make anything from simple outline maps of geographic regions to stylish, antiqued, magazine-style maps. You can even use it to generate street maps from satellite imagery. CartoDB's geocoding functionality is so well-implemented that you can drill down to a location using individual addresses, postal codes, or even IP addresses.

To get going in CartoDB, you need to first setup a user account. You can do that through the CartoDB homepage (at http://cartodb.com/).

For more advanced users, CartoDB offers the following options:

✔ Link to SQL databases.

✔ Customize Cascading Style Sheets (CSS).

✔ Incorporate other chart types in the form of superimposed graphs, outlines, and three-dimensional surface plots.

Figure 11-6 shows CartoDB's version of the example choropleth map of the in-county moving dataset, and Figure 11-7 shows a bubble map of the same dataset. CartoDB is interactive: It allows you to click features to see attribute information and turn map layers on and off in the same map interface.

Map layers are spatial datasets that represent different features on a map. In shared areas, layers often overlap one another in the same spatial region. To better understand this concept, think again about a map that shows an election outcome. In this type of map, there is a "States" layer and a "Political Party" layer. The states layer shows you the name and spatial boundary of the state. The political party layer is geographically overlaid on top of the states layer and tells you how the majority of voters voted in the election, on a state-by-state basis. Although the layers overlap in physical location, both the states layer and the political party layer are based on separate, individual datasets. This is how layers work in mapping applications.

Figure 11-6:
An interactive choropleth map in CartoDB.

Figure 11-7:
An interactive bubble map in CartoDB.

Visualizing with Open Source: Web-Based Data Visualization Platforms

The sole purpose of a non-collaborative, open-source, web-based data visualization platform is to help you quickly and easily create data visualizations without the need to invest tons of time and money learning how to code them up from scratch. These services do away with the need for specialized or bloated proprietary software packages and let you simply upload your data to get the results you need. Most of these platforms aim to help you create visualizations that you can subsequently use offsite. Some services don't even provide you any storage capacity, so you have to store your data and visualizations on a hard drive, on the cloud, or on some other remote data storage device.

Making pretty data graphics with Google Fusion Tables

Google Fusion Tables is an extension of *Google Drive* — the service for storing and editing office-type documents in the cloud. Google Fusion Tables can create visual communications in a wide range of industries, from information publishing to civil and environmental engineering, sustainable development, and real estate. Even human resource management can use it.

Because Fusion Tables only runs off of data that's stored in *Google Sheets* — Google Drive's spreadsheet application — you must have a Google account with Google Drive (at www.google.com/drive/) and Google Fusion Tables (at www.tables.googlelabs.com/) activated. To easily create data visualizations with Fusion Tables, simply link your Google Sheets to the Google Fusion Tables application and then let the application do all the work. You can use Google Fusion Tables to create pie charts, bar charts, line charts, scatter charts, timelines, and geographic maps. You also have the ability to automatically geotag columns with place names that associate your data with single geographic points. Data that's queried from Google Fusion Tables can even be mapped as points on a Google Map.

You can also use Google Fusion Tables to plot polygon data on top of Google Maps, but this task is a bit more challenging because Google Maps doesn't play well with polygon mapping.

For all the benefits it offers, Fusion Tables has one major drawback — it has a steep learning curve. If you're really committed to using the application,

though, Google offers a free online code lab (at `https://sites.google
.com/site/geoapiscodelabs/home/getting-started-with-the-
fusion-tables-api`) from which you can figure out Fusion Tables
at your own pace. If you become a more advanced user of Fusion Tables,
you can bolster Fusion Tables' capabilities with a powerful API — an applica-
tion-programmer interface that tells software applications how they should
interact with one another.

Using iCharts for web-based data visualization

iCharts offers a web-based visual analytics platform that allows everyone to
create, embed, and share interactive charts. The product provides cloud-
based, fully interactive analytics that can be connected to live data using a
variety of connectors, including an iCharts API, Google Sheets, Google Big
Query, NetSuite, and so on. iCharts' visual analytics are fully embeddable and
have built-in SEO optimization and social sharing features. You can use iCharts to visualize your data through a variety of built-in chart types, including
bar charts, column charts, pie charts, line charts, free form charts, and so on.

In addition to the free offering targeted to individuals (such as bloggers), the
company currently offers paid plans focused on the following scenarios:

- **Visual Content Marketing:** Media companies and publishers can create,
  publish, and share interactive visualizations that allow them to offer a
  richer experience to their audiences and expand their brand reach.

- **Embedded Visual Analytics:** Companies of any size can embed iCharts
  within their enterprise systems to quickly visualize their data in real-
  time, without any IT support or data extraction / aggregation.

If you would like to get started using iCharts, the first thing you need to do
is create an account (at `www.icharts.net`). To see what iCharts can do,
check out Figure 11-8, which shows an iCharts version of a bar chart.

Using RAW for web-based data visualization

RAW is a unique and unusual web application that you can use to make artistic and creative visualizations from your dataset. RAW's layout provides you
a very simple drag-and-drop interface that you can use to make unique and
interesting styles of data visualizations with just a few clicks of the mouse.

If you want to get funky and cool with your data visualization, but you don't have the time or money it takes to learn how to code this sort of thing for yourself, then RAW is the perfect data visualization alternative.

Like I said, RAW is funky. It doesn't even offer standard bar chart visualizations. It does, however, offer clustered force diagrams, Voronoi tessellations, Reingold-Tilford trees, and other less-well-known chart types.

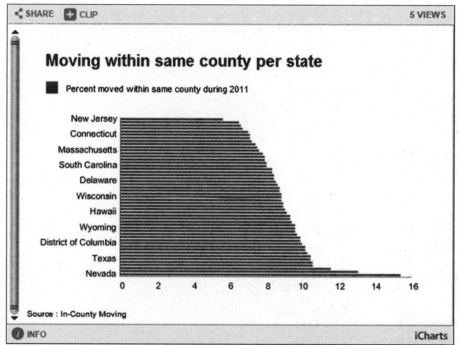

Figure 11-8:
A bar chart in iCharts.

To use RAW, first go to the RAW homepage (at `http://raw.densitydesign.org/`) and then navigate to the "USE IT NOW!" button. You don't even need to create an account to use the application, just copy and paste your raw data into the application and then choose the optimal chart types for that data. RAW makes it easy to choose between chart types by telling you the precise number of quantitative attributes, categorical attributes, and labels that are required to generate each plot.

This service wasn't designed for novices, but its simple, straightforward interface makes it a fun, user-friendly application for playing with your data and figuring out how to generate unique chart types. Even if you don't know a convex hull from a hexagonal bin, you can play around with settings, drag columns from place to place, and view how those changes affect the overall visualization. With enough practice, you may even end up using some of the visualization strategies that you learn from RAW in other contexts.

You can have fun getting cool and funky with visualization design, but you should always make sure that your visual result is easy to understand for the average viewer.

Figure 11-9 shows a circle packing diagram of the in-county moving dataset I created in RAW. (**_Note:_** This is just about the only type of visualization RAW offers that would work with such a simple dataset!)

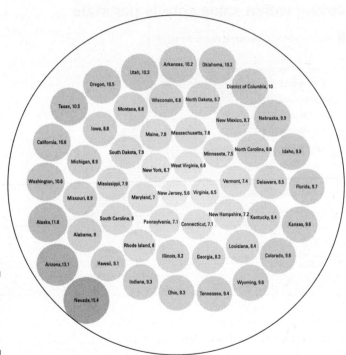

Figure 11-9:
A circle packing diagram.

Knowing When to Stick with Infographics

Although the contextual difference between an infographic and a data visualization is often clear, even data visualization professionals can sometimes have a hard time distinguishing the two. A good rule of thumb is that if the data graphics are primarily produced in an automated fashion using a data-graphing application, then it's a data visualization. But if you use a custom graphic-design tool, such as Photoshop or Illustrator, to produce the final product, then it's an infographic.

This categorization gets a bit more complicated, though. An infographic often incorporates one or more charts, making it more difficult to determine the manner in which the visualization was produced. Complicating the issue, online infographic design applications, such as Piktochart and Infogr.am, have dual functionality that allows for automated data graphing and customizable, artistic graphic design.

An even broader rule of thumb is that if the visualization looks artfully designed, then it's an infographic, but if it looks rather plain and analytical, then it's a data visualization.

Although infographics can be dynamic or static, when you're designing a graphic for print, a slide for PowerPoint, or an image for social media syndication, just stick with static infographics. If you want to tell a story with your data or create data art, then use an infographic.

You can easily directly embed static graphics into a social media post. Social content that has an embedded graphic tends to get more attention and engagement than social content that is posted as text-only.

Applications used to create infographics provide many more creative alternatives than do traditional data visualization applications. In fact, this is as good a time as any to introduce you to a few of the better applications that are available for infographic design. Read on for all the details.

Making cool infographics with Infogr.am

Infogr.am is an online tool that you can use to make aesthetically appealing, vertically stacked-card infographics — a visualization that's comprised of a series of cards, stacked vertically on top of one another, each with its own set of data graphics. Since the cards are stacked vertically, one on top of the other, the end infographic is often longer than it is wide.

Infogr.am offers a variety of trendy color schemes, design schemes, and chart types. With Infogr.am, you can import your own images to make your infographic that much more personalized. Infogr.am also provides you with sharing capabilities so that you can spread your infographic quickly and easily across social channels or via private email.

You can use Infogr.am to create stylish infographics that display bar charts, column charts, pie charts, line charts, area charts, scatter charts, bubble charts, pictorials, hierarchial charts, tables, progress displays, word clouds, tree maps, or even financial charts. To get started using Infogr.am, just head over to the home page (at `https://infogr.am/`) and register for an account. It's freemium plan is robust enough to supply all of your more basic infographic-making needs.

Figure 11-10 shows a bar chart of the (by now familiar) in-county moving dataset in Infogr.am.

If you want to check out some great Infogr.am examples before you get started, you can view a live feed of featured infographics at Infogr.am's Featured Infographics page (`http://infogr.am/featured`).

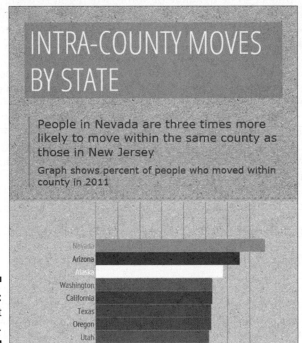

Figure 11-10:
A bar chart
in Infogr.am.

Making cool infographics with Piktochart

The Piktochart web application provides an easy-to-use interface that people like you and I can use to quickly create beautiful infographics. Piktochart offers a very large selection of attractive templates, but be warned that only members who have paying accounts can access most of these templates. These templates are a great option if you want to save time and money on design but need to produce documents in an infographic format. Piktochart offers more creative flexibility than other comparable web applications, which makes Piktochart useful in a wide range of industries, from non-profit grassroots to media and entertainment.

You can use Piktochart to make either static or dynamic infographics, and you can also link your infographics to Google Sheets for live updating. Piktochart offers the usual array of chart types, in addition to some more infographic-oriented types, such as Venn diagrams, gauges, and matrixes.

If you use the free version of Piktochart to create your infographic, then be warned that your infographic will be made available to the public. If you signup for a paid account, however, you have the option of keeping your work private. You can register for Piktochart through the application's homepage at `http://piktochart.com/`.

Using Piktochart, you can create infographics that display bar charts, triangle charts, line charts, area charts, scatter charts, pie charts, Venn diagrams, matrixes, pyramids, gauges, donuts, swatches, and icons. Figure 11-11 shows a Piktochart version of a bar chart of the example in-county moving dataset.

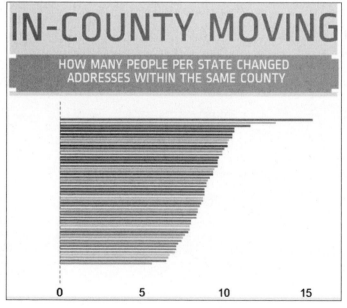

Figure 11-11: A bar chart in Piktochart.

Chapter 12

Exploring Best Practices in Dashboard Design

In This Chapter

▶ Designing a dashboard for its users

▶ Seeing the big picture

▶ Getting down to details

▶ Letting no dashboard go untested

*B*ig data, data engineering, and data science are revolutionizing business. While more and more data is collected at faster and faster rates, the demand for clear and meaningful data insights increases, as well. Organizational decision makers need information delivered quickly, and in a concise and easy-to-understand format.

In this context, data analytics dashboards are one of the more popular methods for delivering such information. Acting as a (hopefully) user-friendly software interface, such dashboards can provide a single-page, easy-to-understand summary of information that's vital to organizational and managerial decision making. A dashboard can also serve as a portal through which users can drill down to obtain more detailed information when needed.

Although dashboards have the potential to be highly effective communication mediums, their usefulness is heavily dependent on the designers' implementation of strategic and thoughtful design principles. In this chapter, I introduce you to the best practices of dashboard design, and explain why those practices are important.

As with any type of design, you can find a lot of good and bad dashboard examples out there. Bad design is usually the direct result of a poorly scoped purpose. Dashboards, like all visualizations, have to be designed for a specific audience to serve a specific function. If you don't define the audience and function clearly in advance, the dashboard probably can't succeed.

The term *dashboard* was adopted from the automobile panel. Don't let the metaphorical title "dashboard" shape your image of the analytics dashboard, though. Dashboards that incorporate illustrations of gauges and odometers are considered old-fashioned and clunky today. These design elements consume a lot of screen space, deliver very little information, and create needless visual clutter on a layout that should be clear, concise, and to the point. Use cleaner, more compact elements instead.

Focusing on the Audience

Dashboards are all about communication, and the golden rule in communication is *know your audience.* One of the most common errors in dashboard design happens when a designer tries to make a dashboard be all things to all people. This designer inevitably uses every type of doodad and gewgaw to visualize every possible item of interest, thus creating a dashboard that's so cluttered and unfocused that it's nearly impossible to use.

A business intelligence dashboard for upper management should have an entirely different focus than that of a small-business e-commerce dashboard. Focus less attention on what your audience *might want* to know and more attention on what your audience *needs* to know. Focus on what's useful to your audience in an at-a-glance resource. Set up your dashboard in such a way that users keep coming back precisely because your dashboard is the one that delivers actionable, timely insights that they can turn to for quick and easy decision support. If the insights aren't actionable, or if they're too hard to understand, your target audience won't adopt the dashboard as a decision-support instrument. This is generally just how things turn out.

One important, yet often overlooked, best practice in dashboard design is to plan your dashboard as if every user is seeing it for the very first time. To secure the comfort of your users, your dashboard must be self-explanatory and intuitive. For this reason, you need to keep your dashboards simple. Use icons, as well as text; label everything; use tooltips, where appropriate; and never expect a user to read a Help file before getting started.

Starting with the Big Picture

In design, there are large-scale issues and smaller, more detail-oriented issues. The space limitations implicit in dashboard design require that you hold strong focus on purpose and carefully integrate and harmonize both large-scale and detail elements to fulfill that purpose. Most industry-standard best practices for dashboard design have been established through trial and error procedures. When conceptualizing your dashboard's design, it also helps to study what clients and managers have found most useful and helpful in their previous dashboards. Here are a few best practices to keep in mind when designing the overall, big-picture layout of your dashboard (in the next section, I drill down to the detail level):

- **Keep it on a single page.** Dashboards are supposed to be an at-a-glance resource, and you can glance at only one page at a time. Therefore, when designing a dashboard, find a way to fit everything on that one page. Also, don't get sucked into the trap of thinking that you need to fit tons of stuff on that page — leave out everything but the most important information.

- **Let it breathe.** *White space* — the blank white space on a screen where no text or images are placed — is very important in design. If you pack everything in closely, the eye has trouble focusing on anything. Carefully chosen whitespace can guide your users to focus on only the most important parts of the dashboard.

- **Give the layout a natural flow.** Your dashboard should flow from top to bottom and left to right. This logical progression intuitively makes sense to users. The progression can be from more specific to more general, it can follow a workflow pathway, or it can simply follow some path of dependencies between one concept and another.

Of course, reading from top to bottom, and from left to right, is the standard practice of western cultures. If you're Japanese, then you'd read from right to left, and should design a visualization that naturally flows in that direction. What's important is that you design your dashboard so that it makes the most intuitive sense for your particular audience, according to their specific cultural norms.

- **Provide a method to drill down to more specific information.** The dashboard should function as an overall summary of the desired information, but if you're including something of particular interest to your audience, then users probably want to explore that area more fully. A good dashboard makes getting more information a near-effortless process. Unlike a static snapshot, dashboards can provide an interactive experience where users can click different parts of the data graphics in order to be presented with a more detailed version (what's known as *drilling down*). For example, a dashboard shows a Sales Stats by Region section and, when you click any given region, a Sales Stats by County pop-up window appears to provide you with the more detailed information.

✔ **Choose alerts wisely.** Get feedback from end users to determine what's important enough to warrant an alert function. For example, for dashboards that track stock valuations, having a stock price fall below a certain value threshold for an allotted period of time should trigger a dashboard alert. Because no two users' needs are the same, alerts can be a difficult balancing act. If you flag everything, then you're really flagging nothing because people will quickly begin to ignore all of the constant alerts. On the other hand, you don't want to let important situations slide by unnoticed. Prepare for a lot of tweaking when configuring alert functionalities.

✔ **Less is more.** The dashboard should be attractive and aesthetically appealing, but it mustn't be over-designed. In every design decision, make sure to focus on utility and usefulness as the top criteria. Let the dashboard's form naturally follow from a simple and functional approach.

Getting the Details Right

After you have your dashboard conceptualized — you know who your audience is, of what they need to be informed, and what elements need to go where on the page — you need to get into the nitty-gritty details. Even if everything was perfect up until this point, your dashboard can still fail to deliver if you haven't taken time to think about the look and feel of the individual elements that comprise it. The following list describes a set of best practices that are helpful when planning the details of your design:

✔ **Less is more.** Even though this was the last bullet point in the preceding section, I'm reusing it here because it's vitally important in designing dashboard details, as well as in overall dashboard design. Real estate on the dashboard is at a premium, and user time and attention isn't guaranteed. Make it as easy as possible for users to get what they need by presenting everything as simply as possible. Although green, yellow, and red traffic lights or thermometer bulbs might work in an infographic, they're much too distracting on a dashboard. Use simple bars and dots instead.

✔ **Stay current.** *Flat design* — a modern minimalistic design approach that restricts designers to only using 2-dimensional elements, and to placing those elements in an exceptionally clean and clutter-free visual layout — is all the rage these days. The greatest advantage of this style is that it makes user interaction simple and easy. If a flat design approach works with your data, you can increase your hipness factor by making use of it.

Keeping your source data current is also extremely important. When you're designing a dashboard to support other people's decision making, timeliness is everything — if you haven't equipped your dashboards with real-time updating, then they must at least be based on current, up-to-date sources.

- **Use color sparingly.** Choose a simple, muted color palette that's easy on the eyes without being monotone and boring. Reserve your vibrant colors for alerts and notifications — you need them to stand out from the background.

- **Stay horizontal.** Since most people from western cultures read words horizontally, our eyes can better follow representations of data when they're laid out horizontally, as well. Make bar charts left to right instead of up and down, and arrange items in lines instead of vertical stacks. A couple of data graphic innovations are quite useful for designing effective dashboards — sparklines and bullet graphs:

  - *Sparklines:* Invented by data visualization pioneer Edward Tufte, sparklines consist of tiny line or bar charts that are presented in the same space and at the same size as words, either in a table or a paragraph. Sparklines offer a very compact and effective way of presenting trends on a dashboard. (See Figure 12-1 for an example.)

  - *Bullet graphs:* A simple and elegant alternative to the old-fashioned thermometers and progress bars of yesteryear. Figure 12-2 shows a bullet graph that represents a danger zone, where the number of new customers in a time period is below 250. In this graphic, the acceptable zone is 250 to 400, and the good zone is above 400. Instead of using gaudy red, yellow, and green colors, this graphic nicely presents the information by using subtle shades of gray. In this graphic, the current status shows 300 new customers, with a goal of 450.

Figure 12-1:
Sparklines are a very effective way to communicate data insights.

Revenues

Expenses

Figure 12-2:
Bullet
graphs
offer an
aesthetically
appealing
alternative
to progress
bars.

Testing Your Design

No matter how careful and strategic your dashboard design, you're bound to come up against trouble when the product goes live. Developing and releasing a preliminary version of the dashboard is just the first step. Dashboard designers must be prepared to see it through until they're certain the product works, and works well.

You can't please everyone, and you may have to juggle and prioritize a list of complaints, but true testing comes from observing how the dashboard works in action. Because dashboards are almost always web-based nowadays, you can easily get some hard statistics about their performance and usability. Log files can tell you about visitor counts, session durations, and user click patterns. You can even incorporate A/B testing by shuffling items around to see which layout is most effective.

You can't prepare for all potential scenarios in advance, and with something as complex and subjective as dashboard design, you're better off adopting a flexible design approach. That way, you have a better chance of designing a product that end users will actually use, and isn't that the point?

Chapter 13

Making Maps from Spatial Data

*A*dvanced statistical methods are great tools when you need to make predictions from spatial datasets, and everyone knows that data visualization design can help you present your findings in the most effective way possible. That's all fine and dandy, but wouldn't it be great if you could combine the two approaches?

I'm here to tell you that it can be done. The key to putting the two together involves envisioning how one could map spatial data — *spatial data visualization,* in other words. Whether you choose to use a proprietary or open-source application, the simplest way to make maps from spatial datasets is to use Geographic Information Systems (GIS) software to help you do the job. This chapter introduces the basics of GIS and how you can use it to analyze and manipulate spatial datasets.

The proprietary GIS software, ESRI ArcGIS for Desktop, is the most widely used map-making application. It can be purchased through the ESRI website (at www.esri.com/software/arcgis/arcgis-for-desktop). But if you don't have the money to invest in this solution, you can use open-source QGIS (at www.qgis.org) to accomplish the same goals. GRASS GIS (at http://grass.osgeo.org/) is another good open-source alternative to proprietary ESRI products. In practice, all of these software applications are simply referred to as *GIS*.

Getting into the Basics of GIS

People use GIS for all sorts of purposes. Some simply want to make beautiful maps, while others could care less about aesthetics and are primarily interested in using GIS to help them make sense of significant patterns in their spatial data. Whether you're a cartographer or a statistician, GIS offers a little bit for everyone. In the following sections, I cover all the basic concepts you need to know about GIS so that you can get started making maps from your spatial data.

To get a handle on some basic concepts, imagine that you have a dataset that captures information on snow events. When most people think of snow events, they may think of making a snowman, or of scary avalanches, or of snow skiing. When a GIS person thinks of a snow event, however, she more likely thinks about snow fall rates, snow accumulation, or in what city it snowed the most. A spatial dataset about snow might provide just this kind of information.

Check out the simple snow dataset shown in Figure 13-1. Although this table provides only a small amount of information, you can use the data in this table to make a simple map that shows what cities have snow and what cities don't.

Although you can use this data to make a simple map, you need to have your location data in a numerical format if you want to go deeper into GIS analysis. Imagine that you go back to the table from Figure 13-1 and add 3 columns of data — one column for latitudinal coordinates, one column for longitudinal coordinates, and one column for number of road accidents that occur at the locations where these coordinates intersect. Figure 13-2 shows what I have in mind.

ID	Snow	Location
1	No	Valley City
2	Yes	Grand Forks
3	Yes	Jamestown
4	No	Aberdeen

Figure 13-1:
A sample of basic spatial data.

ID	Snow (mm)	City	Latitude	Longitude	Road accidents (last 24 h)
1	0	Valley City	46.96	-98.01	2
2	120	Grand Forks	47.95	-97.01	5
3	140	Jamestown	46.92	-98.23	6
4	0	Aberdeen	45.98	-98.47	3
5	150	Miles City	45.74	-98.71	6
6	80	Dickinson	45.79	-96.98	6
7	0	Minot	49.16	-97.76	2
8	20	Bismark	46.91	-98.01	2

Figure 13-2: Spatial data described through coordinates and additional attributes.

When you have spatial data coordinates that specify position and location, you can use GIS to store, manipulate, and perform analysis on large volumes of data. For the snow example, you could use GIS to calculate how much snow has fallen and accumulated in each city or to determine the cities where it's particularly dangerous to drive during snow events.

To do all that neat stuff, you need to bone up on some core GIS concepts that are central to helping you understand spatial databases, GIS file formats, map projections, and coordinate systems. The following sections help you accomplish that task.

Understanding spatial databases

The main purpose of a spatial database is to store, manage, and manipulate attribute, location, and geometric data for all records in a feature's database. With respect to GIS, an *attribute* is a class of fact that describes a feature, *location* describes the feature's location on Earth, and *geometric data* describes the feature's *geometry type* — either a point, a line, or a polygon.

So for example, imagine that you want to make a map of all Dunkin Donuts restaurants that also sell Baskin-Robbin's Ice Cream. The feature you're mapping is "Dunkin Donuts restaurants", the attribute is "Baskin-Robbins Vendor? (Y/N)", the location fields tell you where these restaurants are located, each store is represented by its own *record* in the database, and the geometric data tells you that these restaurants must be represented by points on the map.

A spatial database is similar to a plain relational database, but in addition to storing data on qualitative and quantitative attributes, spatial databases store data about physical location and feature geometry type, as well. Every record in a spatial database is stored with numeric coordinates that represent where that record occurs on a map and each feature is represented by only one of the three following geometry types:

- ✔ Point
- ✔ Line
- ✔ Polygon

Whether you want to calculate the distance between two places on a map or determine the area of a particular piece of land, you can use spatial database querying to quickly and easily make automated spatial calculations on entire sets of records at one time. Going one step further, you can use spatial databases to perform almost all the same types of calculations on — and manipulations of — attribute data that you can in a plain relational database system.

Understanding file formats in GIS

To facilitate different types of analysis and outputs, GIS accommodates two main file formats — raster and vector. Since these are the main two file format types used in GIS, both proprietary and open-source GIS applications have been specifically designed to support each.

Raster data is broken up and plotted out along a two-dimensional grid structure so that each grid cell gets its own attribute value. (See Figure 13-3.) Although most people know that rasters are used to store image data in digital photographs, very few people know that the raster file format is useful for storing spatial data, as well.

Raster files can be used to store data for only one attribute at a time. In GIS, data for a single attribute is stored and plotted in a two-dimensional grid, where the horizontal dimension represents longitude and the vertical dimension represents latitude. Digital photographs and Doppler weather radar maps are two common examples of raster files in the modern world.

Figure 13-3:
Raster and vector representations of different geometric features used in GIS.

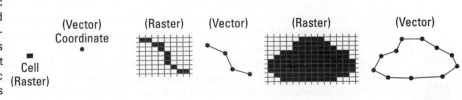

Vector format files, on the other hand, store data as either points, lines, or polygons on a map. (Refer to Figure 13-3.) Point features are stored as single point records plotted in geographic space, while line and polygon features are stored as a series of vertices that comprise each record plotted in geographic space. For data in vector format, GIS can easily handle tens of attributes for each record stored in the spatial database. Google Maps, modern digital graphics, and engineering computer-aided design (CAD) drawings are some prime examples of vector graphics at use in the real world.

To conceptualize the raster versus vector idea, imagine that you have some graphing paper and a pencil, and you want to draw a map of a street cul-de-sac that's in your neighborhood. You can draw it as a series of polygons — one representing the area covered by the street, and the others representing the parcels that abut the street. Or, you can fill in the squares of the graph paper, one after the other, until you cover all the areas with one, single multi-colored surface.

Vector format data is like drawing the street and parcels as a set of separate *polygons*. Raster data format is like making one *surface* by coloring the entire area around the cul-de-sac, so that all street areas and the adjoining parcel areas are covered in their own representative color. The difference between the two methods is shown in Figure 13-4.

Figure 13-4:
A street and neigh-borhood represented as vector polygons and as a raster surface.

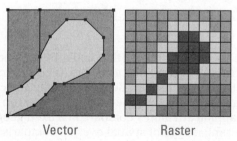

Vector   Raster

If you use GIS to create maps that show municipal boundaries, land cover, roads, attractions, or any other distinct spatial features, as shown in Figure 13-5, then this type of spatial data is best stored in the vector file format. If you need to perform complex spatial analysis of multiple attributes for each feature in your dataset, then keep your data in vector format. Vector data covers only the spatial areas where each discreet feature from your dataset is located on Earth. But with vector data, you get a lot of options on what attributes of that feature you want to analyze or display on a map.

Figure 13-5:
An address
location
map rep-
resented
as vector
format
points and
polygons.

The easiest way to analyze several attributes (that could be derived from one or several features) that spatially overlap one another over a particular piece of land is to put your data into raster format. Because a raster file can represent only one attribute at a time, you'd layer several rasters on top of each other to see how the overlapping attributes compare in a fixed geographic region. While you can do a similar type of spatial overlap comparison using vector files, raster files are going to give you a full and comprehensive coverage for each set of attribute values across an entire study area.

For example, to quantify volume data across a fixed area of land, raster files are definitely the way to go. Consider the snow example once again. Your attribute in this example is snow height. Given that your raster data provides you all height data for the snow (on a pixel-by-pixel basis) in a particular fixed region, you can use that to calculate the volume of snow on the ground in that area: Simply multiply the area of each pixel by the difference between the average snow surface height and the average ground elevation at that location. To find the area of snow that has accumulated in a fixed area, sum up the volume of snow that has fallen in each pixel of that area, as shown in Figure 13-6.

When you work with spatial data that's in vector format, you're focusing on *features*. You're doing things like drawing separate line features, cutting existing features, or performing a buffering analysis to get some determination about features that are within a certain proximity of the feature you're studying. When you work with spatial data that's in raster format, you're focusing on *surfaces*. You're working with a raster surface that covers the entire spatial area you're studying, and describes the quantities, intensities, and changes in value of one attribute across an entire study area.

It's possible to convert a vector feature to a raster surface — but, you can only convert one attribute at a time. For example, imagine you have a vector file that represents gas stations with "Leaking Underground Storage Tanks," represented as points on a map. The attribute table for this layer has data on the following four attributes — "Year Tank Was Installed," "Year Leak Was Detected," "Tank Depth," and "Contaminant Concentrations." When you convert all of this data from vector to raster, you get four separate raster files, one for each attribute. The vector point format is converted to a raster surface that covers the entire study area and displays the attribute values, or lack thereof, on a pixel-by-pixel basis.

Figure 13-6: Interpolated surface of snow depth represented in a raster with low resolution.

Understanding map projections and coordinate systems

Map projections and coordinate systems give GIS a way to accurately represent a round Earth on a flat surface, translating the Earth's arced three-dimensional geometry into flat two-dimensional geometry.

Projections and coordinate systems *project* spatial data. That is to say, they forecast and predict accurate spatial positions and geographic scale, depending on where those features are located on Earth. Although projection and coordinate systems are able to project most features rather accurately, they don't offer a one-size-fits-all solution. If features in one region are projected perfectly at scale, then features in another region are inevitably projected with at least a slight amount of distortion. This distortion is sort of like looking at things through a magnifying glass — you can see the object in the center of the lens very accurately and clearly, but the objects on the outer edge of the lens always appear distorted. No matter where you move the magnifying glass, this fact remains unchanged. Similarly, you can't represent *all* features of a rounded world accurately and to-scale on a flat map.

In GIS, the trick to getting around this distortion problem is to narrow your study area, focus on only a small geographic region, and use the map projection or coordinate system that's most accurate for this region.

Coordinate systems are referencing systems that are used to *define* a feature's location on Earth. There are two types of coordinate systems:

✔ **Projected Coordinate Systems:** Also called *map projections*, projected coordinate systems are mathematical algorithms that you can use to transform the location of features on a round Earth to equivalent positions represented on a flat surface instead. The three common projection types are cylindrical, conical, and planar.

✔ **Geographic Coordinate Systems:** A coordinate system that uses sets of numbers and/or letters to define every location on Earth. In geographic coordinate systems, location is often represented by latitude/longitude, decimal degrees, or degrees-minutes-seconds (if you're familiar with old fashioned surveying nomenclature).

Figure 13-7 shows these three types in all their glory.

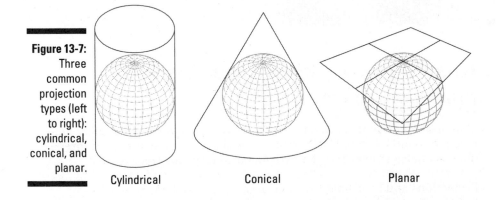

Figure 13-7:
Three common projection types (left to right): cylindrical, conical, and planar.

Cylindrical   Conical   Planar

Now that you know what types of coordinate systems are out there, it's time to take a look at how you'd make practical use of them. This is the easy part!

In almost all cases, when you import a spatial dataset into GIS, it comes in with its own pre-defined coordinate system. The GIS software then adopts that coordinate system and assigns it to the entire project. When you add additional datasets to that project in the future, they may be using that same coordinate system or an alternative one. In cases where the new data is coming in with a coordinate system that's different from that of the project, the GIS software will transform the incoming data so that it is represented correctly on the map.

So, as an example of how all this works in practice, to determine how much agricultural land has been contaminated during a tanker spill at the Mississippi Delta, you import a spatial dataset that's called "Contaminated Land". The "Contaminated Land" file already has a pre-defined coordinate system — State Plane Coordinate System Mississippi, West MS_W 4376 2302. When you import the dataset, GIS automatically detects its coordinate system, assigns that coordinate system to the project you've started, and will transform any subsequently added spatial datasets, so that they come in with correct scale and positioning. It's that easy!

Information about a dataset's default map projection and coordinate system is stored in its mctadata description. The default map projection and coordinate system are the fundamental reference systems from which you can re-project the dataset for your specific needs.

Analyzing Spatial Data

After you've imported your data, it's time to get into spatial data analysis. In the following sections, you find out how to use various querying, buffering, overlay, and classification methods to extract valuable information from your spatial dataset.

Querying spatial data

In GIS, you can query spatial data in two ways — attribute querying and spatial querying. *Attribute querying* is just what it sounds like: You use this querying method when you want to summarize, extract, manipulate, sort, or group database records according to relevant attribute values. If you want to make sense of your data by creating order from its attribute values, then use attribute querying.

Spatial querying, on the other hand, is all about querying data records according to their physical location in space. Spatial querying is based solely on the location of the feature and has nothing to do with the feature's attribute values. If your goal is to make sense of your data based on its physical location, then use spatial querying.

Learning to quickly and fluidly switch between attribute and spatial querying can help you to quickly make sense of complex problems in GIS. A situation where this is true would be if you have a spatial point dataset that represents disease risk. If you want to find the average disease risk of people over the age of 50 that live within a 2-mile distance of a major power center, then you could use spatial and attribute querying to quickly generate some results. The first step would be to use spatial querying to isolate data points, so that you're analyzing only those people that live within the 2-mile radius. From this reduced dataset, you'd next use attribute querying to isolate the records of people that are over the age of 50, and then perform a quick mathematical operation to get the average value for disease risk from that subset.

You can either query the spatial database directly using SQL statements or use the simple built-in interfaces to query your data for you. Sometimes the quickest way to query results is to write the SQL statement yourself, but if your query is simple, then you might as well make your life easy and use the point-and-click interface instead.

Referring back to the snow example, if you want to generate a list of all cities where snow depth was greater than 100mm, you simply use attribute querying to select all records that have a snow value that's greater than 100mm. But if you decide you want to generate a list of cities with more than 100mm of snow that are located within 100 miles of Grand Forks, you'd use both an attribute and a spatial query.

Buffering and proximity functions

Within a GIS project, you can select or extract spatial features based on their physical *proximity*, or nearness, to a point, line, or polygon by using buffering and proximity functions. Buffering and proximity functions are fundamental, basic spatial querying methods.

Proximity analysis is a spatial querying operation you can use to select and extract features that are within a user-defined distance from your target feature. You can use proximity analysis to calculate distances between features or to calculate the shortest route in a network. *Buffering* is a proximity operation that you can use to select and extract spatial features that are within a user-defined distance of your target feature. Figure 13-8 shows a schematic of a Buffer Zone Y that encompasses all areas within distance d of a target Polygon X. You can use Buffer Zone Y to isolate, extract, and analyze all spatial features within the d distance of Polygon X.

Figure 13-8:
Buffered
features
at two
different
distances.

Using layer overlay analysis

One of the most powerful features of a GIS platform is its capability to overlay and derive meaning from multiple layers of data. By using *layer overlay analysis,* you can apply multiple operations to multiple layers of data that overlap the same spatial area.

Union, intersection, non-intersection, and *subtraction* are a few fundamental overlay operations. *Union* operations combine the total area of all features being overlain, whereas *intersection* operations retain only the areas of overlap between the features being overlain. *Non-intersection* operations are the reverse of intersection operations — they represent the areas of non-overlap between the features being overlain. Lastly, you can use a *subtraction* operation to subtract an area from one feature based on the area of other features that overlay it. I know this all sounds rather obscure, but it's not so bad. Take a look at Figure 13-9 to see how these operations work.

Overlay analysis is commonly used in suitability studies to determine which sites are best suited to support a particular function or type of business. For example, if you have to plan a new town settlement, you can use GIS to overlay spatial data layers and analyze the land's proximity to potable water sources, suitable terrain, suitable soil type, bodies of water, and so on. By overlaying these layers, you generate a map that shows which regions are more or less suitable to support the planned settlement.

Vector format data is often a bit too big and clunky for complex overlay analyses. To reduce computing requirements, consider converting your vector data to raster data and then using overlay operations to make sense of the layers. This type of overlay analysis is called *raster algebra.*

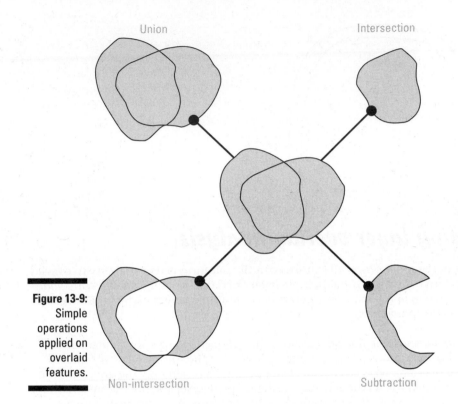

Union

Intersection

Non-intersection

Subtraction

Reclassifying spatial data

In GIS, *reclassification* is the act of changing or reclassifying the values of cells in a raster file, or the values of an attribute in a vector file. Although you can use layer overlay operations to analyze more than one layer at a time, you have to perform reclassification on a layer-by-layer basis. You can use reclassification if you want to reassign a new set of values to existing cells (in rasters) or attribute values (in vectors), but you need the newly assigned values to be proportional to and consistent with the current values and groupings of those cells or attribute values. Reclassification is applied to vector or raster data layers that generally represent attributes of the Earth's surface (in other words, elevation, temperature, land cover type, soil type, and so on).

To fully grasp the concept of reclassifying data in a raster layer, imagine a raster surface where every cell is assigned a depth of snow. Simply by creating new groupings of depth ranges, you could easily reclassify this source data to uncover new snow depth patterns in the study area.

To illustrate the concept of vector layer reclassification, consider that you have a vector polygon layer that depicts land cover across your study area. In this layer, you have polygons that represent lakes, rivers, agricultural land, forests, grassland, and so on. Now imagine that you want to know where only the water and vegetation are located in this study area. You can simply repackage your map by reclassifying all Lake and River polygons as Water and all Agricultural, Forest, and Grassland polygons as Vegetation. With this reclassification, you can identify water from vegetation areas without needing to give the map more than a sweeping glance.

Getting Started with Open-Source QGIS

Earlier sections in this chapter focus on the basic concepts involved in GIS and spatial data analysis. The following sections let you finally get your hands dirty. I show you how to set up your interface, add data, and specify display settings in QGIS. To follow along, you must first start by downloading and installing QGIS (from `http://qgis.org/en/site/forusers/index.html`) and then download the following spatial dataset:

- Cartographic Boundary File, State-County-Census Tract, 1:500,000 (at `http://goo.gl/3zUuIL`)

Getting to know the QGIS interface

The main window of QGIS contains a lot of toolbars and menus, as shown in Figure 13-10. The toolbar on the far left is used to add data. You can add vector layers, raster layers, comma-delimited tables, and several other data types. The toolbar at the very top contains many tools that allow you to navigate through the map that you're creating. You can use the two toolbars below the topmost toolbar to manipulate and analyze data. Then, you have the three embedded windows running down the left side of the main window:

- **Browser:** Allows you to browse through your files and add data.
- **Layers:** Shows you what layers are active in your map.
- **Shortest Path:** Calculates the shortest path between two points on a map.

You won't use the Browser or Shortest Path window in this chapter, so you can close those windows by clicking the X that appears in the top-right corner of each window.

Figure 13-10:
The default
QGIS setup.

Your screen should now look something like Figure 13-11.

Adding a vector layer in QGIS

To continue your exploration of the QGIS interface, add a vector layer containing the borders for all counties in the United States to your map by following these steps:

1. **Click the Add Vector Layer icon in the toolbar on the left of your screen.**

   An Add Vector Layer dialog box appears onscreen, as shown in Figure 13-12.

2. **Click the Add Vector Layer dialog box's Browse button.**

3. **In the Open an OGR Supported Vector Layer dialog box that appears, navigate to the folder where you choose to store the GIS data that you downloaded for this tutorial.**

4. **Choose the** `county.shp` **file, click OK, and then click Open.**

A layer named County appears in the Layers menu, as shown in Figure 13-13.

Figure 13-11:
Your new
QGIS setup.

Displaying data in QGIS

This county.shp file (a vector file) displays all counties in the United States. All these polygons have Attribute data connected to and stored in the dataset's Attribute table. To see what I mean, take a look at what kind of information this table contains. Follow these steps:

1. **Right-click the County layer in the Layers window and choose Open Attribute Table from the pop-up menu that appears.**

   The Attribute Table window containing all the data appears, as shown in Figure 13-14.

   Each record in this table represents a single polygon. Every record has its own row, and each attribute has its own column. Within the QGIS Layer Properties settings, you can set up your record attributes so that they display different colors, are grouped in certain ways, and do a lot of other nifty things.

Figure 13-12:
Adding a
vector layer
to QGIS.

Figure 13-13:
A layer
added into
QGIS.

	STATEFP	COUNTYFP	COUNTYNS	AFFGEOID	GEOID	NAME	LSAD	ALAND	AWATER
0	01	001	00161526	0500000US01001	01001	Autauga	06	1539584443	25773561
1	01	009	00161530	0500000US01009	01009	Blount	06	1670041814	15077461
2	01	023	00161537	0500000US01023	01023	Choctaw	06	2365954803	19059247
3	01	033	00161542	0500000US01033	01033	Colbert	06	1534878355	80029923
4	01	049	00161550	0500000US01049	01049	DeKalb	06	2012664422	4121499
5	01	089	00161570	0500000US01089	01089	Madison	06	2076115375	28770709
6	01	109	00161581	0500000US01109	01109	Pike	06	1740741440	2336918
7	01	133	00161592	0500000US01133	01133	Winston	06	1587615096	48922725
8	02	016	01419965	0500000US02016	02016	Aleutians West	05	11370496382	25190642141
9	02	090	01419969	0500000US02090	02090	Fairbanks North...	04	19006935117	272298859
10	02	270	01419985	0500000US02270	02270	Wade Hampton	05	44240303572	6712008910
11	04	007	00040471	0500000US04007	04007	Gila	06	12323010025	97111871
12	04	021	00025447	0500000US04021	04021	Pinal	06	13897002061	22331517
13	05	013	00063758	0500000US05013	05013	Calhoun	06	1627959476	9926129
14	05	017	00069160	0500000US05017	05017	Chicot	06	1668799972	120391647
15	05	073	00066864	0500000US05073	05073	Lafayette	06	1368208572	43539042
16	05	099	00069169	0500000US05099	05099	Nevada	06	1600189832	7257493
17	05	145	00069906	0500000US05145	05145	White	06	2680081964	18326633
18	06	003	01675840	0500000US06003	06003	Alpine	06	1912243146	12557256
19	06	005	01675841	0500000US06005	06005	Amador	06	1539947370	29470575
20	06	011	01675902	0500000US06011	06011	Colusa	06	2980373007	14581043
21	06	015	01682074	0500000US06015	06015	Del Norte	06	2606517997	578525673
22	06	025	00277277	0500000US06025	06025	Imperial	06	10817387352	790204642
23	06	027	01804637	0500000US06027	06027	Inyo	06	26368506526	119060126
24	06	033	00277281	0500000US06033	06033	Lake	06	3254241507	188959508
25	06	043	00277286	0500000US06043	06043	Mariposa	06	3752425637	36268140
26	06	079	00277304	0500000US06079	06079	San Luis Obispo	06	8543653416	820437991
27	06	089	01682610	0500000US06089	06089	Shasta	06	9778188422	186530228
28	06	099	00277314	0500000US06099	06099	Stanislaus	06	3870792977	51176485
29	06	105	00277317	0500000US06105	06105	Trinity	06	8234308383	73407838
30	08	001	00198116	0500000US08001	08001	Adams	06	3023994956	41935475
31	08	005	00198118	0500000US08005	08005	Arapahoe	06	2066561712	19528620

Figure 13-14:
An Attribute table in QGIS.

The attribute STATEFP contains a unique number for each state. You can use this number to do things like represent all counties in the same state with the same color. The attribute ALAND represents the size of each county. You can use the data that belongs to this attribute category to do things like assign darker colors to larger counties.

Say that you're interested in only the counties that fall within the state of Colorado. Therefore, you need to tell QGIS what polygons should be shown.

2. **Close the Attribute Table window by clicking the red X in the top-right corner, and then double-click the County layer in the Layers window on the left.**

   The Layer Properties window appears, as shown in Figure 13-15.

3. **Click the window's General tab (active by default) and scroll down until you find the Feature Subset section.**

4. **In the Feature Subset section, click the Query Builder button.**

   The Query Builder dialog box appears, as shown in Figure 13-16.

   The Fields box displays only those fields that are available in the Attribute table of the county.shp file.

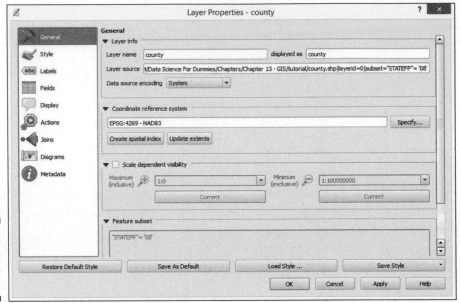

Figure 13-15:
Layer prop-
erties in
QGIS.

5. **Double-click the STATEFP entry in the Fields box of the Query Builder dialog box.**

   The STATEFP field appears in the Provider Specific Filter Expression box located near the bottom of the Query Builder dialog box.

6. **Type = '08' after the "STATEFP" entry in the Provider Specific Filter Expression box.**

   The final expression should look like

   ```
   "STATEFP" = '08'
   ```

   STATEFP contains codes that represent the states in America, and in that code, 08 stands for Colorado.

7. **Click OK, and then click OK again.**

   The main Layer Properties window reappears.

8. **Right-click the County layer in the Layers window and choose Zoom to Layer from the pop-up menu that appears.**

Figure 13-16:
Query
Builder in
QGIS.

You can make these kinds of queries as complicated as you need. You can choose to display only polygons for which the value in a specific column is larger or smaller than a given value, or you can combine different arguments for different fields. QGIS relies on SQL queries.

The map shown in Figure 13-17 displays only the counties that are in Colorado.

Figure 13-17:
A basic
vector layer
mapped in
QGIS.

Part IV
Computing for Data Science

Check out your options for data science programming languages at www.dummies.com/extras/datascience.

In this part . . .

- ✔ Find out how Python is being used for data science projects.

- ✔ Look at your open source data science options. (Can you say R?)

- ✔ See how SQL can be put to new (data science) uses.

- ✔ Explore old programs (Excel) and new (KNIME).

Chapter 14

Using Python for Data Science

*P*ython is a versatile programming language that's been widely adopted across the data science sector over the last decade. Although popular programming languages like Java and C++ are better for developing stand-alone desktop applications, Python is terrific for processing, analyzing, and visualizing data. For this reason, it has earned a reputation of excellence in the data science field. In fact, Python has become so popular it seems to have stolen ground from R — the other free, widely adopted programming language for data science applications. Python's status as one of the more popular programming languages out there can be linked to the fact that a) it's relatively easy to master and b) it allows users to accomplish several tasks with just a few lines of code.

In this chapter, I first introduce you to the fundamental concepts of programming with Python. Learning these concepts helps you familiarize yourself with the principal components of the language. Next, I present the information you need to know to set up a standard working environment in Python. I also introduce some of the best Python libraries for manipulating data, performing statistical computations, creating data visualizations, and doing other related tasks. Lastly, I walk you through some scenarios designed to illustrate how Python can best help you analyze your data.

Understanding Basic Concepts in Python

You can use Python to do anything, from simple mathematical operations to data visualization, and even predictive analytics. An example of a basic math operation in Python is listed below, while Figure 14-1 shows an example — taken from Python's MatPlotLib library — of a more advanced output.

```
>>> 2.5+3
5.5
```

Figure 14-1:
An example
output from
Python's
MatPlotLib
library.

Regardless of the task at hand, it's always important to learn the fundamentals about a language before attempting to delve into its more specialized libraries.

Python is an object-oriented programming language. That means that everything in Python is considered an object. In Python, an *object* is everything that can be assigned to a variable or that can be passed as an argument to a function. The following are all considered objects in the Python programming language:

- ✔ Numbers
- ✔ Strings
- ✔ Lists
- ✔ Tuples
- ✔ Sets

- Dictionaries
- Functions
- Classes

Additionally, numbers, strings, lists, tuples, sets, and dictionaries function as plain Python's basic data types — *plain* here means Python without any external extensions added to it. (I'll introduce you to the external Python libraries NumPy, SciPy, and MatPlotLib in the section "Getting on a First-Name Basis with Some Useful Python Libraries," later in this chapter; by adding these libraries, additional data types become available to you, as well.)

In Python, a *function* does basically the same thing as it does in plain math — it accepts data inputs, processes them, and outputs the result. Output results depend wholly on what the function was programmed to do. *Classes,* on the other hand, are prototypes of objects that are designed to output additional objects.

If your goal is to write fast, reusable, easy-to-modify code in Python, then you must utilize functions and classes. Using functions and classes helps to keep your code efficient and organized.

Introducing Python data types

If you do much work with Python, you need to know how to work with different data types. The main data types in Python are

- Numbers
- Strings
- Lists
- Tuples
- Sets
- Dictionaries

Numbers and strings are the most basic data types. You can incorporate them inside other, more complicated data types. All Python data types can be assigned to variables.

In Python, numbers, strings, lists, tuples, sets, and dictionaries are classified as both object types and data types.

Numbers in Python

The numbers data type represents numeric values that you can use to handle all types of mathematical operations. Numbers come in the following formats:

- ✔ **Integers:** A whole number format
- ✔ **Long:** A whole number format with an unlimited digit size
- ✔ **Float:** A real number format, written with a decimal point
- ✔ **Complex:** An imaginary number format, represented through the root square of –1

Strings in Python

Strings are probably the most often used data type in Python — and in every other programming language, as well. Simply put, *strings* are one or more characters written inside quotes. The following code represents a string:

```
>>> variable1="This is a sample string"
>>> print(variable1)
This is a sample string
```

In this code snippet, the string is assigned to a variable, and the variable subsequently acts like a storage container for the string value.

To print out what's contained inside the variable, simply use the predefined function, print.

Python coders often refer to lists, tuples, sets, and dictionaries as data structures rather than data types. *Data structures* are basic functional units that organize data so that it can be used efficiently by the program or application with which you're working. From their perspective, lists, tuples, sets, and dictionaries are structures, but keep in mind that they're still comprised of one or more basic data types (numbers and/or strings, for example).

Lists in Python

Lists are sequences of numbers and/or strings. To create a list, you simply need to enclose the elements of the list (divided by commas) within square brackets. Here's an example of a basic list:

```
>>> variable2=["ID","Name","Depth","Latitude","Longitude"]
>>> depth=[0,120,140,0,150,80,0,10]
>>> variable2[3]
'Latitude'
```

Every element of the list is automatically assigned an index number, starting from 0. You can access each element using this index, and the corresponding value of the list will be returned. If you need to store and analyze long arrays of data, it's better to use lists because storing your data inside a list makes it fairly easy to extract statistical information. The following code snippet is an example of a simple computation to pull the mean value from the elements of the depth list created in the preceding code:

```
>>> sum(depth)/len(depth)
62.5
```

In this example, the average of the list elements is computed by first summing up the elements, via the sum function, and then dividing them by the number of the elements contained in the list. See, it's as simple as 1-2-3!

Tuples in Python

Tuples are just like lists, except that you can't modify their content after you create them. Also, to create tuples, you need to use normal brackets instead of squared ones. Here's an example of a tuple:

```
>>> depth=(0,120,140,0,150,80,0,10)
```

In this case, you can't modify any of the elements like you would with a list. If you want to make sure your data stays in a read-only format, use tuples.

Sets in Python

A *set* is another data structure that's similar to a list. In contrast to lists, however, elements of a set are unordered. This disordered characteristic of a set makes them impossible to index, and thus, they're not a commonly used data type.

Dictionaries in Python

Dictionaries are data structures that consist of pairs of keys and values. In a dictionary, every value corresponds to a certain key, and consequently, each value can be accessed using that key. The following code shows a typical key/value pairing:

```
>>> variable4={"ID":1,"Name":"Valley City","Depth":0,
        "Latitude":49.6, "Longitude":-98.01}
>>> variable4["Longitude"]
-98.01
```

Putting loops to use in Python

When working with lists in Python, you typically access a list element by using the element index number. In a similar manner, you can access other elements of the list by using their corresponding index numbers. The following code snippet illustrates this concept:

```
>>>variable2=["ID","Name","Depth","Latitude","Longitude"]
>>> print(variable2[3])
Latitude
>>> print(variable2[4])
Longitude
```

Don't let the index numbering system confuse you. Every element of the list is automatically assigned an index number starting from 0 — *not* starting from 1. That means the fourth element in an index actually bears the index number 3.

When you're analyzing considerable amounts of data and you need to access each element of a list, this technique becomes very inefficient. In these cases, you should use a looping technique instead.

You can use *looping* to execute the same block of code multiple times for a sequence of items. Consequently, instead of manually accessing all the elements one by one, you simply create a loop to automatically iterate through each element of the list.

There are two types of loops you can use in Python — the for loop and the while loop. The most often used looping technique is the for loop — a looping technique especially designed to iterate through sequences, strings, tuples, sets, and dictionaries. The following code snippet illustrates a for loop iterating through the variable2 list created in the preceding code:

```
>>> for element in variable2:print(element)
ID
Name
Depth
Latitude
Longitude
```

The other available looping technique in Python is the while loop. Use a while loop to perform actions while a given condition is true.

Looping is crucial when you work with long arrays of data, such as is the case when working with raster images. Looping allows you to apply certain actions to all data or to apply those actions to only predefined groups of data.

Getting to know functions and classes

Functions and classes are crucial building blocks of almost every programming language. They provide a way to build organized, reusable code.

Having fun with functions

Functions are blocks of code that take an input, process it, and return an output. Function inputs can be numbers, strings, lists, objects or functions. There are two types of functions in Python, built-in functions and custom functions. *Built-in* functions are functions that are predefined inside Python. You can use them by just typing their names. The following code snippet is an example of the built-in function `print`:

```
>>> print("Hello")
Hello
```

`print` is a highly used built-in function that prints out a given input. The code behind `print` has already been written by the people who created Python. Now that this code stands in the background, you don't need to know how to code it yourself; you just simply need to call the `print` function. The people who created the Python library couldn't guess every possible function to satisfy everyone's needs, but they managed to provide users a way to create and reuse their own functions when need be.

In the section "Introducing Python data types," earlier in this chapter, the code snippet from that section (also listed below) was used to calculate the average of elements in a list:

```
>>> depth=[0,120,140,0,150,80,0,10]
>>> sum(depth)/len(depth)
62.5
```

The preceding data actually represents snow and snow depth records from multiple point locations. As you can see, the points where snow depth measurements were collected have an average depth of 62.5 units. These are depth measurements taken at only one time, though. In other words, all the data bears the same timestamp. When modeling data using Python, you oftentimes see scenarios in which you have sets of measurements taken at different times. This is known as *time-series* data. An example of time-series data is illustrated in the following code snippet:

```
>>> december_depth=[0,120,140,0,150,80,0,10]
>>> january_depth=[20,180,140,0,170,170,30,30]
>>> february_depth=[0,100,100,40,100,160,40,40]
```

You could make the average of December, January, and February in the same way you averaged values in the previous list, but that would be cumbersome. This is where custom functions come in handy:

```
>>> def
        average(any_list):return(sum(any_list)/len(any_
        list))
```

The code above defines a function named `average`. `average` takes any list as input and calculates the average of the list's elements. The function is not executed yet, but the preceding code defines what the function does when it later gets some input values. In this snippet, `any_list` is just a variable that's later assigned the given value when the function is executed. To execute the function, all you need to do is pass it a value. In this case, the value is a real list with numerical elements:

```
>>> average(february_depth)
72
```

Executing a function is very straightforward. You can use functions to do the same thing repeatedly, as many times as you need, for different input values. The beauty here is that, once constructed, you can reuse functions without having to rewrite the calculating algorithm.

Keeping cool with classes

Although *classes* are blocks of code that put together functions and variables to produce other objects, they're slightly different from functions. The set of functions and classes tied together inside a class describes the blueprint of a certain object. In other words, classes spell out what has to happen in order for an object to be created. After you come up with a class, you can generate the actual object instance by calling a class instance. In Python, this is referred to as *instantiating* an object — creating an instance of that class, in other words.

Functions that are created inside of a class are called *methods,* and variables within a class are called *attributes* — methods describe the actions that generate the object, and attributes describe the actual object properties.

To better understand how to use classes for more efficient data analysis, consider the following scenario: Imagine that you have your snow depth data from different locations and times, and that you're storing it online on an FTP server. The dataset contains different ranges of snow-depth data, depending on the month of the year. Now imagine that every monthly range is stored in a different location on the FTP server.

Your task is to use Python to fetch all the monthly data and then analyze the entire dataset, so you need to use different operations on the data ranges. First, download the data from within Python by using an FTP handling library, such as `ftplib`. Then, to be able to analyze the data in Python, you need to store it in proper Python data types (in lists, tuples, or dictionaries, for example). After you fetch the data and store it as recognizable data types in a Python script, you can then apply more advanced operations that are available through specialized libraries such as NumPy, SciPy, and MatPlotLib.

In this scenario, you want to create a class that creates a list containing the snow-depth data for each month. Every monthly list would be an object instance generated by the class. The class itself would tie together the FTP downloading functions and the functions that store the downloaded records inside the lists. You can then instantiate the class for as many months as you need to carry out a thorough analysis. Code to do something like this is shown in Listing 14-1.

Listing 14-1: Defining a Class in Python

```
class Download:
    def __init__(self,ftp=None,site,dir,fileList=[]):
        self.ftp =ftp
        self.site=site
        self.dir=dir
        self.fileList=fileList
        self.Login_ftp()
            self.store_in_list()
    def Login_ftp(self):
        self.ftp=ftplib.FTP(self.site)
        self.ftp.login()
    def store_in_list(self):
        fileList=[]
        self.ftp.cwd("/")
        self.ftp.cwd(self.dir)
        self.ftp.retrlines('NLST',fileList.append)
        return fileList
```

Defining a class probably looks intimidating right now, but I simply want to give you a feeling for the basic structure and point out the class methods involved.

Delving into Listing 14-1, the keyword `class` defines the class, and the keyword `def` defines the class methods. The `__init__` function is a default function that you should always define when creating classes because you use it to declare class variables. The `Login_ftp` method is a custom function that you define to log in to the FTP server. After you log in through the

Login_ftp method and set the required directory where the data tables are located, you then store the data in a Python list using the custom function store_in_list.

After you finish defining the class, you can use it to produce objects. You just need to instantiate the class, as follows:

```
>>> Download("ftpexample.com","ftpdirectory")
```

And that's it! With this brief snippet, you just declared the particular FTP domain and the internal FTP directory where the data is located. After you execute this last line, a list appears, giving you data that you can manipulate and analyze as needed.

Getting on a First-Name Basis with Some Useful Python Libraries

In Python, a *library* is a specialized collection of scripts that were written by someone else to perform specialized sets of tasks. To use specialized libraries in Python, you must first go through the installation process. (For more on installing Python and its various libraries, check out the "Using Python to Analyze Data — An Example Exercise" section, later in this chapter.) After you install your libraries onto your local hard drive, you can import any library's function into a project simply by using the import statement. You must be sure to import the library into your Python project before attempting to call its functions in your code. So for example, if you want to import the ftplib library, you write the following:

```
>>> import ftplib
```

After you import the library, you can use its functionality inside any of your scripts. Simply use dot notation to access the libraries' various functions and classes. An example of dot notation is as follows:

```
>>> ftplib.any_ftp_lib_function
```

There are countless libraries that you can use to accomplish different tasks in Python, but the Python libraries most commonly used in data science are NumPy, SciPy, and MatPlotLib. The NumPy and SciPy libraries were specially designed for scientific uses. The MatPlotLib library was designed for creating data visualizations in Python.

Saying hello to the NumPy library

NumPy is the Python package that primarily focuses on working with _n_-dimensional array objects, and SciPy is a collection of mathematical algorithms and sophisticated functions that extends the capabilities of the NumPy library. When working with plain Python — a Python without any external extensions (such as libraries) added to it — you're confined to storing your data in one-dimensional lists. But if you extend Python by using the NumPy library, you're provided a basis from which you can work with _n_-dimensional arrays. (Just in case you were wondering, _n-dimensional_ arrays are arrays of one or multiple dimensions.)

To enable NumPy in Python, you must first install and import the library. After that, you can generate multi-dimensional arrays.

To see how generating n-dimensional arrays works in practice, first start by checking out the following code snippet, which shows how you'd create a one-dimensional NumPy array:

```
import numpy
>>> array_1d=numpy.arange(8)
>>> print(array_1d)
[0 1 2 3 4 5 6 7]
```

After importing `numpy`, you can use it to generate _n_-dimensional arrays, such as the one-dimensional array shown above. One-dimensional arrays are referred to as _vectors_. You can also create multi-dimensional arrays using the `reshape` method:

```
>>> array_2d=numpy.arange(8).reshape(2,4)
>>> print(array_2d)
[[0 1 2 3]
 [4 5 6 7]]
```

The preceding code is a two-dimensional array, otherwise known as a _2 × 4 matrix_. Using the `arange` and `reshape` method is just one way to create NumPy arrays. You can also generate arrays from lists and tuples.

In the snow dataset that I introduce in the "Getting to Know Functions and Classes" section, earlier in this chapter, I store my snow-depth data for different locations inside three separate Python lists — one list per month:

```
>>> december_depth=[0,120,140,0,150,80,0,10]
>>> january_depth=[20,180,140,0,170,170,30,30]
>>> february_depth=[0,100,100,40,100,160,40,40]
```

It would be more efficient to have the measurements stored in a better-consolidated structure. For example, you could easily put all those lists in a single NumPy array by using the following code:

```
>>>depth=numpy.array([december_depth,january_
        depth,february_depth])
>>> print(depth)
[[   0 120 140   0 150  80   0  10]
 [  20 180 140   0 170 170  30  30]
 [   0 100 100  40 100 160  40  40]]
```

Using this structure allows you to pull out certain measurements more efficiently. For example, if you want to calculate the average of the snow depth for the first location in each of the three months, you'd need to extract the first elements of each horizontal row (values 0, 20, and 0, to be more precise). You can do the extraction in one line of code by applying slicing and then calculating the mean through the NumPy mean function. Here's an example:

```
>>> numpy.mean(depth[:,0])
6.666666666666667
```

Beyond using NumPy to extract information from single matrices, you can use it to interact with different matrices, as well. You can use NumPy to apply standard mathematical operations between matrices, or even to apply non-standard operators, such as matrix inversion, summarize, and minimum/maximum operators.

Array objects have the same rights as any other objects in Python. You can pass them as parameters to functions, set them as class attributes, or iterate through array elements to generate random numbers.

Getting up close and personal with the SciPy library

The SciPy library adds some specialized scientific functions to Python for more specific tasks in data science. To use SciPy's functions within Python, you must first install and import the SciPy library.

Some sticklers out there consider SciPy to be an extension of the NumPy library. That's because SciPy was *built on top of* NumPy — it uses NumPy functions, but adds to them.

SciPy offers functionalities and algorithms for a variety of tasks, including vector quantization, statistical functions, discrete Fourier transform algorithms, orthogonal distance regression, airy functions, sparse eigenvalue solvers, maximum entropy fitting routines, *n*-dimensional image operations, integration routines, interpolation tools, sparse linear algebra, linear solvers, optimization tools, signal-processing tools, sparse matrices, and other utilities that are not served by other Python libraries. Impressive, right? And yet that's not even a complete listing of the available SciPy utilities. If you're dying to get a hold of a complete list, run the following short code snippet in Python:

```
>>> import scipy
>>> help(scipy)
```

You need to first download and install the SciPy library before you can use this code.

The `help` function used in the preceding code returns a script that lists all utilities that comprise SciPy and documents all of SciPy's functions and classes. This information helps you understand what's behind the prewritten functions and algorithms that make up the SciPy library.

SciPy is still under development. Because it's changing and growing on a regular basis, it's a good idea to regularly check the `help` function to see what's changed.

Bonding with MatPlotLib for data visualization

Generally speaking, data science projects usually culminate in visual representations of objects or phenomena. In Python, things are no different. After taking baby steps (or some not-so-baby steps) with NumPy and SciPy, you can use Python's MatPlotLib library to create complex visual representations of your dataset or data analysis findings. MatPlotLib, when combined with NumPy and SciPy, creates an excellent environment in which to work when solving problems using data science.

Looking more closely at MatPlotLib, I can tell you that it is a two-dimensional plotting library you can use in Python to produce figures from data. You can use MatPlotLib to produce plots, histograms, scatter plots, power spectra, and a variety of other data graphics. What's more, because the library gives you full control of your visualization's symbology, line styles, fonts, and colors, you can even use MatPlotLib to produce publication-quality data graphics.

As is the case with all other libraries in Python, to work with MatPlotLib, you first need to install and import the library into your script. After you complete those tasks, it's pretty easy to get started producing graphs and charts.

To illustrate how to use MatPlotLib, consider the following NumPy array (which I came up with in the "Saying hello to the NumPy library" section, earlier in this chapter):

```
>>> print(depth)
[[   0 120 140    0 150   80   0   10]
 [  20 180 140    0 170 170   30   30]
 [   0 100 100   40 100 160   40   40]]
```

With the following few lines of code, using just a `for` loop and a MatPlotLib function — pyplot — you can easily plot all the measurements in a single graph within Python:

```
>>> import matplotlib.pyplot as plt
>>> for month in depth:
        plt.plot(month)
>>> plt.show()
```

This code instantly generates the line chart you see in Figure 14-2.

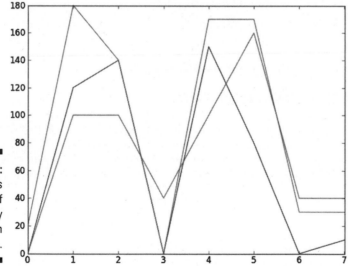

Figure 14-2: Time-series plot of monthly snow-depth data.

Each line in the graph represents the depth of snow at different locations in the same month. The preceding code you use to build this graph is really simple. If you want to make a better representation, you could add color or text font attributes to the `plot` function. Of course, you can also use other types of data graphics, depending on which types best show the data trends you want to display. What's important here is that you know when to use each of these important libraries and you understand how you can use the Python programming language to make data analysis both easy and efficient.

Using Python to Analyze Data — An Example Exercise

Most of Python's recent growth has been among users from the science community, which means most users probably didn't study computer science in school, yet find programming to be a skill they must have in order to work in their respective fields. Python's uncomplicated, human-readable syntax and its welcoming user community has created a large and dedicated user base. The following sections get you started in analyzing data using Python.

For the following exercises, I refer to a hypothetical classroom dataset, but I want to start out by showing you where to go to do an easy install and setup of a good Python programming environment. From there, I show you how to import the classroom data CSV file into Python, how to use Python to calculate a weighted grade average for students in the class, and how to use Python to generate an average trendline of student grades.

Installing Python on the Mac and Windows OS

The Mac comes with a basic version of Python preinstalled, and Windows doesn't ship with Python at all. Whether you're on the Mac or a Windows PC, I recommend downloading a free Python distribution that gives you easy access to as many useful modules as possible. I've tried several distributions, and the one I recommend is Anaconda by Continuum Analytics (available from `https://store.continuum.io/cshop/anaconda`). This Python distribution comes with 197 packages, including NumPy, SciPy, and MatPlotLib. I really like how Anaconda also comes with the pandas package (short for PANel DAta analySis) because this package allows you to make and manipulate a *tabular data frame* — sort of like an Excel table, but better.

In order to do anything of any magnitude in Python, you also need a programming environment. Anaconda comes with the IPython programming environment, which I recommend you to use. IPython runs right in your web browser and allows you to write code in separate cells and then see the results for each step. To open IPython in your web browser, after installing Anaconda, just navigate to and open the IPython Notebook program. That program automatically launches the web-browser application. (See Figure 14-3.)

Figure 14-3:
The IPython
program-
ming
environ-
ment.

When you're using data science to solve problems, you aren't writing the programs yourself. Rather, you're using prebuilt programming tools and languages to interact with your data.

When you download your free Python distribution, you have a choice between downloading version 2 or version 3. In 2010, the Python language was completely overhauled to make it more powerful in ways that only computer scientists would understand. The problem is that the new version is not *backwards-compatible* — in other words, Python 2 scripts aren't compatible with a Python 3 environment. Python 2 scripts need syntax changes to run in Python 3. This sounds like a terrible situation, and while it's not without controversy, most *pythonistas* — Python users — are fine with it.

I highly recommend you use the final Python 2 release, version Python 2.7.8. As of late 2014, that version is being used by the vast majority of non-CompSci Python users. It performs great for data science, it's easier to learn than Python 3, and sites like GitHub have millions of snippets and scripts that you can copy to make your life easier.

Loading CSV files

To load data from a comma-separated values (CSV) file, use the pandas library. I walk you through the process in the code shown in Listing 14-2. Before getting started, make sure to place your data file — the `class_grades.csv` file, to be precise — in the IPython Notebooks folder. By default, IPython always looks at the IPython Notebooks folder to find any external files that are called by your code.

Just in case you don't know about commenting yet, in Python, a coder can insert his or her comments on the code by prefixing all comment lines with a *hash symbol* — a # symbol. All comments are invisible to the application — they aren't acted upon — but they are visible to the programmers and their buddies (and to their enemies, for that matter).

Figure 14-4 shows you what IPython comes up with when fed this code.

Listing 14-2:   Example Code for Loading a CSV File into Python

```
import pandas as pd
import numpy as np
import matplotlib.pyplot as plt
from scipy import stats
# This loads the modules I'll use throughout this
         notebook, giving each a short alias.

%matplotlib inline
# This will show charts below each cell instead of in a
         separate viewer.

grades = pd.read_csv('class_grades.csv')
# That's it, you're done!

print grades.head()
```

If you want to limit your code output to the first five rows only, then you can use the head() function.

Calculating a weighted average

Okay, so you fed IPython a lot of student grades kept in a CSV file in the preceding section. The question is, how do you want these grades calculated?

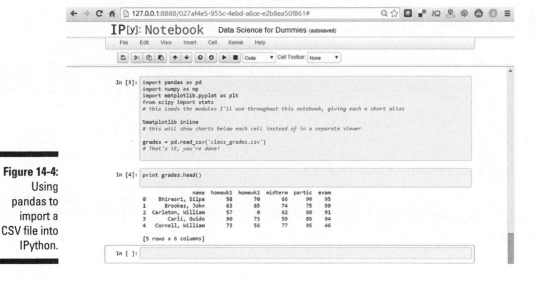

Figure 14-4:
Using
pandas to
import a
CSV file into
IPython.

How do you want to weigh each separate component of the grade?

I'm just going to make a command decision and say that final grades are to be calculated as follows:

- Each homework assignment = 10 percent
- Midterm = 25 percent
- Class participation = 10 percent
- Final exam = 45 percent

With pandas, you can easily calculate each student's weighted final grade. Listing 14-3 shows you how it's done.

**Listing 14-3:   Example Code for Calculating a
                 Weighted Average in Python**

```
import pandas as pd
import numpy as np
import matplotlib.pyplot as plt
from scipy import stats
%matplotlib inline
grades = pd.read_csv('class_grades.csv')
grades['grade'] = np.round((0.1 * grades.homewk1 + 0.1 *
          grades.homewk2 + 0.25 * grades.midterm + 0.1 *
          grades.partic + 0.45 * grades.exam), 0)

# This creates a new column called 'grade' and populates
          it based on the values of other columns,
          rounded to an integer.

print grades.tail()
```

Figure 14-5 shows the results of your new round of coding.

If you want to limit your code output to the last five rows only, then you can use the `tail()` function.

Just for fun, you can calculate letter grades with a `letter_grade` function and `if` commands. The code is shown in Listing 14-4, and the results are shown in Figure 14-6.

Figure 14-5: Calculating a weighted average in IPython.

Listing 14-4:   Using a `letter_grade` Function and `if` Command in Python

```
def calc_letter(row):
    if row.grade >= 90:
        letter_grade = 'A'
    elif row['grade'] > 75:
        letter_grade = 'B'
    elif row['grade'] > 60:
        letter_grade = 'C'
    else:
        letter_grade = 'F'
    return letter_grade
# See how in Python there are no "then" statements, no
        braces, and few brackets or parentheses. Flow
        is determined by colons and indents.

grades['ltr'] = grades.apply(calc_letter, axis=1)
# "apply" with axis=1 applies a function to an entire
        column using values from the same row.
print grades
```

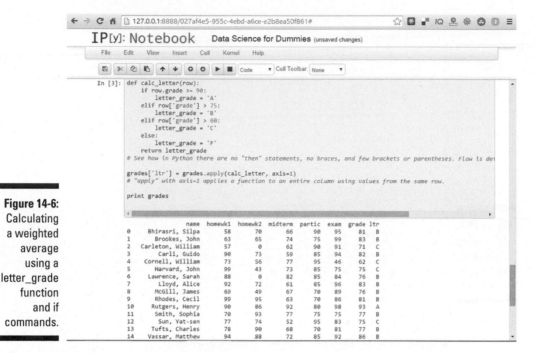

Figure 14-6:
Calculating
a weighted
average
using a
letter_grade
function
and if
commands.

Drawing trendlines

Using SciPy, you can easily draw a *trendline* — a line on a chart that indicates the overall trend of a dataset. Popular kinds of trendlines include best-fit, regression, or ordinary least squares lines. In this section, I show you how to track the progress of any student in our hypothetical class, from the beginning of the semester to the end. For this example, I've created a trendline for the first student, Silpa Bhirasri. You can generate a trendline for any student, however, simply by plugging his or her name in for the student variable.

To use SciPy, you first need to make a basic Python ordered list (denoted by numbers or strings in square brackets), then turn those numbers or strings into a NumPy array. This new NumPy array allows you to run calculations on all the values at once, instead of needing to write code to run over each of the values separately. Lastly, you calculate the best-fit line for *y*-values (the *x*-values are always the same as the original series) and draw the chart in the

IPython Notebook using four lines of code in the MatPlotLib library. Listing 14-5 puts it all together for you.

Listing 14-5: Example Code for Creating a Trendline in Python

```
student = 'Bhirasri, Silpa'

y_values = [] # create an empty list
for column in ['homewk1', 'homewk2', 'midterm', 'partic',
        'exam']:
    y_values.append(grades[grades.name == student]
        [column].iloc[0])
# Append each grade in the order it appears in the
        dataframe.
print y_values

x = np.array([1, 2, 3, 4, 5])
y = np.array(y_values)
slope, intercept, r, p, slope_std_err = stats.
        linregress(x, y)
# This automatically calculates the slope, intercept,
        Pearson correlation, coefficient (r), and two
        other statistics'I won't use here.

bestfit_y = intercept + slope * x
# This calculates the best-fit line to show on the chart.

plt.plot(x, y, 'ko')
# This plots x and y values; 'k' is the standard printer's
        abbreviation for the color 'blacK', and 'o'
        signifies markers to be circular.
plt.plot(x, bestfit_y, 'r-')
# This plots the best fit regression line as a 'r'ed
        line('-').

plt.ylim(0, 100)
# This sets the upper and lower limits of the y axis.
# If it were not specified, the minimum and maximum values
        would be used.

plt.show() # since the plot is ready, it will be shown
        below the cell
print 'Pearson coefficient (R) = ' + str(r)
```

Figure 14-7 shows the trendline for Student Bhirasri, Silpa.

From the trendline, you can see that Mr. Bhirasri's grades steadily improved all semester, with a little dip at the midterm. At about 0.93, the Pearson correlation coefficient is high, indicating his grades improved, and it's close to a linear progression. For more on the Pearson coefficient, check out Chapter 18.

Figure 14-7:
A trendline generated in IPython.

Pearson coefficient (R) = 0.932202116916

Chapter 15

Using Open Source R for Data Science

R is an open source, free statistical software system that, like Python, has been widely adopted across the data science sector over the last decade. In fact, there is somewhat of a never-ending squabble between data science types about which programming language is actually best suited for data science. Practitioners that favor R generally do so because of its advanced statistical programming and data visualization capabilities — capabilities that simply can't be replicated in Python. When it comes to data science practitioners, specifically, R's user base is broader than Python's. (For more on Python, see Chapter 14; note that the R programming language and the packages that support it are downloadable from `http://cran.r-project.org`.)

Introducing the Fundamental Concepts

R is not as easy to learn as Python, but it can be more powerful for certain types of advanced statistical analyses. Although R's learning curve is somewhat steeper than Python's, the programming language is nonetheless relatively straightforward. All you really need to do is closely study the basic vocabulary used to describe the language and, after you master that, it shouldn't be too hard to get a grasp on how the software works.

Mastering R's basic vocabulary

Although the vocabulary associated with R may seem exotic at first, you can quickly master it through practice. You can run R in non-interactive or interactive mode. *Non-interactive mode* is when you run your R code by executing it as an .r *file* — the .r file extension is the extension that's assigned to script files created for execution by the R program— straight from the command line. In interactive mode, you're generally working in a software application that interacts with you by prompting you to enter your data and R code. In an R *session,* within interactive mode you can import datasets or enter in your raw data directly; assign names to variables and data objects; and use functions, operators, and built-in iterators to help you gain some insight into your source data.

R is an *object-oriented* language, which just means the different parts that comprise the language belong to *classes* — each class with its own specific definition and role. A specific example of a class is known as an *instance* of that class and so inherits the class's characteristics. Classes are *polymorphic,* which means the subclasses of a class can have their own set of unique behaviors and yet share some of the same functionality of the parent class. To illustrate this, consider R's print function — print( ). Because this function is polymorphic, it works slightly differently depending on the class of the object it's told to print. Thus, this function and many others perform the same general job in many classes but differ slightly according to class. In the section "Observing how objects work," later in this chapter, I elaborate on object-oriented programming and its advantages, but for now I want to introduce objects, their names, and their definitions.

R works with the following main object types:

✔ **Vectors:** A *vector* is an ordered list of the same mode — character (alphanumeric), numeric, or Boolean. Vectors can have any number of dimensions. For instance, the vector A = ["a", "cat", "def"] is a three-dimensional vector of mode character. B = [2, 3.1, -5, 33] is a four-dimensional vector of mode numerical. To identify specific elements of these vectors, you could enter the following codes at the prompt in interactive mode in order to get R to generate the following returns: A[[1]] = "a", or A[[2]] = "cat", or A[[3]] = "def", or B[[1]] = 2, or B[[2]] = 3.1, or B[[3]] = -5, or B[[4]] = 33. R views a single number as a vector of dimension one. Because they can't be broken down further in R, vectors are also known as *atomic vectors* (which are not the same as *generic vectors* that are actually list objects, as I discuss under "Lists"). R's treatment of atomic vectors gives the language tremendous advantages with respect to speed and efficiency (as I describe in the section "Iterating in R," later in this chapter).

✔ **Matrices:** Think of a *matrix* as a collection of vectors. A matrix can be of any mode (numerical, character, or Boolean), but the entire matrix has to be of the same mode. A matrix is also characterized by its number of dimensions. Unlike a vector, a matrix has only two dimensions — number of rows and number of columns.

✔ **Lists:** A *list* is a list of items of arbitrary modes, including other lists or vectors.

Lists are sometimes also called *generic vectors,* since some of the same operations that are performed on vectors can be performed on lists as well.

✔ **Data frames:** A *data frame* is a type of list that's analogous to a table in a database. Technically speaking, a data frame is a list of vectors, each of which is the same length. A row in a table contains the information for an individual record, but elements in the row will most likely not be of the same mode. All elements in a specific column, however, are all of the same mode. Data frames are structured in this same way — each vector in a data frame corresponds to a column in a data table, and each possible index for these vectors is a row.

There are two ways to access members of vectors, matrices, and lists in R. Single brackets [ ] give a vector, matrix, or list (respectively) of the element(s) indexed, while double brackets [[ ]] give a single element. There is some disagreement among R users as to the proper use of [ ] and [[ ]] for indexing. Generally, the double bracket ([[ ]]) has several advantages: For example, it returns an error message if you enter an index that's out of bounds. If, however, you want to indicate more than one element of a vector, matrix, or list, then you should use a single bracket ([ ]).

Now that you have a grasp of R's basic vocabulary, you're probably eager to see how it works with some actual programming. Imagine you're going to use a simple EmployeeRoll dataset and that you're going to enter the dataset into R by hand. You'd come up with something that looks like Listing 15-1.

Listing 15-1: Assigning an Object and Concatenating in R

```
> EmployeeRoll <- data.frame(list(EmployeeName=c("Smith,
        John","O'Bannon, Tom","Simmons,
        Sarah"),Grade=c(10,8,12),Salary=c(100000,75000,
        125000), Union=c(TRUE, FALSE, TRUE)))
> EmployeeRoll
    EmployeeName Grade  Salary Union
1      Smith,John    10  100000   TRUE
2   O'Bannon, Tom     8   75000 FALSE
3 Simmons, Sarah    12  125000   TRUE
```

The combined symbol < - in the first line of Listing 15-1 is called "gets." It assigns the contents on its right to the name on the left. You can think of this relationship in even simpler terms by considering the following statement, which assigns the number 3 to the variable c.

```
> c <- 3
```

Line 1 of Listing 15-1 also exhibits the use of R's concatenate function — c( ) — which is used to create a vector. The concatenate function is being used to form the atomic vectors that comprise the vector list that makes up the EmployeeRoll data frame. Line 2 of Listing 15-1, EmployeeRoll, instructs R to display the object's contents on the screen. (Figure 15-1 breaks out the data in more diagrammatic form.)

One other object within R is vitally important — the function. *Functions* use atomic vectors, matrices, lists, and data frames to accomplish whatever analysis or computation you want done. (In the following section, I discuss functions more thoroughly. For now, just understand their role, in general.) Each analysis you perform in R may be done in one or more sessions, which consist of entering a set of instructions that tells R what you want it to do with the data that you've entered or imported. In each session, you specify the functions of your script. Then, the blocks of code process any input received and then return an output. A function's input (also known as a function's *arguments*) can be any R object or combination of objects — vectors, matrices, arrays, data frames, tables or even other functions. (Note that invoking a function in R is known as *calling* a function.)

Commenting in R is the same as in Python (Python is covered in Chapter 14). As an R coder, you'd insert any comments you may have on the code by prefixing them with a *hash symbol* — the # symbol, in other words.

DATA FRAMES, LISTS, & VECTORS IN R

DATA FRAME   EmployeeRoll

Figure 15-1:
A diagram
of the
relationship   LIST
between   COMPONENTS   EmployeeName   Grade   Salary   Union
atomic
vectors,
lists, and   ATOMIC   Smith, John   10   100000   TRUE
data-frame   VECTORS   O'Bannon, Tom   8   75000   FALSE
objects.   Simmons, Sarah   12   125000   TRUE

                             (*character*) (*numeric*) (*numeric*) (*Boolean*)

Going deeper into functions and operators

You can choose one of two methods when writing your functions — a quick, simple method and a more complex but ultimately more useful method. Of course, you achieve the same result through either approach, but each method is advantageous in its own ways. If you want to call a function and generate a result as simply and as quickly as possible, and if you don't think you're going to want to reuse the function in the future, then use Method 1. If you want to write a function that you can call for different purposes and use with different datasets in the future, then use Method 2 instead.

To illustrate the difference between these two methods, consider again the EmployeeRoll dataset defined in Listing 15-1. Say you want to come up with a function you can use to derive a mean value for employee salary. Using the first, simpler method, you call a single function to handle that task: You simply define an operation by writing the name of the function you want to use, and then include whatever argument(s) the function requires in the set of parentheses following the function name. More specifically, you call the built-in statistical function mean( ) to calculate the mean value of employee salaries, as shown here:

```
> #Method 1 of Calculating the Mean Salary
> MeanSalary1 <- mean(EmployeeRoll$Salary)
> MeanSalary1
[1] 1e+05
```

In this method, the mean( ) function calculates and saves the average salary, 100,000 (or 1e+05, in scientific notation) as an object (a vector, of course!) named MeanSalary1.

The $ symbol refers R to a particular field in the dataset. In this example, it's referring R to the Salary field of the EmployeeRoll dataset.

Method 2 illustrates a more complicated but possibly more useful approach. Instead of defining just a single operation, as in Method 1, Method 2's function can define a series of separate operations if they're needed; therefore, the method can oftentimes get quite complex. In the following code, the statement MeanSalary2 <- function(x) creates a function named MeanSalary2 which takes one argument, x. The statements between the curly braces ({ }) make up this function. The job of {return(mean(x))} is to calculate the mean of some entity *x* and then return that value as a result to the computer screen:

```
> #Method 2 of Calculating the Mean Salary
> #This method allows the user to create a custom set of
        instructions for R that can be used again and
        again.
```

```
> MeanSalary2 <- function(x) {return(mean(x))}
>
> MeanSalary2(EmployeeRoll$Salary)
[1] 1e+05
```

The argument of the function definition isn't the `Salary` field from the `EmployeeRoll` dataset because this type of function can be called and used for different purposes on different datasets and different fields of said datasets. Also, nothing happens when you finish typing the function and press Return after entering the ending curly brace; in the next line, you just get another prompt (`>`). That's because you set the function up correctly. (You know it's correct because you didn't get an error message.) You now can call this function when you actually need it — that's what the last instruction entered at the prompt in the preceding code does. Typing `MeanSalary2(EmployeeRoll$Salary)` is a *function call*, and it replaces the function's placeholder argument `x` with `EmployeeRoll$Salary`; a real object that allows the function to generate a solution.

Of course, the function that's written in Method 2 yields the same mean salary as did the function in Method 1, but the Method 2 function can now be reused for different applications. To illustrate how you'd use this same function on a different dataset, imagine that you have another business with its own payroll. It has five employees with the following salaries: $500,000; $1,000,000; $75,000; $112,000; and $400,000. If you want to call and use the `MeanSalary2` function to find the mean salary of these employees, you could simply write the following:

```
> MeanSalary2(c(500000,1000000,75000,112000,400000))
[1] 417400
```

Just as instructed in Method 2, the `MeanSalary2` function quickly generates a mean value for this new dataset — in this case, $417,400.

The primary benefit of using functions in R is that functions make it easier to write cleaner, more concise code that's easy to read and more readily re-usable. But at the most fundamental level, R is simply using functions to apply operators. Although applying operators and calling functions both serve the same purpose, you can distinguish the two techniques by their differing syntaxes. R uses many of the same operators that are used in other programming languages. Table 15-1 is a list of the more commonly used operators.

Operators act as functions in R. I warned you that learning the vocabulary of R can be tricky!

Table 15-1	A Table of Popular Operators
Operation	*Operator*
plus	+
minus	-
times	*
divide	/
modulo	%%
power	^
greater than	>
greater than or equal to	>=
less than	<
less than or equal to	<=
equals	==
not equals	!=
not (logical)	!
and (logical)	&
or (logical)	|
is assigned; gets	<-
is assigned to	->

This code shows several examples of where operators are used as functions:

```
> "<"(2,3)
[1] TRUE
> "<"(100,10)
[1] FALSE
> "+"(100,1)
[1] 101
> "/"(4,2)
[1] 2
> "+"(2,5,6,3,10)
Error in `+`(2, 5, 6, 3, 10) : operator needs one or two
        arguments
```

In the preceding code, the Boolean operators less than (<) and greater than (>) return a value of either TRUE or FALSE. Also, see the error message that's generated by the last line of code? That error happened because the operator + can take only one or two arguments, and in that example, I provided three arguments more than it could handle.

TIP

You can use the + operator to add two numbers or to add two vectors. In fact, all arithmetic operators in R can accept both numbers and vectors as arguments — for more on arithmetic operators, check out the following section, "Iterating in R".

Iterating in R

Because of the way R handles vectors, programming in R offers you a very efficient way to handle loops and iterations. Essentially, R has built-in iterators that automatically loop over elements without the added hassle of you having to write out the loops yourself. This process is called *vectorization*.

To better conceptualize this idea, imagine that you want to add a constant c = 3 to a series of three numbers that you've stored as a vector, m = [10, 6, 9]. You can use the following code:

```
> c <- 3
> m <- c(10, 6, 9)
> m <- m + c
> m
[1] 13  9 12
```

The preceding method works because of an R property known as *recyclability* — if you're performing operations on two vectors that aren't the same length, R repeats and reuses the smaller vector to make the operation work. In this example, c was a one-dimensional vector, but R reused it to make it into a three-dimensional vector so that the operation could be performed on m. Here's the logic behind this process:

10		3		13
6	+	3	=	9
9		3		12

This method works also because of the vectorization of the + operator, which performs the + operation on the vectors m and c, in effect looping through each of the vectors to add their corresponding elements. Here's another way of writing this process that makes the vectorization of the + operator obvious:

TIP

```
> m <- "+"(m,c)
```

R vectorizes all arithmetic operators, including +, -, /, *, and ^.

When you're using conditional statements within iterative loops, R uses vectorization to make this process more efficient. If you've used other

programming languages, you've probably seen a structure that looks
something like this:

```
for (y = 1 through 5) {     if (3*y <= 4) then z = 1
               else z = 0}
```

This loop iterates the code within the brackets ({ }) sequentially for each
y equal to 1, 2, 3, 4, and 5. Within this loop, for each *y*-value, the conditional
statement 3*y <= 4 generates either a TRUE or a FALSE statement. For
y-values that yield TRUE values, z is set to 1; otherwise, it's set to 0. This loop
thus generates the following:

```
| y | 3*y | 3*y <= 4 | z |
| 1 | 3   | TRUE  | 1 |
| 2 | 6   | FALSE | 0 |
| 3 | 9   | FALSE | 0 |
| 4 | 12  | FALSE | 0 |
| 5 | 15  | FALSE | 0 |
```

Now, check out how you can do this same thing using R:

```
> y <- 1:5
> z <- ifelse(3*y <= 4, 1, 0)
> z
[1] 1 0 0 0 0
```

Much more compact, right? In the preceding R code, the y term represents the
numerical vector [1, 2, 3, 4, 5]. As was the case above, in the R code
the operator <= is vectorized and recyclability is again applied so that the
apparent scalar 4 is treated as a five-dimensional vector [4, 4, 4, 4, 4]
to make the vector operation work. As before, only where y = 1 is the
condition met and, consequently, z[[1]] = 1 and z[2:5] = 0.

In R, you often see something that looks like 1:10. This *colon operator*
notates a sequence of numbers — the first number, the last number, and
the sequence that lies between them. Thus, the vector 1:10 is equivalent to
1, 2, 3, 4, 5, 6, 7, 8, 9, 10 and 2:5 is equal to 2, 3, 4, 5.

Observing how objects work

R's object-oriented approach makes deploying and maintaining code relatively
quick and easy. As part of this object-oriented functionality, objects in R are
distinguished by characteristics known as *attributes*. Each object is defined by
its attributes; more specifically, each object is defined by its class attribute.

As an example, the USDA provides data on the percentages of insect-resistant and herbicide-tolerant corn planted per year, for years ranging from 2000 through 2014. You could take this information and use a linear regression function to predict the percentage of herbicide-tolerant corn planted in Illinois during 2000 to 2014, from the percentage of insect-resistant corn planted in Illinois during these same years. The dataset and function are shown in Listing 15-2.

Listing 15-2: Exploring Objects in R

```
> GeneticallyEngineeredCorn <-
          data.frame(list(year=c(2000, 2001, 2002, 2003,
          2004, 2005, 2006, 2007, 2008, 2009, 2010, 2011,
          2012, 2013, 2014),Insect =c(13,
          12,18,23,26,25,24,19,13, 10, 15, 14, 14, 4, 3),
          herbicide=c(3,3,3,4,5,6,12,15,15,15,15,17,18,7,
          5)))
> GeneticallyEngineeredCorn
   year Insect herbicide
1  2000    13         3
2  2001    12         3
3  2002    18         3
4  2003    23         4
5  2004    26         5
6  2005    25         6
7  2006    24        12
8  2007    19        15
9  2008    13        15
10 2009    10        15
11 2010    15        15
12 2011    14        17
13 2012    14        18
14 2013     4         7
15 2014     3         5
> PredictHerbicide <-
          lm(GeneticallyEngineeredCorn$herbicide ~
          GeneticallyEngineeredCorn$Insect)
> attributes(PredictHerbicide)$names
 [1] "coefficients" "residuals"      "effects"
          "rank"
 [5] "fitted.values" "assign"        "qr"
          "df.residual"
 [9] "xlevels"        "call"          "terms"
          "model"
> attributes(PredictHerbicide)$class
 [1] "lm"
> PredictHerbicide$coef
                   (Intercept)
        GeneticallyEngineeredCorn$Insect
                   10.52165581
          -0.06362591
```

In Listing 15-2, the expression PredictHerbicide <- lm(Genetically Engineered Corn$herbicide ~ GeneticallyEngineeredCorn$ Insect) instructs R to perform a linear regression and assign the results to the PredictHerbicide object. In the linear regression, Genetically EngineeredCorn is defined as the source dataset, the Insect column acts as the independent variable, and the herbicide column as the dependent variable.

R's attribute function allows you to get information about an object's attributes. In this example, typing in the function attribute (PredictHerbicide)$names instructs R to name all of the attributes of the PredictHerbicide object, and the function attribute (PredictHerbicide)$class instructs R to identify the object's classes. You can see from Listing 15-2 that the PredictHerbicide object has 12 attributes and has class lm (which stands for *linear model*).

R allows you to request specifics on each of these attributes; but to keep this example brief, simply ask R to specify the coefficients of the linear regression equation — looking back, you can see that this is the first attribute that's provided for the PredictHerbicide object. To ask R to show the coefficients obtained by fitting the linear model to the data, enter PredictHerbicide$coef, as shown in Listing 15-2, and R returns the following information:

```
 (Intercept)  GeneticallyEngineeredCorn$Insect
10.52165581                          -0.06362591
```

In plain math, the preceding result translates into the equation shown in Figure 15-2.

Translated into mathematical terms, this is equivalent to the following:

Percentage of Genetically Engineered Herbicide-Tolerant Corn = 10.5 – 0.06*Percentage of Genetically Engineered Insect-Resistant Corn

Figure 15-2:
Linear
regression
coefficients
from R,
translated
into a
plain math
equation.

$$(\%_{\text{herbicide-resistant corn}})_{\text{Illinois, 2000-2014}} = 10.52165581 - 0.06362591(\%_{\text{insect-resistance corn}})_{\text{Illinois, 2000-2014}}$$

Thus, the relationship between the two variables appears rather weak, and so the percentage of genetically engineered insect-resistant corn planted wouldn't provide a good predictor of percentage of herbicide-resistant corn planted.

This example also illustrates the polymorphic nature of generic functions in R — that is, where the same function can be adapted to the class it's used with, so that function is applicable to many different classes. The polymorphic function of this example is R's `attributes( )` function. This function is applicable to the `lm` (linear model) class, the `mean` class, the `histogram` class, and many others.

If you want to get a quick orientation when working with instances of an unfamiliar class, R's polymorphic generic functions will come in handy. These functions generally tend to make R a more efficiently mastered programming language.

Previewing R Packages

R has a plethora of easy-to-install packages and functions, many of which are quite useful in data science. In an R context, *packages* are bundles comprised of specific functions, data, and code suited for performing specific types of analyses or sets of analyses. The CRAN site lists the current packages available for download at `http://cran.r-project.org/web/packages`, along with directions on how to download and install them. In the following sections, I discuss some popular packages, and then delve deeper into the capabilities of a few of the more advanced packages that are available.

Pointing out popular statistical analysis packages

The robust R packages can help you do things like forecasting, multivariate analysis, and factor analysis. In this section, I quickly present an overview of a few of the more popular packages that are useful for this type of work.

R's `forecast` package contains various forecasting functions that you can adapt to use for ARIMA, or for other types of univariate time series forecasts. Or perhaps you want to use R for quality management. You can use R's Quality Control Charts package (`qcc`) for quality and statistical process control.

In the practice of data science, you're likely to benefit from almost any package that specializes in multivariate analysis. If you want to carry out logistic regression, you can use R's multinomial logit model (`mlogit`). A *multinomial logit model* is one in which observations of a known class are used to "train" the software so that it can identify classes of other observations whose classes are unknown. (For example, you could use logistic regression to train software so that it can successfully predict customer churn, which you can read about in Chapter 3.)

If you want to use R to take undifferentiated data and identify which of its factors are significant for some specific purpose, you can use factor analysis. To better illustrate the fundamental concept of factor analysis, imagine that you own a restaurant. You want to do everything you can to make sure your customer satisfaction rating is as high as possible, right? Well, factor analysis can help you determine what exact factors have the largest impact on customer satisfaction ratings — those could coalesce into the general factors of ambience, restaurant layout, and employee appearance/attitude/knowledge. With this knowledge, you can work on improving these factors in order to increase customer satisfaction and, with that, brand loyalty.

Few people enter data manually into R. Data is more often either imported from Microsoft Excel or from a relational database. You can find driver packages available to import data from various types of relational databases, including RSQLite, RPostgreSQL, RMySQL, and RODBC, as well as packages for many other RDBMSs. One of R's strengths is how it equips users with the ability to produce publication-quality graphical illustrations or even just data visualizations that can help you understand your data. The `ggplot2` package offers you a ton of different data visualization options — more on this package in the section "Visualizing R statistics with ggplot2," later in this chapter.

For information on additional R packages, take a look through the R Project website at `www.r-project.org`. You can find a lot of existing online documentation to help you identify what packages best suit your needs. Also, coders in R's active community are making new packages and functions available all the time.

Visualizing, mapping, and graphing in R

The preceding sections in this chapter hopefully give you a basic understanding of how functions, objects, and R's built-in iterators work. You hopefully also can think of a few data science tasks that R can help you accomplish. In the following sections, I introduce you to some powerful R packages for data visualization, network graph analysis, and spatial point pattern analysis.

Visualizing R statistics with ggplot2

If you're looking for a very fast and efficient way to produce good-looking data visualizations that you can use to derive and communicate insights from your datasets, then look no further than R's ggplot2 package. This package was designed to help you create all different types of data graphics in R, including histograms, scatterplots, bar charts, box plots, and density plots. It offers a wide variety of design options, as well — including choices in colors, layout, transparency, and line density. ggplot2 is useful if you want to do data showcasing, but it's probably not the best option if you're looking to do data storytelling or data art. (You can read about these data visualization design options in Chapter 9.)

To better understand how the ggplot2 package works, consider the following example: Figure 15-3 shows a simple scatterplot that was generated using ggplot2. This scatterplot depicts the concentrations (in parts per million, or ppm) of four types of pesticides that were detected in a stream between the years 2000 to 2013. The scatterplot could've been designed to show only the pesticide concentrations for each year, but ggplot2 provides an option for fitting a regression line to each of the pesticide types. The regression lines are the solid lines shown on the plot. ggplot2 can also present these pesticide types in different colors. The colored areas enclosing the regression lines represent 95-percent confidence intervals for the regression models.

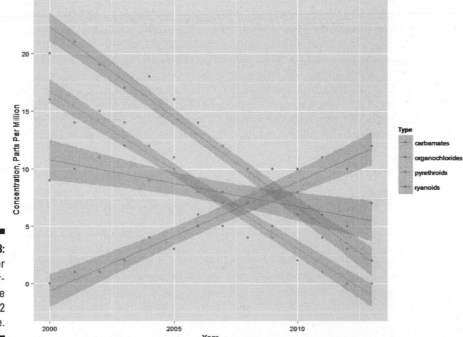

Figure 15-3:
A scatter plot generated in the ggplot2 package.

The scatterplot chart makes it clear that all pesticides except for ryanoids are showing decreasing stream concentrations. Organochlorides had the highest concentration in 2000, but then exhibited the greatest decrease in concentration over the 13-year period.

Analyzing networks with statnet and igraph

Social networks and social network data volumes have absolutely exploded over the last decade. Therefore, knowing how to make sense of network data has becoming increasingly important for analysts. Social network analysis skills enable you to analyze social networks to uncover how accounts are connected and the ways in which information is shared across those connections. You can use network analysis methods to determine how fast information spreads across the Internet. You can even use network analysis methods in genetic mapping to better understand how one gene affects and influences the activity of other genes, or in hydraulic modeling to know how to best design a water distribution or sewer collection system.

Two R packages were explicitly written for network analysis purposes — statnet and igraph. You can use either statnet or igraph to collect network statistics or statistics on network components. Figure 15-4 shows an example output from network analysis in R, generated using the statnet package. This output is just a simple network in which the direction of the

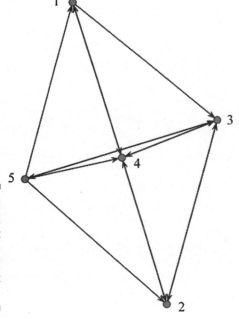

Figure 15-4:
A network diagram that was generated using the statnet package.

arrows shows the direction of flow within the network, from one vertex to another. The network has five vertices and nine *faces* — connections between the vertices.

Mapping and analyzing spatial point patterns with spatstat

If you want to analyze spatial data in R, you can use the spatstat package. This package is most commonly used in analyzing point pattern data, but you can also use it to analyze line patterns, pixels, and linear network data. By default, the package installs with geographical, ecological, and environmental datasets you can use to support your analyses, if appropriate. With its space-time point pattern analysis capabilities, spatstat can help you visualize a spatiotemporal change in one or several variables over time. The package even comes with three-dimensional graphing capabilities. Because spatstat is a geographic data analysis package, it's commonly used in ecology, geosciences, and botany, or for environmental studies, although the package could easily be used for location-based studies that relate to business, logistics, sales, marketing, and more.

Chapter 16

Using SQL in Data Science

SQL, or *Structured Query Language,* is a standard for creating, maintaining, and securing relational databases. It's a set of rules that you can use to quickly and efficiently query, update, modify, add, or remove data from large and complex databases. You use SQL to do these tasks, rather than doing them using Python or Excel, because SQL is the simplest, fastest way to get the job done. It offers a very plain and standardized set of core commands and methods that are hard to mess up when performing these tasks. In this chapter, I introduce you to some basic SQL concepts and explain how you can use SQL to do cool things like query, join, group, sort, and even text-mine structured datasets.

Getting Started with SQL

Although you can use SQL to work with structured data that resides in relational database management systems, you can't use standard SQL as a big-data–handling solution because you can't handle big data using relational database technologies. Much more on big data and big data handling solutions is covered in Chapter 2's discussion of data engineering pipelines and infrastructure. But for now, suffice it to say that SQL is simply a tool you can use to manipulate and edit structured data tables. It's nothing super innovative, but it can be helpful to use SQL for the data querying and manipulation tasks that often arise in the practice of data science. In the following sections, I introduce the basics about relational databases, SQL, and database design.

Getting a handle on relational databases and SQL

Although the name Structured Query Language suggests that SQL is a programming language, don't be misled. SQL is not a programming language like R or Python. Rather, it's a language of commands and syntax that you can use only to create, maintain, and search relational database systems. SQL supports a few common programming forms, like conditionals and loops, but to do anything more complex, you'd have to import your SQL query results into another programming platform, and then do the more complex work there.

SQL has become so ubiquitous in the data field, passionate users are commonly found debating whether SQL should be pronounced "ess-queue-el" or "sequel." Most users that I've met lean towards the latter.

One fundamental characteristic of SQL is that you can use it on only structured data that sits in a relational database. SQL database management systems (DBMSs) optimize their own structure with minimal user input, which enables blazing-fast operational performance.

An *index* is the lookup table you create to index (and point to) data in tables of a database. Although SQL DBMSs are known for their fast structured database querying capabilities, this speed and effectiveness is heavily-dependent on good indexing. Good indexing is vital for fast data retrieval in SQL.

Similar to how different web browsers comply with, add to, and ignore different parts of the HTML standard in different ways, SQL rules are interpreted a bit differently, depending on whether you're working in open-source or with commercial vendor software applications. Because not every SQL solution is the same, it's a good idea to know something about the benefits and drawbacks of some of the more popular SQL solutions on the market. Here are the three most popular open-source SQL implementations among data scientists:

- ✔ **SQLite:** This software is more limited than other SQL implementations, especially when it comes to user management and performance-enhancing customizations, but it's a fantastic place to get started when you're first learning SQL.

- ✔ **MySQL:** MySQL is by far the most popular open-source version of SQL. It offers a complete and powerful version of SQL, and it's used on the backend of millions of websites.

- ✔ **PostgreSQL:** This software adds object-oriented elements to SQL's relational language; that makes it popular with programmers who want to integrate SQL objects into their own platform's object model.

Other powerful commercial SQL implementations, such as Oracle and Microsoft SQL Server, are great solutions, as well; but they're designed for use in business, rather than as a data science tool.

As you might guess from the name, the most salient aspect of *relational* databases is that they're relational: They're comprised of related tables. To illustrate the idea of a relational database, imagine an Excel spreadsheet with rows, columns, and predefined relationships between shared columns. Now, imagine having an Excel workbook with many worksheets (tables), and every worksheet has a column with the same name as a column in one or more other worksheets. Because these worksheets have a shared relationship, if you use SQL, then you can use that shared relationship to look up data in all related worksheets. This type of relationship is illustrated in Figure 16-1.

The *primary key* of a table is a column of values that uniquely identifies every row in that table. A good example of primary keys would be ISBN numbers for a table of books or Employee ID numbers for a table of employees. A *foreign key* is a column in one table that matches the primary key of another and is used to link tables together.

Keeping the focus on terminology, remember that proper database science often associates particular meanings to particular words, as you can see in this list:

- **Columns:** Called fields, keys, and attributes
- **Rows:** Called records
- **Cells:** Called values

Foreign Key

Lake Name	Max Water Depth (ft)	Average Annual Depth Change (in)
Lake Monroe	...	...
Lake Lilly	...	...
Lake Conway	...	...

Primary Key

Lake Name	Alkalinity (mEq/L)	Total Dissolved Solids (ppm)	Phosphates (u g/L)
Lake Monroe	...	...	...
Lake Lilly	...	...	...
Lake Conway	...	...	...

Foreign Key

Lake Name	Subdivision Name	Taxing District
Lake Monroe	...	...
Lake Lilly	...	...
Lake Conway	...	...

Figure 16-1: A relationship between data tables that share a column.

Database science has a lot of synonyms. For simplicity's sake, I try to stick to using the words *column, row,* and *cell.* And because *primary key* and *foreign key* are such standard terms, I use those to describe these two special column types.

The main benefits of using relational database management systems (RDBMSs, for short) is that they're fast, they have a pretty large storage and handling capacity (compared to spreadsheet applications such as Excel), and they're an ideal tool to help you maintain *data integrity* — the consistency and accuracy of data in your database. If you need to make quick and accurate changes and updates to your datasets, you can use SQL and a RDBMS.

Let the following scenario serve as an illustration. The table shown below describes films and lists the ratings that viewers have given each one.

id	title	genre	rating timestamp	rating
1	The Even Couple	NULL	2011-08-03 16:04:23	4
2	The Fourth Man	Drama	2014-02-19 19:17:16	5
2	The Fourth Man	Drama	2010-04-27 10:05:36	4
3	All About Adam	Drama	2011-04-05 21:21:05	4
3	All About Adam	Drama	2014-02-21 00:11:07	3
4	Dr. Yes	Thriller	NULL	NULL

What happens if you find out that *All About Adam* is really a comedy? If the table was in a simple spreadsheet, then you'd have to go into the data table, find all instances of the film, and then manually change the genre value for that record. That's not so hard in this sample table because there are only two records related to that film. But even here, if you forgot to change one of these records, this inconsistency would cause a loss of data integrity, which can cause all sorts of unpredictable problems for you down the road.

In contrast, the relational database solution is simple and elegant. Instead of one table for this example, you'd have three:

Film	id	title
	1	The Even Couple
	2	The Fourth Man
	3	All About Adam
	4	Dr. Yes

Genre	id	genre
	2	Drama
	3	Drama
	4	Thriller

Rating	timestamp		id	rating
	2011-08-03 16:04:23		1	4
	2014-02-19 19:17:16		2	5
	2010-04-27 10:05:36		2	4
	2011-04-05 21:21:05		3	4
	2014-02-21 00:11:07		3	3

The primary key for the Film and Genre tables is id. The primary key for the Rating table is timestamp — because a film can have more than one rating, id is not a unique field and, consequently, it can't be used as a primary key. In this example, if you want to look up and change the genre for *All About Adam,* you'd use Film.id as the primary key and Genre.id as the foreign key. You'd simply use those keys to query the records you need to change and then apply the changes systematically. This systematic approach eliminates the risk of stray errors.

Understanding database design

If you want to ensure your database will be useful to you for the foreseeable future, then you need to invest time and resources into excellent database design. If you want to create databases that offer fast performance and error-free results, then your database design needs to be as flawless as possible. Before you enter any data into a data table, you need to carefully consider what tables and columns you want to include, what kinds of data those tables will hold, and what relationships you want to create between those tables.

Every hour you spend planning your database and anticipating future needs can save you countless hours down the road, when your database might hold a million records. Poorly planned databases can easily turn into slow, error-ridden monstrosities. You want to avoid them at all costs.

There are a few principles to keep in mind when designing databases. More specifically, when designing your database, you should be mindful of the three following considerations:

✓ Data types
✓ Constraints
✓ Normalization

The next few sections take a closer look at each topic.

Defining data types

When creating a data table, one of the first things you have to do is to define the data type of each column. Your data type can be designated from any of the following options:

Text types: If your column is to contain text values, you can classify it as a Character data type with a fixed length, or a Text data type of indeterminate length.

✔ **Numerical types:** If your column is to hold number values, you can classify it as a Numerical data type. These can be stored as integers or floats.

✔ **Date types:** If your column is to hold date- or time-based values, you can designate this as a Date data type or Date-Time data type.

Text data types are handy, but they're terrible for searches. If you plan to query a column, make sure to assign that column a fixed length.

Considering constraints

Properly designed constraints are also an important consideration. In the context of SQL, constraints can be thought of as rules that are used to control what type of data can be placed in a table. When considering constraints, the first thing you need to do is to decide whether each column is allowed to hold a NULL value. (NULL is not the same as blank or zero data; it means there is a total absence of data in a cell.

So, for example, if you have a table of products you're selling, you probably don't want to allow a NULL in the Price column. For the Product Description column, however, since some of your products may have really long descriptions, you might allow some of the cells in this column to contain NULL values.

Within any data type, you can also constrain exactly what type of input values the column accepts. Imagine that you have a text field for Employee ID, which must contain values that are exactly two letters followed by seven numbers, like SD0154919. Because you don't want your database to accept a typo, you'd define a constraint that requires all values entered into the cells of the Employee ID column to have exactly two letters followed by seven numbers.

Normalizing your database

Finally, you need to deal with *normalization* — structuring your database so that any changes, additions, or deletions to the data have to be done only once and won't result in anomalous, inconsistent data. There are many different degrees and types of normalization (at least seven), but a good, robust, normalized SQL database should have at least the following properties:

✔ **Primary keys:** Each table has a *primary key,* which is a unique value for every row in that column.

✔ **Non-redundancy of columns:** No two tables have the same column, unless it's the primary key of one and the foreign key of the other.

✔ **No multiple dependencies:** Every column's value must depend only on one other column, whose value does not in turn depend on any other column. This means that *calculated values* — values like the total for an invoice, for example — must be done on the fly for each query and should not be hard-coded into the database. This also means that ZIP codes should be stored in a separate table because a ZIP code depends on three columns — address, city, and state.

✔ **Column indexes:** In SQL, an *index* is a lookup table that points to data in tables of a database. When you make a *column index* — an index of a particular column— each record in that column is assigned a unique key value that's indexed in a lookup table. Column indexing enables faster data retrieval from that column.

It's an excellent idea to create a column index for frequent searches, or to be used as a search criterion. This takes up memory, but it increases your search speeds tremendously. It's easy to set up, too. Just tell your SQL DBMS to index a certain column, and then the system sets it up for you.

If you're concerned that your queries are slow, first make sure you have all the indexes you need before trying other, perhaps more involved, trouble-shooting efforts.

✔ **Subject-matter segregation:** Another feature of good database design involves each table containing data for only one kind of subject matter. This is not exactly a normalization principle, per se, but it helps to achieve a similar end.

Consider again the film rating example:

```
Film    id   title
        1    The Even Couple
        2    The Fourth Man
        3    All About Adam
        4    Dr. Yes

Genre   id   genre
        2    Drama
        3    Drama
        4    Thriller

Rating  timestamp             id   rating
        2011-08-03 16:04:23   1    4
        2014-02-19 19:17:16   2    5
        2010-04-27 10:05:36   2    4
        2011-04-05 21:21:05   3    4
        2014-02-21 00:11:07   3    3
```

I could've designated Genre to be a separate column in the Film table, but it's better off in its own table because that allows for the possibility of missing data values (NULLs). Look at the Film table shown above. Film 1 has no genre assigned to it. If the Genre column were included in this table, then Film 1 would have a NULL value there. Rather than have a column that contains a NULL value, it's much easier to make a separate Genre data table. The primary keys of the Genre table don't align exactly with those of the Film table, but they don't need to when you go to join them.

NULL values can be quite problematic when you're running a SELECT query. When you're querying based on the value of particular attribute, any records that have a null value for that attribute will not be returned in the query results. Of course these records would still exist, and they may even fall within the specified range of values that you've defined for your query, but if the record has a null value, then it will be omitted from the query results. In this case, you're likely to miss them in your analysis.

Using SQL and Its Functions in Data Science

Any data scientist worth her salt must address many challenges, both when dealing with the data and when dealing with the science. SQL takes some of the pressure off when you're dealing with the data, saving precious time and effort that's required to store and query data. When you're working with complex datasets, storing and querying data can sometimes be the most time-consuming tasks. In the following sections, I explain how SQL is able to play so well with others, and I introduce some of its more useful functions and capabilities.

Integrating SQL, R, Python, and Excel into your data science strategy

Some data scientists are resistant to learning SQL because of the so-called cognitive overhead. They think, "I've already memorized a bunch of commands for dealing with data in R or Python. Won't it be confusing to switch over to a whole new language?" In the case of SQL, no, it's really not that confusing, and the small hassle is worth it. Although the SQL standard is lengthy, a user commonly needs fewer than 20 commands, and the syntax is human-readable. Making things even easier, SQL commands are written in ALL CAPS, which helps to keep the language distinct and separate from other programming languages in your mind.

If you want to integrate SQL capabilities into your R or Python workflow, every DBMS has a library or module that you can use. Generally, it's a good idea to take advantage of SQL's speed by doing as much work in SQL as possible, and then accessing the SQL database from within your scripting language only when necessary. In this type of procedure, you'd translate query results into native R or Python data forms only when you finish with SQL and have all the data you need.

You can also integrate Microsoft Excel with your work in SQL. You can use MySQL to import your databases into Excel using the Data Ribbon (the Ribbon's Other Sources button, to be precise), or you can save your Excel tables as text files and import them into the DBMS. If you're not working in MySQL, look around online and you'll be sure to find plug-ins for integrating other DBMSs into Excel, as well. Some plug-ins are even free.

Using SQL functions in data science

When working with SQL commands, you use *functions* to perform tasks and *arguments* to more narrowly specify those tasks. To query a particular set from within your data tables, for example, use the SELECT function. To combine separate tables into one, use the JOIN function. To place limits on the data that your query returns, use a WHERE argument. As I said, fewer than 20 commands are commonly used in SQL. This section introduces SELECT, JOIN, WHERE, GROUP, MAX(), MIN(), COUNT(), AVG(), and HAVING.

The most common SQL command is the SELECT function. You can use this function to generate a list of search results based on designated criteria. To illustrate, imagine the film-rating scenario. This time, you have a tiny database of movie ratings that contains the three tables — Film, Genre, and Rating.

To generate a printout of all data from the Rating table, use the SELECT function. Any function with SELECT is called a *query,* and SELECT functions accept different arguments to narrow down or expand the data that is returned. Since an asterisk (*) represents a wildcard, the asterisk in SELECT * tells the *interpreter* — the SQL component that carries out all SQL statements — to show every column in the table. You can then use the WHERE argument to limit the output to only certain values. For example, here is the complete Rating table:

```
Rating   timestamp              id   rating
         2011-08-03 16:04:23    1    4
         2014-02-19 19:17:16    2    5
         2010-04-27 10:05:36    2    4
         2011-04-05 21:21:05    3    4
         2014-02-21 00:11:07    3    3
```

If you want to limit your ratings to those made after a certain time, you'd use code like that shown in Listing 16-1.

Listing 16-1: Using SELECT, WHERE, and DATE() to Query Data

```
SELECT * FROM Rating
WHERE Rating.timestamp >= date('2014-01-01')
timestamp              id    rating
2014-02-19 19:17:16    2     5
2014-02-21 00:11:07    3     3
```

In Listing 16-1, the DATE() function turns a string into a date that can then be compared with the timestamp column.

You can also use SQL to join columns into a new data table. Joins are made on the basis of shared (or compared) data in a particular column (or columns). There are several ways you can execute a join in SQL, but the ones I list below are probably the most popular:

- ✔ **Inner join:** The default JOIN type. It returns all records that lay in the intersecting regions between the tables being queried.

- ✔ **Outer join:** Returns all records that lay outside of the overlapping regions between queried data tables.

- ✔ **Full outer join:** Returns all records that lay both inside and outside of the overlapping regions between queried data tables — in other words, all records for both tables are returned.

- ✔ **Left join:** Returns all records that reside in the leftmost table.

- ✔ **Right join:** Returns all records that reside in the rightmost table.

You should be sure to differentiate between an inner join and an outer join because these functions handle missing data in different ways. As an example of a join in SQL, if you want a list of films that includes genres, you use an inner join between the Film and Genre tables to return only the results that intersect (overlap) between the two tables.

To refresh your memory, here are the two tables you're interested in:

```
Film    id    title
        1     The Even Couple
        2     The Fourth Man
        3     All About Adam
        4     Dr. Yes

Genre   id    genre
        2     Drama
        3     Drama
        4     Thriller
```

Listing 16-2 shows how you'd use an inner join to get the information you want.

Listing 16-2:   An Inner JOIN Function

```
SELECT Film.id, Film.title, Genre.genre
FROM Film
JOIN Genre On Genre.id=Film.id
id    title            genre
2     The Fourth Man   Drama
3     All About Adam   Drama
4     Dr. Yes          Thriller
```

In Listing 16-2, I name specific columns (Film.title and Genre.genre) after the SELECT command. I do this to avoid creating a duplicate id column in the table that results from the JOIN — one id from the Film table and one id from the Genre table. Since the default for JOIN is inner, and inner joins return only records that are overlapping or shared between tables, Film 1 is omitted from the results (due to its missing genre value).

If you want to return all rows, even ones with NULL values, simply do a full outer join, like what is shown in Listing 16-3.

Listing 16-3:   A Full Outer JOIN

```
SELECT Film.id, Film.title, Genre.genre
FROM Film
FULL JOIN Genre On Genre.id=Film.id
id    title             genre
1     The Even Couple   NULL
2     The Fourth Man    Drama
3     All About Adam    Drama
4     Dr. Yes           Thriller
```

To aggregate values so you can figure out the average rating for a film, use the GROUP statement. [GROUP statement commands include MAX(), MIN(), COUNT() or AVG().] Listing 16-4 shows one way you could aggregate values.

In Listing 16-4, the average rating of films was returned; the AS statement was used in SELECT to rename the column to make sure it was properly labeled. The Film and Ratings tables had to be joined, and because *Dr. Yes* had no ratings and an inner join was used, that film was left out.

To narrow the results even further, add a HAVING clause at the end, as shown in Listing 16-5.

The code in Listing 16-5 limits the data that your query returns, so that you get only records of titles that have an average rating greater than or equal to 4.

Listing 16-4:   Using a GROUP Statement to Aggregate Data

```
SELECT Film.title, AVG(rating) AS avg_rating
FROM Film
JOIN Rating On Film.id=Rating.id
GROUP BY Film.title

title                avg_rating
All About Adam       3.5
The Even Couple      4.0
The Fourth Man       4.5
```

Listing 16-5:   A HAVING Clause to Narrow Results

```
SELECT Film.title, AVG(rating) AS avg_rating
FROM Film
JOIN Rating On Film.id=Rating.id
GROUP BY Film.title
HAVING avg_rating >= 4

title                avg_rating
The Even Couple      4.0
The Fourth Man       4.5
```

It should be noted that, while SQL can do some very basic text mining, packages like the Natural Language Toolkit in Python (NLTK, at www.nltk.org/), or General Architecture for Text Engineering (GATE, at https://gate.ac.uk/) are needed to do anything more complex than word and collocation counting. These more advanced packages can be used for preprocessing of data to extract linguistic items such as parts of speech or syntactic relations, which can then be stored in a relational database for later querying.

Mining text with SQL

In this era of big data, more and more analysis is being done on larger and larger amounts of raw text — from books to government procedures, and even Twitter feeds. You can use the `tm` and `nltk` packages in R and Python, respectively, to process such data, but as scripting languages, they can be rather slow. That's why users commonly do some text mining in SQL. If you want to generate quick statistics on word counts and frequencies, you can use SQL to your advantage.

When the first SQL standard was published, the originators likely had no idea it would be used for these purposes, but the boundaries of SQL are being pushed and expanded all the time. This flexibility is yet another reason SQL maintains its place as an indispensable tool among data science practitioners.

Chapter 17

Software Applications for Data Science

*I*n this day and age, when it seems like everything is going to the cloud, standard installable desktop applications are fewer and farther between. Nonetheless, there are still a few programs out there that you can install on your computer and use for data science tasks. In this chapter, I explain how you can use Microsoft Excel to perform some basic tasks to help simplify your project work in data science. I also introduce a free, open-source analytics platform called KNIME and discuss how you can use that to perform advanced data science tasks without having to learn how to code.

Making Life Easier with Excel

Microsoft Excel holds its own special place among data science tools. It was originally designed to act as a simple spreadsheet. Over time, however, it's become most people's first choice in data analysis software. In response to user demands, Microsoft has been adding more and more analysis and visualization tools with every release. As Excel advances, so do its data munging and data science capabilities. Excel 2013 includes easy-to-use tools for charting, pivot tables, and macros. It also supports scripting in Visual Basic so that you can design scripts to automate repeatable tasks.

The benefit of using Excel in a data science capacity is that it offers a really fast and easy way to get up close and personal with your data. If you want to browse every data point in your dataset, you can quickly and easily do this using Excel. Most data scientists start in Excel and eventually add other tools and platforms when they find themselves pushing against the boundaries of the things Excel is designed to do. Still, even the best data scientists out there keep Excel as an important tool in their tool belt. When working in data science, you might not use Excel on a daily basis, but knowing how to use it can make your job easier.

Although you have many different tools available to you when you want to see your data as one big forest, Excel is a great first choice when you need to look at the trees. Excel attempts to be many different things to many different kinds of users. Its functionality is well-compartmentalized to avoid overwhelming new users, while still providing so-called "power users" the more advanced functionality they crave. In the following sections, I show you how you can use Excel to quickly get to know your data. I also introduce Excel pivot tables and macros, and how you can use those to greatly simplify your data cleanup and analysis tasks.

Using Excel to quickly get to know your data

If you're just starting off with an unfamiliar dataset and you need to spot patterns or trends as quickly as possible, then use Excel. Excel offers very effective features for just such purposes. Its main features for a quick-and-dirty data analysis are

- **Filters:** Filters are great for sorting out all records that are irrelevant to the analysis at hand.

- **Conditional formatting:** Specify a condition, and Excel flags records that meet that condition. By using conditional formatting, you can easily detect outliers and trends in your tabular datasets.

- **Charts:** Charts have long been used to visually detect outliers and trends in data, so charting is an integral part of almost all data science analyses.

To see how these features work in action, consider the sample dataset depicted in Figure 17-1. A closer look reveals that it tracks sales figures for three employees over six months.

Salesperson	Month	Total Sales
Abbie	Jan	$ 10,144.75
Abbie	Feb	$ 29,008.52
Abbie	Mar	$ 208,187.70
Abbie	Apr	$ 21,502.13
Abbie	May	$ 23,975.73
Abbie	Jun	$ 20,172.20
Brian	Jan	$ 9,925.44
Brian	Feb	$ 9,183.93
Brian	Mar	$ 12,691.39
Brian	Apr	$ 19,521.37
Brian	May	$ 16,579.38
Brian	Jun	$ 14,161.52
Chris	Jan	$ 2,792.18
Chris	Feb	$ 5,669.46
Chris	Mar	$ 4,909.24
Chris	Apr	$ 8,731.14
Chris	May	$ 11,747.29
Chris	Jun	$ 13,856.17

Figure 17-1:
The full dataset that tracks employee sales performance.

Fooling with filters in Excel

To narrow your view of your dataset to only the data that matters for your analysis, use Excel filters to filter irrelevant data out of the data view. Simply select the data and click the Home tab's Sort & Filter button, and then choose Filter from the options that appear. A little drop-down option then appears in the header row of the selected data, and from this drop-down you can select what classes of records you'd like to be have filtered from the selection. Using the Excel Filter functionality allows you to very quickly and easily sort or restrict your view to only the subsets of the data that interest you the most.

Take another look at the full dataset, as shown in Figure 17-1. Say you wanted to view only data related to Abbie's sales figures. If you select all records in the "Salesperson" column and then activate the filter functionality (as described above), from the drop-down menu that appears, you can specify that the filter isolates only all records named "Abbie," as shown in Figure 17-2. When filtered, the table is reduced from 18 rows down to only 6 rows.

With this particular example, that change doesn't seem so dramatic, but when you have hundreds, thousands, or even a million rows, this feature comes in very, very handy.

Excel lets you store only up to 1,048,576 rows per worksheet.

Figure 17-2:
The sales performance dataset, filtered to show only Abbie records.

Salesperson	Month	Total Sales
Abbie	Jan	$10,144.75
Abbie	Feb	$29,008.52
Abbie	Mar	$208,187.70
Abbie	Apr	$21,502.13
Abbie	May	$23,975.73
Abbie	Jun	$20,172.20

Conditional formatting to spot outliers and trends in tabular data

To quickly spot outliers in your tabular data, use Excel's Conditional Formatting feature. For example, imagine there was a data entry error and Abbie's March Total Sales showed $208,187.70 but was really supposed to be $20,818.77. You're not quite sure where the error is located, but you know it must be a pretty big one because the figures seem off by about $180,000.

To quickly show such an outlier, select all of the records in the Total Sales column and then click the Conditional Formatting button on the Ribbon's Home tab. When the button's menu appears, choose the Data Bars option. Doing so brings up the red data bar scales you see in Figure 17-3. With data bars turned on, the bar in the $208,187.70 cell is so much larger than any of the others that you can easily see the error.

If you want to quickly discover patterns in your tabular data, you can choose the Color Scales option (rather than the Data Bars option) from the Conditional Formatting menu. After correcting Abbie's March Total Sales figure to $20,818.77, select all cells in the Total Sales column and then activate the Color Scales version of conditional formatting. Doing so brings up what you see in Figure 17-4. From the red-white-blue heat map, you can see that Abbie has the highest sales and Brian has been selling more than Chris. (Okay, you can't see the red-white-blue in my black-and-white figures, but you can see light-versus-dark contrast.)

Salesperson	Month	Total Sales
Abbie	Jan	$ 10,144.75
Abbie	Feb	$ 29,008.52
Abbie	Mar	$ 208,187.70
Abbie	Apr	$ 21,502.13
Abbie	May	$ 23,975.73
Abbie	Jun	$ 20,172.20
Brian	Jan	$ 9,925.44
Brian	Feb	$ 9,183.93
Brian	Mar	$ 12,691.39
Brian	Apr	$ 19,521.37
Brian	May	$ 16,579.38
Brian	Jun	$ 14,161.52
Chris	Jan	$ 2,792.18
Chris	Feb	$ 5,669.46
Chris	Mar	$ 4,909.24
Chris	Apr	$ 8,731.14
Chris	May	$ 11,747.29
Chris	Jun	$ 13,856.17

Figure 17-3: Spotting outliers in a tabular dataset with conditional formatting data bars.

Excel charting to visually identify outliers and trends

Excel's Charting tool gives you an incredibly easy way to visually identify both outliers and trends in your data. An XY (Scatter) chart of the original dataset from Figure 17-1 yields the scatter plot shown in Figure 17-5. As you can see, the outlier is overwhelmingly obvious when the data is plotted on a scatter chart.

Alternatively, if you want to visually detect trends in your dataset, you can use Excel's Line Chart feature. The data from Figure 17-4 is shown as a line chart in Figure 17-6.

As you can clearly see from the line chart in Figure 17-6, Chris's sales performance is very low. He's in last place among the three, but he's gaining some momentum. Because he seems to be improving, maybe management would want to wait a few months before making any firing decisions based on sales performance data.

Salesperson	Month	Total Sales
Abbie	Jan	$ 10,144.75
Abbie	Feb	$ 29,008.52
Abbie	Mar	$ 20,818.77
Abbie	Apr	$ 21,502.13
Abbie	May	$ 23,975.73
Abbie	Jun	$ 20,172.20
Brian	Jan	$ 9,925.44
Brian	Feb	$ 9,183.93
Brian	Mar	$ 12,691.39
Brian	Apr	$ 19,521.37
Brian	May	$ 16,579.38
Brian	Jun	$ 14,161.52
Chris	Jan	$ 2,792.18
Chris	Feb	$ 5,669.46
Chris	Mar	$ 4,909.24
Chris	Apr	$ 8,731.14
Chris	May	$ 11,747.29
Chris	Jun	$ 13,856.17

Figure 17-4: Spotting outliers in a tabular dataset with color scales.

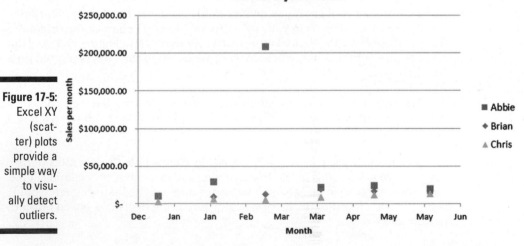

Figure 17-5: Excel XY (scatter) plots provide a simple way to visually detect outliers.

Sales by month

Figure 17-6:
Excel line
charts make
it easy to
visually
detect
trends in
data.

Reformatting and summarizing with pivot tables

Excel developed the pivot table to make it easier for users to extract valuable insights from large sets of spreadsheet data. If you want to generate insights by quickly restructuring or reclassifying your data, use a pivot chart. One of the main differences between a traditional *spreadsheet* and a *dataset* is that spreadsheets tend to be wide (with a lot of columns) while datasets tend to be long (with a lot of rows). Figure 17-7 clearly shows the difference between a long dataset and a wide spreadsheet.

Long format:

Salesperson	Month	Total Sales
Abbie	Jan	$ 10,144.75
Abbie	Feb	$ 29,008.52
Abbie	Mar	$ 208,187.70
Abbie	Apr	$ 21,502.13
Abbie	May	$ 23,975.73
Abbie	Jun	$ 20,172.20
Brian	Jan	$ 9,925.44
Brian	Feb	$ 9,183.93
Brian	Mar	$ 12,691.39
Brian	Apr	$ 19,521.37
Brian	May	$ 16,579.38
Brian	Jun	$ 14,161.52
Chris	Jan	$ 2,792.18
Chris	Feb	$ 5,669.46
Chris	Mar	$ 4,909.24
Chris	Apr	$ 8,731.14
Chris	May	$ 11,747.29
Chris	Jun	$ 13,856.17

Wide format:

Salesperson	Jan	Feb	Mar	Apr	May	Jun
Abbie	$10,144.75	$29,008.52	$208,187.70	$21,502.13	$23,975.73	$20,172.20
Brian	$ 9,925.44	$ 9,183.93	$ 12,691.39	$19,521.37	$16,579.38	$14,161.52
Chris	$ 2,792.18	$ 5,669.46	$ 4,909.24	$ 8,731.14	$11,747.29	$13,856.17

Figure 17-7:
A long
dataset
and a wide
spread-
sheet.

The way that Excel is designed leads many users to intuitively prefer the wide format — which makes sense because it's a spreadsheet application. To counter this preference, however, Excel offers the table feature so that you can quickly convert between long and wide formats. You can also use pivot tables to quickly calculate subtotals and summary calculations on your newly formatted and rearranged data tables.

 Creating pivot tables is super easy. All you need to do is select all the cells that comprise the table that you seek to analyze. Then go to the Insert tab and click the Pivot Table button on that tab. This will lead you to a Create PivotTable dialog box that will allow you to define where you want Excel to construct the pivot table. Select OK and Excel will automatically generate a PivotTables Fields interface on the page you've specified. From this interface, you can specify what fields you want to have included in the pivot table and how you want them to be laid out.

The table shown in Figure 17-8 was constructed using the long-format sales-performance data shown in Figure 17-7. It's an example of the simplest possible pivot table that can be constructed, but even at that, it automatically calculates subtotals for each column, and those subtotals automatically update when you make changes to the data. What's more, pivot tables come with *pivot charts* — data plots that automatically change when you make changes to the pivot table filters based on the criteria you're evaluating.

Figure 17-8:
Creating a wide data table from the long dataset via a pivot table.

Total_Sales	Month ⏷						
Salesperson ⏷	Jan	Feb	Mar	Apr	May	Jun	Grand Total
Abbie	$10,144.75	$29,008.52	$20,818.77	$21,502.13	$23,975.73	$20,172.20	$125,622.10
Brian	$9,925.44	$9,183.93	$12,691.39	$19,521.37	$16,579.38	$14,161.52	$82,063.03
Chris	$2,792.18	$5,669.46	$4,909.24	$8,731.14	$11,747.29	$13,856.17	$47,705.48
Grand Total	$22,862.37	$43,861.91	$38,419.40	$49,754.64	$52,302.40	$48,189.89	$255,390.61

Automating Excel tasks with macros

Within Excel, macros act as a set of functions and commands that you can use to automate tasks. If you want to save time and hassle by automating Excel tasks that you find yourself repeating on a routine basis, then use macros.

Macros are pre-scripted routines that are written in Visual Basic for Applications (VBA). You can use macros to decrease the amount of manual processing you need to do when working with data in Excel. To access macros, first activate Excel's Developer Tab from within the Options menu on the File tab. (When the Options menu opens, choose Customize Ribbon from your choices on the left and then click to select the Developer check box in the column on the right.) Using the Developer tab, you can either record a macro, import one that was created by someone else, or code up your own in VBA.

To illustrate macros in action, imagine you have a column of values and that you want to insert an empty cell between each one of the values. Excel has no easy, out-of-the-box way to do this insertion. Using Excel macros, however, you could ask Excel to record you while you step through the process one time, and then assign a key command to this recording to create the macro. After you create the macro, every time you need to repeat the same task in the future, just run the macro by pressing the key command, and the script performs all the required steps for you. (See Figure 17-9.)

Before macro:

one
two
three
four
five
six
seven
eight
nine
ten

After macro:

one
two
three
four
five
six
seven
eight
nine
ten

Figure 17-9:
Using a macro to insert empty cells between values.

When you use a macro, specify whether the cells that the macro is changing are *relative* or *absolute*. With relative macros, every action and movement you make is recorded as relative to the cell that was selected when you began the recording. When you run the macro in the future, it will run in reference to the cell that's selected, acting as if that cell were the same cell that you had initially selected when you recorded the macro. In absolute macros, after you start recording the macro, every action and movement you make after recording will be repeated when you run the macro in the future, and those actions or movements will not be made in any relative reference to whatever cell was active when you started recording. The macro routine will be repeated exactly as you recorded it.

In the preceding example, I specified the cells as *relative*. If I had specified them as *absolute,* the macro would have kept adding a space between only the one and two values every time you run the macro.

Macro commands are not entered into Excel's Undo stack. If you use a macro to change or delete data, you're stuck with that change. Test your macros first and save your worksheets before using them so you can revert to the saved file if something goes wrong.

Power Excel users often graduate to programming their own macros using VBA. As a full-fledged programming language, the possibilities of Excel paired with VBA are almost endless. Still, here's one important thing to consider: If you're going to invest time learning a programming language, do you need to work within the confines of Excel's spreadsheet structure? If not, you might consider learning a scientific-computing language like R or Python. Those languages are open source, have a more user-friendly syntax, and are much more flexible and powerful.

Using KNIME for Advanced Data Analytics

If you don't know how to code but still want the benefits that custom predictive analytics has to offer, you can download and install KNIME and use its visual environment to access these features. KNIME offers services, solutions, and open-source software to fulfill the advanced analytics requirements of today's data-driven business enterprise. The company's purpose is to provide an open platform that meets the data-mining and analytics needs of the masses.

If you want data-mining software that you can install on your PC and use for predictive analytics, look no further than KNIME Analytics Platform. KNIME is easy to use, so even beginners who don't know how to code can use the program — but for more advanced users, KNIME offers plug-ins that you can use to integrate Weka's pre-constructed analysis modules or run your R and

Python scripts from within the application. Beginners and advanced users alike can use KNIME predictive analytics to do things like

- ✔ **Upsell and cross-sell.** You can use KNIME to build cross-selling and upselling models that enable you to increase sales by making optimal recommendations of other products which customers are likely to be interested in purchasing as well.

- ✔ **Churn reduction.** You can use KNIME to mine your customer data and identify which of your customers you're most likely to lose and why.

- ✔ **Sentiment and network analysis.** You can use KNIME to analyze the sentiment of people and organizations in your social networks. This information helps you to identify those areas of your business that are performing well and what areas may need some work.

- ✔ **Energy usage prediction and auditing.** You can use KNIME software to do time series analyses and build regression models from energy usage data.

If you're curious about KNIME and how you can use it to increase revenues and streamline business workflows, the good news is that KNIME's Analytics Platform is available free of charge. In the following sections, I discuss how KNIME can be used to reduce churn, perform sentiment analysis, and predict energy usages.

Reducing customer churn via KNIME

I talk a bit about customer churn in Chapter 20, where I spell out how you can use clustering techniques to keep customer loyalty. Within KNIME, you use the k-means algorithm to perform this type of churn analysis. (For more on the k-means algorithm, see Chapter 5.) If you want to use KNIME to help reduce customer churn, it offers a cool churn analysis workflow (see www.knime.org/knime-applications/churn-analysis) that shows exactly how to go about using the platform to perform this type of analysis.

Using KNIME to make the most of your social data

As I discuss in Chapter 20, you can use sentiment analysis to monitor and early-detect your customer satisfaction rates. KNIME offers a social media clustering workflow (see www.knime.org/knime-applications/social-media-sentiment-analysis) and a text processing plug-in (see https://tech.knime.org/knime-text-processing) that you can use against your social media data in order to keep a close eye on how customers and potential customers are feeling about your brand and offerings.

In Chapter 20, I also discuss the benefits that strategic social networking can bring to your business. If you want to identify and forge alliances with thought leaders and online social influencers who operate in your target niche, use KNIME's Social Media Leader/Follower Analysis workflow and network analysis plug-in. (See `www.knime.org/knime-applications/ social-media-leaderfollower-analysis` for more on this plug-in.)

Using KNIME for environmental good stewardship

Everyone knows that energy usage predictions and audits are essential to responsible energy planning. Within KNIME, you use time-series analysis and auto-regressive modeling to generate a predictive model from historical data and data trends. (For more on time-series analysis and regression models, see Chapter 5.) If you want to use KNIME to build predictive models for energy usage, you can use the Energy Usage Prediction (Time Series Prediction) workflow (see `www.knime.org/knime-applications/ energy-usage-prediction`) that the platform provides at its public workflow server (see `www.knime.org/example-workflows`).

Part V

Applying Domain Expertise to Solve Real-World Problems Using Data Science

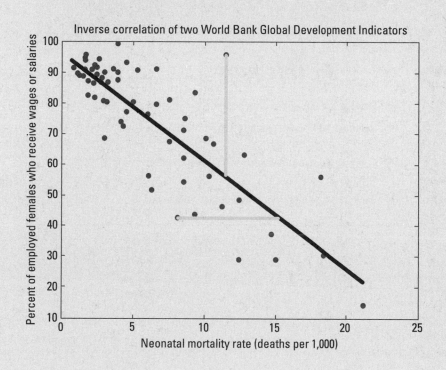

Inverse correlation of two World Bank Global Development Indicators

To see how data science is being used to better our world, check out
www.dummies.com/extras/datascience.

In this part . . .

✔ Explore the impact of data science on journalism.

✔ Use data science techniques to illuminate environmental issues.

✔ Turbocharge your e-Commerce growth with the help of data science.

✔ Look at data science's crime busting potential.

Chapter 18

Using Data Science in Journalism

*Y*ou're not interested in yesterday's news, right? Well, neither is anyone else. That's why traditional media is in a sink-or-swim situation. The journalism field and traditional media industry have undergone countless changes since the explosion of the Internet. Although the industry was once dominated by print and television, the growth of digital media technologies continues to introduce irreversible changes.

As the adoption of digital media like Twitter, Facebook, and blogs continues to grow, media's response-time requirements get shorter and shorter. If you've already heard about the latest news through social media — or through word-of-mouth from someone who heard it on social media — then why would you spend time reading it in a paper or watching it on TV? It's most likely that, if you're at all tech-savvy, then digital media has already reshaped your expectations for how you want to receive your news and when.

In a quest to stay relevant, many traditional media venues have turned to the same technological advances that previously threatened to annihilate them. This adoption of more advanced digital technologies resulted in the birth of data journalism as an independent field. Data journalism — also known as *data-driven journalism* — is proving to be a potent marriage between public trust in traditional journalism and the power of data.

Modern data journalists — the experts who craft all the cool data-driven stories you see out there — must be masters at collecting, analyzing, and presenting data. In its simplest form, data journalism can be described as a process involving three distinct steps:

1. **Data collection:** Can involve web-scraping and the configuration of automated data feeds. (*Web-scraping* is a process that involves setting up automated programs to scour and extract the data you need straight from the Internet.)

2. **Data analysis:** Can involve trend-spotting, outlier analysis, and contextual evaluation

3. **Data presentation:** Involves data-visualization design and the drafting of concise, well-written story narratives

Exploring the Five Ws and an H

For as long as newsrooms have been around, reporters have been on a mission to cover answers to questions about *who*, *what*, *when*, *where*, *why*, and *how*. The tools have changed and the data sources have grown, but this only provides journalists with deeper and more insightful answers to their questions. In this digital media era, traditional journalists can't survive if they're unable to quickly find sufficient answers to these questions — they simply won't be fast enough or relevant enough to compete with other, more data-savvy journalists. Indeed, for any journalist to stay competitive in her field, she has to learn at least basic data science skills and to use those skills to help her develop, design, and publish content that consistently demonstrates competitive readership and engagement rates.

It's critical to emphasize here, at the beginning of the chapter, that data journalists have an ethical responsibility to always represent data accurately. A data journalist should never distort the message of the data to fit a story they want to tell. Readers rely on data journalists to provide honest and accurate representations, thus amplifying the level of ethical responsibility that the journalist must assume. Data journalists must first find out what the data really says, and then either tell just that story (even if it wasn't the first idea for the story) — or in the alternative, drop the storyline, if the data doesn't support it.

Checking out who

When most people think of data, questions about *who* don't readily come to mind. In data journalism, however, answers to questions about *who* are profoundly important to the success of any data-driven story. You must consider who created and maintains your source datasets to determine whether those datasets are a credible basis for a story. If you want to write a story that appeals to your target readership, then you must consider who comprises that readership and the most pressing needs and concerns of those people.

Considering who made your data

The answer to the question, "Who made your data?" is the most fundamental and important answer to any of the five W questions. No story can pass the litmus test unless it's been built upon highly credible sources. If your sources aren't valid and accurate, you could spend countless hours producing what, in the end, amounts to a worthless story.

You must be scrupulous about knowing who made your data sources because you need to be able to validate those sources' accuracy and credibility. You definitely don't want to go public with a story you generated from non-credible sources because if anyone questions the story's validity, then you have no ground on which to stand.

News is only as good as its source, so make sure to protect your own credibility by reporting on data from only credible sources. Also, it's important to use as many relevant data sources as can be acquired, to avoid bias or an accusation of cherry-picking.

If you want to create a meaningful, credible data-driven story that gets a maximum amount of attention from your audience, then you can use the power and clout of reputable data sources to make your stories and headlines that much more compelling. In any type of data journalism piece you publish, it's critical that you disclose your data sources. You don't have to provide a live web link back to those sources, but you should at least make a statement about where you got your information, in case people want to investigate further on their own.

Pinpointing who is your audience

Really research and get to know your target audience before planning your story so that you can make sure you craft something that's of maximum interest and usefulness to them. You can take the same interesting, high-quality story and present it in countless different lights — with some lights being much, much more compelling than others.

To present your story in a way that most attracts your reader's attention, spend some serious time researching your target audience and what presentation styles work well with readers of that group. One way to begin getting to know your readers is to gather data on stories that have performed well with that audience in the recent past.

If you search social bookmarking sites — StumbleUpon, for example, (http://stumbleupon.com), or Digg (http://digg.com), or Delicious (http://delicious.com) — or just mine some Twitter data, then you can quickly generate a list of headlines that perform well with your target audience. Just get in there and start searching for content that's based on the same topic as that of your own. Identify what headlines seem to have the best performance — the highest engagement counts, in other words — among them.

After you have a list of related headlines that perform well with your target audience, note any similarities between them. Identify any specific keywords or hashtags that are getting the most user engagement. Leverage those as main draws to generate interest in your article. Lastly, examine the *emotional value* of the headlines — the emotional pull that draws readers in to read the piece, in other words. Speaking of emotions, news articles generally satisfy at least one of the following core human desires:

- ✔ **To learn:** Often closely tied to a desire for profit, but not always.

- ✔ **To protect:** The desire to protect one's property, income, and well-being, or that of friends and family.

- ✔ **For money, stuff, and property:** A person's innate desire to have things that bring him comfort, safety, security, and status.

- ✔ **For self-esteem:** People are sometimes interested in knowing about topics that help them feel good about themselves. These topics often include ideas about philanthropy, charity, service, or grassroots causes for social change.

Ask yourself what primary desires your headlines promise to satisfy. Then craft your headlines in a way designed to appeal most strongly to that desire. Try to determine what type of articles perform the best with your target audience or what your target audience most strongly seeks when looking for new content to consume. With that info in hand, make sure to exact-target your writing and headlines in a way that clearly meets a core desire among your target audience.

Taking a hard look at why your story matters

The human capacity to question and understand why things are the way they are is a clear delineation point between the human species and other highly cognitive mammals. Answers to questions about *why* help you to make better-informed decisions. These answers help you to better structure the world around you and help you develop reasoning beyond what you need for mere survival.

In data journalism, as in all other types of business, answers to the question *why* help you predict how people and markets respond. These answers help you know how to proceed to achieve an outcome of most probable success. Knowing why your story matters helps you write and present it in a way that achieves the most favorable outcomes — presumably, that your readers enjoy and take tremendous value from consuming your content.

Asking why to generate and augment a storyline

No matter what topic you're crafting a story around, it's incredibly important to generate a storyline around the wants and needs of your target audience. After you know who your audience is and what needs they most often try to satisfy through consuming content (which I talk about in the section "Pinpointing who is your audience," earlier in this chapter), then use that knowledge to help you craft your storyline. If you want to write a story and design a visualization that exact-targets the needs and wants of your readership, then take the time to pinpoint why people would be interested in your story and create a story that directly meets that desire in as many ways as possible.

Looking at why your audience should care

People care about things that matter to them and that affect their lives. Generally, people want to feel happy and safe. They want to have fulfilling relationships. They want to have good status among their peers. People like to learn things, particularly things that help them earn more money. People like possessions and things that bring them comfort, status, and security. People like to feel good about themselves and what they do. This is all part of human nature.

The above-described desires summarize *why* people care about anything; from the readers of your story to the person down the street. People care because it does something for them, it fills one of their core desires. Consequently, if your goal is to publish a high-performing, well-received data journalism piece, make sure to craft it in a way that really fulfills one or two core desires of your target readership. To better understand your audience and what they most desire in the content they consume, flip back to the section "Checking out who," earlier in this chapter.

Getting to the point of what you're saying

The *what,* in data journalism, refers to the gist of your story. In all forms of journalism, a journalist absolutely must be able to get straight to the point. Keep it clear, concise, and easy to understand.

When crafting data visualizations to accompany your data journalism piece, make sure that the visual story is easy to discern at a moment's glance.

If it takes longer than that, the data visualization is not focused enough. The same thing goes with your writing. No one wants to drag through loads of words trying to figure out *what* you're trying to say. Readers appreciate it when you make their lives easier by keeping your narrative clear, direct, and to the point.

The more people have to work to understand your content, the less they tend to like it. If you want to provide readers with information they enjoy consuming, make sure that your writing and data visualizations are clear and to the point.

Considering when

As the old adage goes, timing is everything. It's a valuable skill to know how to take old data and refurbish it so that it's interesting to a modern readership. Likewise, in data journalism, it's imperative to keep an eye on contextual relevancy and know when it's the optimal time to craft and publish a particular story.

Integrating when as context to your story

If you want to craft a data journalism piece that really garners a lot of respect and attention from your target audience, consider *when* — over what time period — your data is relevant. Stale, outdated data usually doesn't help your story make breaking news, and unfortunately you can find tons of old data out there. But if you're skillful with your data, you can create data mashups that take trends in old datasets and present them in ways that are interesting to your present-day readership.

For example, take gender-based trends in 1940s employment data and do a *mashup* — integration, comparison, or contrast — of that data and employment data trends from the five years just previous to the current one. You could then use this combined dataset to support a really dramatic story about how much things have changed or how very little things have changed, depending on the angle you're after with your piece.

Returning once again to the issue of ethical responsibilities in journalism, as a data journalist, there's a fine line between finding datasets that most persuasively support your storyline, and finding facts that support a factually-challenged story you're trying to push. Journalists have an ethical responsibility to convey an honest message to their readers. When building a case to support your story, make sure not to take things too far — in other words, don't take things into the realm of fiction. There are a million facts that could be presented in countless ways to support any story you're looking to tell. Make sure your story is based in reality, and is not just some divisive or fabricated story that you're trying to promote because you think your readers will like it.

You may sometimes have trouble finding interesting or compelling datasets to support your story. In these situations, look for ways to create data mashups that tie your less-interesting data into some data that's extremely interesting to your target audience. Use the combined dataset as a basis for your data-driven story.

Knowing when your audience cares the most

If your goal is to publish a data journalism piece that goes viral, then you certainly want to consider the story's *timeliness* — when would be primetime to publish an article on this particular topic.

For obvious reasons, you're not going to do well by publishing a story in 2014 about who won the 1984 election for U.S. President; everyone knows, and no one cares. Likewise, if there's a huge media scandal going on that has already piqued the interest of your readership, then it's not a bad idea to ride the tailwinds of that media hype and publish a related story. The story would likely perform pretty well, if it's interesting.

As a recent example, you could have created a data journalism piece on Internet user privacy assumptions and breaches thereof, and then published it in the days just after the Edward Snowden/NSA controversy news broke. Keeping relevant and timely publishing schedules is one way to ensure that your stories garner the attention they need to keep you employed.

Placing where your story matters

Data and stories are always more relevant to some places than others. From where is a story derived and where is it going — if you keep these important facts in mind, the publications you develop are more relevant to their intended audience.

The *where* aspect in data journalism is a bit ambiguous because it can refer to a geographical location or a digital location, or both.

Looking for where your story is happening

You need to focus on where your story is most relevant so that you can craft the most compelling story by reporting on the most relevant trends.

If your story is *location independent* — you're reporting on a trend that's irrelevant to location — of course you want to use data sources that most clearly demonstrate the trend upon which you're reporting. Likewise, if you're reporting a story that's tied to a specific geographic location, you probably want to report statistics that are generated from regional areas that demonstrate the greatest degree of extremes — either as greatest value fluxes or as greatest value differences for the parameters on which you're reporting.

Sometimes, you find multiple geographic or digital locations that exemplify extreme trends and unusual outliers. In other words, you find more than one excellent information source. In these cases, consider using all of them by creating and presenting a *data mashup* — a combination of two or more data sources that are analyzed together in order to provide readers with a more complete view of the situation at hand.

Figuring out where to publish your story

Another important question to consider in data journalism is, "Where do you intend to publish your story?" This *where* can be a geographical place, a particular social media platform, or certain series of digital platforms that are associated with a particular brand — Facebook, Twitter, Pinterest, and Instagram accounts, as well as blogs, that are all tied together to stream data from one branded source.

Just as you really need to have a firm grasp on who your audience is, you really want to be careful that you understand the implications of where your publication is distributed. Spelling out where you'll be publishing helps you conceptualize to whom you're publishing, what you should publish, and how you should present that publication. If your goal is to craft high-performing data journalism articles, your headlines and storylines should cater to the interests of the people that are subscribed to the channels in which you're distributing. Since the collective interest of the people at each channel may slightly differ, make sure to adapt to those differences before posting your work.

Looking at how to develop, tell, and present your story

By really thinking through the *how* of a story, you are putting yourself in position to craft better data-driven stories. Looking at your data objectively and considering factors like how it was created helps you to discover interesting insights that you can include in your story. Also, knowing how to quickly find stories in potential data sources helps you to quickly sift through the staggering array of options.

And, how you present your data-driven story determines much about how well that story is received by your target audience. You could have done everything right — really taken the time to get to know who your audience is, boiled your story down so that it says exactly what you intend, published it at just the right time, crafted your story around what you know about why people care, and even published it to just the right venue — but if your data visualization looks bad, or if your story layout makes it difficult for readers to quickly gather useful information, then your positive response rates are likely to be low.

Integrating how as a source of data and story context

You need to think about how your data was generated because that line of thinking often leads you into more interesting and compelling storylines. Before drawing up a final outline for your story, brainstorm about how your source data was generated. If you find startling or attention-grabbing answers that are relevant to your story, consider introducing those in your writing or data visualization.

Knowing how to find stories in your data

If you know how to quickly and skillfully find stories in datasets, you can use this set of skills to save time when you're exploring the array of stories that your datasets offer. If you want to quickly analyze, understand, and evaluate the stories in datasets, then you need to have solid data analysis and visualization skills. With these skills, you can quickly discover which datasets to keep and which to discard. Getting up to speed in relevant data science skills also helps you quickly find the most interesting, relevant stories in the datasets you select to support your story.

Knowing how to present your data-driven story

How you present your data-driven story determines much about whether it succeeds or fails with your target audience. Should you use an infographic? A chart? A map? Should your visualization be static or interactive? You have to consider countless aspects when deciding how to best present your story. (For much more on data visualization design, check out Chapter 9.)

Collecting Data for Your Story

A data-journalism piece is only as good as the data that supports it. To publish a compelling story, you must find compelling data on which to build. That isn't always easy, but it's easier if you know how to use *scraping* and *auto-feeds* to your advantage.

Scraping data for your story

Web-scraping involves setting up automated programs to scour and extract the exact and custom datasets that you need straight from the Internet so you don't have to do it yourself. The data you generate from this process is commonly called *scraped* data. Most data journalists scrape source data for their story because it's the most efficient way to get datasets for unique stories. Datasets that are easily accessible have usually already been exploited and mined by teams of data journalists who were looking for stories. To generate unique data sources for your data-driven story, scrape the data yourself.

If you find easy-to-access data, beware that most of the stories in that dataset have probably been told by a journalist who discovered that data before you.

To illustrate how you'd use data scraping in data journalism, imagine the following example: You're a data journalist living in a U.S. state that directly borders Mexico. You've heard rumors that the local library's selection of Spanish-language children's books is woefully inadequate. You call the library, but they fear negative publicity and won't share any statistics with you about the topic.

Because the library won't budge on their data-sharing, you're forced to scrape the library's online catalog to get the source data you need to support this story. Your scraping tool is customized to iterate over all possible searches and keep track of the results. After scraping the site, you discover that 25 percent of children's books at the library are Spanish-language books. Spanish-speakers make up 45 percent of the primary-school population; is this difference significant enough to form the basis of a story? Maybe, maybe not.

To dig a little deeper and possibly discover a reason behind this difference, you decide to scrape the catalog once a week for several weeks, and then compare patterns of borrowing. When you find that a larger proportion of Spanish books are being checked out, this indicates that there is, indeed, a high demand for children's books in Spanish. This finding, coupled with the results from your previous site scrape, give you all the support you need to craft a compelling article around the issue.

Setting up your data alerts

To generate hot stories, data journalists must have access to the freshest, newest data releases that are coming from the most credible organizations. To stay on top of what datasets are being released where, data journalists subscribe to alert systems that send them notifications every time potentially important data is released. These alert systems often issue notifications via RSS feeds or via email. It's also possible to set up a custom application like DataStringer (https://github.com/pudo/datastringer) to send push notifications when significant modifications or updates are made to source databases.

After you subscribe to data alerts and get a pretty solid idea about the data-release schedule, you can begin planning for data releases in advance. For example, if you're doing data journalism in the business analytics niche and know that a particularly interesting quarterly report is to be released in one week, you can use the time you have before its release to formulate a plan on how you'll analyze the data when it does become available.

Many times, after you're alerted to important new data releases, you still need to scrape the source site in order to get that data. In particular, if you're pulling data from a government department, you're likely to need to scrape the source site. Although most government organizations in western countries are legally obligated to release data, they aren't required to release it in a format that's readily consumable. Don't expect them to make it easy for you to get the data you need to tell a story about their operations.

Finding and Telling Your Data's Story

Every dataset tells a story, but not every story is newsworthy. To get to the bottom of a data-driven story, you need an analytical mind, plus basic skills in data science and a solid understanding of journalistic procedure for developing a story.

Spotting strange trends and outliers

One very quick way to identify interesting stories in your dataset is to do a quick spot-check for unusual trends or extreme outliers. These anomalies usually indicate that some external force is affecting a change that you see reflected in the data.

If you want to do a quick-and-dirty spot-check for easy-to-identify stories, you can simply throw your data into an *x, y* scatter plot and visually inspect the result for obvious trends and outliers. After you spot these anomalies, look into reasons behind why the data behaves oddly. In doing so, you can usually uncover some pretty juicy stories.

Illustrating this fact, consider the World Bank Global Development Indicator (GDI) open dataset, available for review at http://data.worldbank.org. Looking at this data, you can easily see a clear correlation between a country's

Gross Domestic Product and the life expectancy of its citizens. The reason for this correlation is obvious — more affluent people can afford better healthcare.

But say you're searching through the hundreds of GDI indicators for the year 2013, and you come across something less obvious — the survival rate of newborns is reasonably well-correlated with the percentage of employed females who receive wages or salaries instead of only performance-based remuneration, as illustrated in Figure 18-1.

The relationship in this data is a little murky. Although you naturally expect two metrics based on health and economic well-being to be related, after analyzing your data a bit, you find a Pearson correlation coefficient of 0.86. That's quite high. Is there a story here? Does this qualify as a newsworthy trend? An effective and time-efficient way to explore answers to this question is to try to find the exception that proves the rule. In Figure 18-2, the simple least-squares best-fit line is in black, and the two data points that most differ (horizontally and vertically) from this line are indicated with light grey lines.

A *Pearson coefficient* is a statistical correlation coefficient that measures the linear correlation between two variables. A high (nearer to 1) or low (nearer to -1) Pearson correlation coefficient indicates a high degree of correlation between the variables. The closer the coefficient is to zero, the smaller the correlation between the variables. The maximum value for a Pearson coefficient is 1 and the minimum is –1.

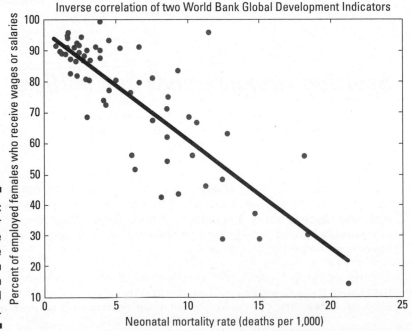

Figure 18-1:
A scatter plot of the inverse correlation between two GDI indicators.

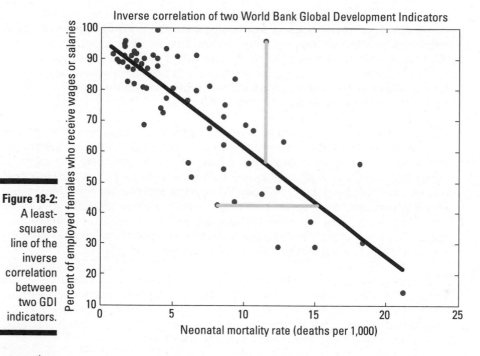

Figure 18-2:
A least-squares line of the inverse correlation between two GDI indicators.

TIP

You could also look for your exceptions at the largest perpendicular distance from the line, but it's a little more difficult to calculate. The topmost point in Figure 18-2 would fulfill that criterion.

Examining context to understand data's significance

By pinpointing strange trends or outliers in your dataset, you can subsequently focus in on those patterns and look for the interesting stories about the external factors that cause them. If you want to cultivate the most thought-provoking story about what's happening in your source dataset, then you need to further investigate, compare, and contrast these factors you've identified. By examining the context in which competing causative factors are creating extreme trends and outliers, you can then begin to get a solid understanding of your data's significance.

For example, think back to the World Bank Global Development Indicator (GDI) in the preceding section. The topmost point in Figure 18-2 represents the country of Jordan. For a given level of child mortality, Jordan has an unusual number of women with predictable income. If you dig a little deeper into factors that might account for this outlier, you see that the overall employment rate for women in Jordan is among the lowest in the world. In a country where few women work, the women that do work in Jordan are earning relatively stable wages or salaries. This might indicate that the precariously paid work is being given mostly to men. Maybe the underlying story here is about gender roles in Jordan? If so, what conclusions could you draw by looking at another outlier country in the dataset — Peru, for example?

Well, because only 41 percent of Peruvian women are employed with a stable income, Peru is near the bottom ranks in terms of employed women with stable incomes. Perhaps this is to be expected in a country with so much agriculture by hand. And, in all honesty, Peruvian men aren't much better off either, indicated by the fact that only 51 percent of them are reporting stable employment. But the Peruvian neonatal mortality rate is unusually low. Does Peru have an exceptionally well-funded healthcare system? Not really — it spends less, per capita, on healthcare than most of its neighbors. So what could be the cause for the low neonatal mortality rate?

Introducing contextually relevant datasets, the Social Institutions and Gender Index (SIGI) data ranks Peru low on the scale for economic gender equality, but quite high — ranked at 17th — on an overall scale for gender equality that includes legal, societal, and educational metrics (`http://genderindex.org/country/peru`). Perhaps there's a story there!

Although the possible stories identified in this exercise are not exceptionally dramatic or earth-shaking, that's okay — not all stories have to be.

You shouldn't expect to find a ground-breaking story in a dataset as accessible as World Bank's open data. Again, the more accessible a dataset is, the more likely it is that the dataset has been thoroughly picked over and exploited by other data journalists.

Emphasizing the story through your visualization

When it comes to data-visualization design, you always want to pick the colors, styles, and data graphic types that most dramatically convey the visual story you're trying to tell. You want to make your visual stories as clear, concise, and easy to understand as possible. In making selections among visual elements for your data visualization, find the best way to visually convey your story without requiring your audience to have to strain and work to understand it.

Looking back to the World Bank Global Development Indicator (GDI) example from the preceding sections, imagine that you decide to go with the Peru story. Because the SIGI dataset is so relevant to the Peru story, you need to make a thorough study of that dataset, as well as any other datasets you've identified to be relevant. Time-series data on different statistics is likely to be very informative because it should indicate several relevant metrics — the proportion of total income earned by women, survival rates of pregnant mothers, legal-based gender equality metrics, and so on.

After you gather and appraise the most relevant metrics that are available to you, pick and choose the metrics whose datasets show the most extreme trends. Subtle changes in data don't lend themselves to dramatic and easy-to-understand visual stories. After you select the most dramatic metrics to use in telling your story, it's time to decide the best way to represent that story visually.

For the Peruvian example, imagine that its legal system's gender-based equality metric is the most striking statistic you've found in all the data that covers the topic of women's status in that country. The dramatic impact of that metric makes it a very good choice for the fundamental basis of your visual story. With that impact in mind, you decide to use a static infographic to show how the Peruvian legal system is more equitable when it comes to gender than that of its neighboring countries. Whatever story you decide to cover, just be sure that the visualizations you create are well *branded* — be sure to pick a common color palette, font type, and symbol style to unify your visualizations.

 Solid visual branding practices govern that you make subtle associations between each of your related visualizations by using color, font type, or symbol style. If you choose to brand with color choices, for instance, then independent of the data graphics you use to display data on a metric, make sure to always use the same color to represent that metric across every graphic you employ.

Creating compelling and highly focused narratives

As you well know, no one wants to wade through a bunch of needless, complicated words to try to figure out what your story says. It's frustrating, and it simply takes too much work. Presuming that your purpose for creating a data-driven story is to publish something that has impact and value in the lives of your readers, you must work hard to whittle your narrative down to its simplest, most-focused form. Failure to do so decreases the impact and performance of your data-driven story.

Narrow each of your stories down to its hook and lede before going any further into the process of writing a full narrative. In journalism, a *hook* is a dramatic angle that cultivates interest in potential readers and draws them into your piece. A *lede* is the first sentence of your story — it introduces the story and shows readers why the story is newsworthy. After you go through your story and flesh out a hook, a lede, and a full narrative, you always need to go back through your piece once or twice and cut unnecessary words or restructure sentences so that they most directly express the ideas you seek to convey.

Referring back to the Peru example from the preceding sections, gender equality is a very broad subject. So, start by creating a *hook* — in this case, the hook could be a description of the most dramatic metrics indicating that Peruvian women are far better off than women in neighboring South American countries. Next, get to work on the *lede* — perhaps something like, "In Peru, economically disadvantaged women experience the highest chance of dying during childbirth, yet their children have among the highest chances of surviving." Lastly, go back through and clean things up so that your lede is as clear and easy to understand as possible. So for this example, you might rewrite the lede so that it reads, "Poor Peruvian mothers have the greatest childbirth mortality rates of any South America women, yet oddly, Peruvian infants demonstrate the highest chances of surviving childbirth."

Bringing Data Journalism to Life: Washington Post's The Black Budget

Any chapter on data science in journalism would be utterly incomplete without a solid case study to demonstrate the power of data journalism in action. The *Washington Post* story "The Black Budget" is one incredible example of such a piece. (Check it out for yourself at www.washingtonpost.com/wp-srv/special/national/black-budget.)

When former NSA contractor Edward Snowden leaked a trove of classified documents, he not only unleashed a storm of controversy among the public, but among the data journalists who were tasked with analyzing the documents for stories. The challenge for data journalists in this case was that they had to discover and disclose data insights that were relevant to the public without compromising the safety of ordinary citizens.

Among the documents leaked by Snowden was the so-called *Black Budget* for fiscal year 2013, a 178-page line-by-line breakdown of the funds that were earmarked for 16 various U.S. federal intelligence agencies. Through the

Washington Post's "The Black Budget," the American public was informed that $52.6 billion taxpayer dollars had been spent on mostly covert federal intelligence services in 2013 alone.

The *Washington Post* did a phenomenal job in its visual presentation of the data. The opening title is a somber visual pun: The words *The Black Budget* are written in a huge black box contrasted only with gray and white. This layout visually implies the serious and murky nature of the subject matter. The only touch of color is a navy blue, which conjures a vaguely military image and barely contrasts with the black. This limited palette is continued throughout the visual presentation of the data.

Washington Post data journalists used unusual blocky data graphics — an unsettling, strangely horizontal hybrid of a pie chart, a bar graph, and a tree map — to hint at the surreptitious and dangerous nature of the topic, as well as the shady manner in which the information was obtained.

The data graphics used in the piece exhibited a low *data-to-ink ratio* — in other words, only a little information is conveyed with a lot of screen space. Although normally a low data-to-ink ratio indicates bad design, in "The Black Budget," the data-to-ink ratio very effectively hints that there are mountains of data underneath the layers being shown, and that these layers remain undisclosed so as not to endanger intelligence sources and national security.

Traditional infographic elements used in this piece include stark, light-gray seals of the top five intelligence agencies, only two of which the average person would have ever heard of. Simple bar charts outlined funding trends, and people-shaped icons represented the army of personnel involved in intelligence gathering.

A lot of thought went into the collection, analysis, and presentation of this story. Its ensemble is an unsettling, yet overwhelmingly informative, piece of data journalism. Although this sort of journalism was in its infancy even just a decade ago, now the data and tools required for this type of work are widely available for journalists to use to quickly develop high-quality data-journalism articles.

Chapter 19

Delving into Environmental Data Science

....

In This Chapter

▶ Modeling the environmental-human interaction

▶ Using statistical modeling for natural resources in the raw

▶ Using statistics to predict for location-dependent environmental phenomenon

....

*B*ecause data science can be used to successfully reverse-engineer business growth and increase revenues, many of its more noble applications often slide by completely unnoticed. Environmental data science is one such application. Environmental data science is the use of data science techniques, methodologies, and technologies to address or solve problems that are related to the environment. It falls into three main categories — environmental intelligence, natural resource modeling, and spatial statistics to predict environmental variation. In this chapter, I discuss each type of environmental data science and how it's being used to make a positive impact on human health, safety, and the environment.

Modeling Environmental-Human Interactions with Environmental Intelligence

The purpose of environmental intelligence (EI) is to convert raw data into insights that can be used for data-informed decision making about matters that pertain to environmental-human interactions. EI solutions are designed to support the decision making of community leaders, humanitarian response decision makers, public health advisors, environmental engineers, policy makers, and more. If you want to collect and analyze environmentally-relevant data in order to produce content crucial for your decision-making process, like real-time maps, interactive data visualizations, and tabular data reports, then look into an EI solution.

In the following sections, I discuss the type of problems being solved by using EI technologies and what organizations are out there using EI to make a difference. I explain the ways in which EI is similar to business intelligence (BI) and the reasons why it qualifies as applied data science despite those similarities. I end the section with a real-world example of how EI is being used to make a positive impact.

Looking at the types of problems solved

EI technologies are used to monitor and report on interactions between humans and the natural environment to provide decision makers and stakeholders real-time intelligence about on-the-ground happenings, in hopes of avoiding preventable disasters and community hardships through proactive, data-informed decision making. EI technologies are being used to achieve the following types of results:

✔ **Making more responsible energy consumption plans:** EI technology is just what you need to audit, track, monitor, and predict energy consumption rates. Here, energy is the natural resource, and people's consumption of energy is the human interaction. (Note that you can use KNIME to help you build this type of EI solution right on your desktop computer; check out Chapter 17 for more on KNIME.)

✔ **Expediting humanitarian relief efforts:** EI of this type falls into the crisis-mapping category. In *crisis mapping*, EI technology is used to collect, map, visualize, analyze, and report environmental data that is relevant to the crisis at-hand. Crisis mapping provides real-time humanitarian decision support. Here, water supply, sanitation, natural disaster, and hygiene statuses are measures of natural resources, and the effects that these resources have on the health and safety of people is the human interaction.

✔ **Improving water resource planning:** You can use EI technologies to generate predictive models for water consumption, based on simple inference from statistically derived population forecasts, historical water consumption rates, and spatial data on existing infrastructure. Water supply is the natural resource here, and people's consumption of it is the human interaction.

✔ **Combating deforestation:** EI technologies are being used in real-time interactive map-based data visualization platforms to monitor deforestation in remote regions of developing nations. This type of solution utilizes conditional autoregressive modeling, spatial analysis, web-based mapping, data analytics, data cubes, and time series analyses to map, visualize, analyze, and report deforestation in near–real-time. These uses of EI increase transparency and public awareness on this important environmental issue. In this application, forestry and land are the natural resources, and the act of cutting down trees is the human interaction.

Defining environmental intelligence

Although environmental intelligence (EI) and business intelligence (BI) technologies have a lot in common, EI is still considered applied data science. Before going into the reasons for this difference, first consider the following ways in which EI and BI are similar:

✔ **Simple inference from mathematical models:** As discussed in Chapter 3, BI generates predictions based on simple mathematical inference, and not from complex statistical predictive modeling. Many of the more simple EI solutions derive their predictions from simple mathematical inference, as well.

✔ **Data structure and type:** Like BI, many of the simpler EI products are built solely from structured data that sits in a relational SQL database.

✔ **Decision-support product outputs:** Both EI and BI produce data visualizations, maps, interactive data analytics, and tabular data reports as decision-support products.

Much of the EI approach was borrowed from the BI discipline. However, EI evolved away from BI technologies when its features were upgraded and expanded to solve real-world environmental problems. When you look into the data science features that are central to most solutions, the evolution of EI away from standard BI becomes increasingly obvious. Here are a few data science processes you won't find used in BI but will find in EI technology:

✔ **Statistical programming:** The most basic EI solutions deploy time series analysis and autoregressive modeling. Many of the more advanced solutions make use of very complex statistical models and algorithms, as well.

✔ **GIS technology:** Because environmental insights are so location-dependent, it's almost impossible to avoid integrating so-called Geographic Information Systems (GIS) technologies into EI solutions. Not only that, but almost all web-based EI platforms require advanced spatial web programming. (For more on GIS technologies, check out Chapter 13.)

✔ **Web-based data visualization:** Almost all web-based EI platforms offer interactive, near–real-time data visualizations that are built off of the JavaScript programming language.

✔ **Data sources:** Unlike BI, EI solutions are built almost solely from external data sources. These sources oftentimes include data auto-feeds derived from image, social media, and SMS sources. Other external data comes in the form of satellite data, scraped website data, or .pdf documents that need to be converted via custom optical text recognition scripts. In EI, the reported data is almost always real-time updating.

Web-scraping is a process that involves setting up automated programs to scour and extract the data you need straight from the Internet. The data you generate from this type of process is commonly called scraped data.

✔ **Coding requirements:** EI solutions almost always require advanced custom coding. Whether in the form of web programming or statistical programming, extra coding work is required to deliver EI products.

Identifying major organizations that work in environmental intelligence

Because EI is a social-good application of data science, there aren't a ton of funding sources out there, which is probably the chief reason why not many people are working in this line of data science. EI is small, but some dedicated organizations have found a way to earn a living by creating EI solutions that serve the public good. In the following list, I name a few of those organizations, as well as the umbrella organizations that fund them. If your goal is to use EI technologies to build products that support decision making for the betterment of environmental health and safety, one of these organizations will likely be willing to help you with advice or even support services:

✔ **DataKind:** A non-profit organization of data science volunteers who donate their time and skills to work together in the service of humanity, DataKind (www.datakind.org) was started by data science legend Jake Porway. The organization has donated EI support to projects in developing nations and first-world countries alike. DataKind's sponsors include National Geographic, IBM, and Pop! Tech.

✔ **Elva:** A non-governmental organization, Elva (www.elva.org) was built by a small, independent group of international *digital humanitarians* — knowledge workers who use data and disruptive technologies to build solutions for international humanitarian problems. Elva founders gave their time and skills to build a mobile-phone platform, which allows marginalized communities to map local needs and to work with decision makers to develop effective joint-response plans. Elva offers EI support for environmental projects that are centered in underserved, developing nations. Elva is directed by Jonne Catshoek and is sponsored by UNDP, USAID, and Eurasia Partnership.

✔ **Vizzuality:** Here's a business started by the founders of CartoDB — a technology that's discussed further in Chapter 11. Almost all of Vizzuality's projects involve using EI to serve the betterment of the environment. Vizzuality was founded by Javier de la Torre, and some of the organization's bigger clients include Google, UNEP, NASA, the University of Oxford, and Yale University. Check out their website at `www.vizzuality.com`.

✔ **QCRI:** The Qatar Computing Research Institute (QCRI) is a national research institute that's owned and funded by a private non-profit community development foundation in Qatar. The social-innovation section that delivers most of the organization's EI projects is led by the digital humanitarian all-star, Patrick Meier. Some of QCRI's ongoing projects include Artificial Intelligence in Disaster Response (AIDR), a crowd-sourced verification-for-disaster-response platform (Verily), and a do-it-yourself check-in app for mutual aid during disasters (MatchApp). As you might expect, they have their own website, too, at `www.qcri.com`.

Making positive impacts with environmental intelligence

Elva (`www.elva.org`) is a shining example of how environmental intelligence technologies can be used to make a positive impact. Elva is a free, open source platform that facilitates cause mapping and data-visualization reporting for election monitoring, human rights violations, environmental degradation, and disaster risk in developing nations.

In one of its more recent projects, Elva has been working with Internews, an international non-profit devoted to fostering independent media and access to information in an effort to map crisis-level environmental issues in one of the most impoverished, underdeveloped nations of the world, the Central African Republic. As part of these efforts, local human rights reporters and humanitarian organizations are using Elva to monitor, map, and report information derived from environmental data on natural disasters, infrastructure, water, sanitation, hygiene, and human health. The purpose of Elva's involvement on this project is to facilitate real-time humanitarian-data analysis and visualizations to support the decision making of international humanitarian-relief experts and community leaders.

With respect to data science technologies and methodologies, Elva implements the following:

- **Auto-feeds for data collection:** The data that's mapped, visualized, and reported through the Elva platform is actually created by citizen activists on the ground who use SMS and smartphones to report environmental conditions through reports or surveys. The reporting system is built so that all reports come in with the correct structure, are collected by service-provider servers, and then are pushed over to the Elva database.

- **Non-relational database technologies:** Elva uses a non-relational NoSQL database infrastructure to store survey data submitted by smartphone and SMS, as well as other sources of structured, unstructured, and semi-structured data.

- **Open data:** OpenStreetMap powers the map data that the Elva platform uses. You can find out more about OpenStreetMap in Chapter 22, where I focus on *open data* resources — data resources that have been made publically available for use, reuse, modification, and sharing with others.

- **Inference from mathematical and statistical models:** Elva's data analysis methods aren't overly complex, but that's perfect for producing fast, real-time analytics for humanitarian decision support. Elva depends mostly on time series analysis, linear regression, and simple mathematical inference.

- **Data visualization:** Elva produces data visualizations directly from reported data and also from inferential analyses. These are interactive JavaScript visualizations built off of the Highcharts API.

- **Location-based predictions:** Such predictions are based on simple inference and not on advanced spatial statistics, as discussed in the section "Using Spatial Statistics to Predict for Environmental Variation across Space," later in this chapter. Elva staff can infer locations of high risk based on historical time series reported in the region.

Modeling Natural Resources in the Raw

You can use data science to model natural resources in their raw form. This type of environmental data science generally involves some very advanced statistical modeling to better understand natural resources. You model the resources *in the raw* — meaning water, air, and land conditions as they occur in nature — to better understand the natural environment's organic effects on human life.

In the following sections, I explain a bit about the type of natural-resource issues that most readily lend themselves to exploration via environmental data science. Then I offer a brief overview about what data science methods are particularly relevant to environmental resource modeling. Lastly, I present a case in which environmental data science has been used to better understand the natural environment.

Exploring natural resource modeling

Environmental data science can model natural resources in the raw so that we can better understand environmental processes in order to understand how those processes affect life on Earth. After environmental processes are clearly understood, then and only then can environmental engineers step in to design systems to solve problems that these natural processes may be creating. The following list describes what types of natural-resource issues environmental data science can model and predict:

- **Water issues:** Rainfall rates, geo-hydrologic patterns, groundwater flows, and groundwater toxin concentrations
- **Air issues:** The concentration and dispersion of particulate-matter levels and greenhouse gas concentrations
- **Land issues:** Soil contaminant migration and geomorphology, as well as geophysics, mineral exploration, and oil and gas exploration

If your goal is to build a predictive model that you can use to help you better understand natural environmental processes, then you can use natural resource modeling to help you do this. Don't expect natural-resource modeling to be easy, though. The statistics that go into these types of models can be incredibly complex.

Dabbling in data science

Because environmental processes and systems involve so many different interdependent variables, most natural-resource modeling requires the use of incredibly complex statistical algorithms. The following list shows a few elements of data science that are commonly deployed in natural-resource modeling:

- **Statistical programming:** Bayesian inference, multilevel hierarchical Bayesian inference, multi-taper spectral analysis, copulas, Wavelet Autoregressive Method (WARM), Autoregressive Moving Averages

(ARMAs), Monte Carlo simulations, structured additive regression (STAR) models, regression on order statistics (ROS), maximum likelihood estimations (MLEs), or expectation-maximization (EM), among other processes

- ✔ **Mathematical programming:** Linear and nonlinear dimension reduction, wavelets analysis, frequency domain methods, and Markov chains, among other methods

- ✔ **Clustering analysis:** k-nearest neighbor, kernel density, and logspline density estimation, among other methods

- ✔ **Spatial statistics:** Generally, something like probabilistic mapping

- ✔ **GIS technology:** Spatial analysis and map-making

- ✔ **Machine learning:** Minimum variance embedding or multiple-point geostatistics (MP), among other methods

- ✔ **Coding requirements:** Using Python, R, SPSS, SAS, MATLAB, Fortran, and SQL, among other programming languages

Modeling natural resources to solve environmental problems

The work of Columbia Water Center's director, Dr. Upmanu Lall, provides a world-class example of using environmental data science to solve incredibly complex water resource problems. (For an overview of the Columbia Water Center's work, see http://water.columbia.edu.) Dr. Lall uses advanced statistics, math, coding, and a staggering subject-matter expertise in environmental engineering to uncover complex interdependent relationships between global water-resource characteristics, national gross domestic products (GDPs), poverty, and national energy consumption rates.

In one of Dr. Lall's recent projects, he found that in countries with *high rainfall variability* — countries that experience extreme droughts followed by massive flooding — the instability results in lack of stable water resources for agricultural development, more run-off and erosion, and overall decreases in that nation's GDP. The inverse is also true, where countries that have stable, moderate rainfall rates have a better water resource supply for agricultural development, better environmental conditions overall, and higher average GDPs. So, through environmental data science, Dr. Lall has been able to draw strong correlations between a nation's rainfall trends and its poverty rates.

With respect to data science technologies and methodologies, Dr. Lall implements the following:

- ✔ **Statistical programming:** Dr. Lall's arsenal includes multilevel hierarchical Bayesian models, multi-taper spectral analysis, copulas, Wavelet Autoregressive Moving Averages (WARMs), Autoregressive Moving Averages (ARMAs), and Monte Carlo simulations.

- ✔ **Mathematical programming:** Tools here include linear and nonlinear dimension reduction, wavelets analysis, frequency domain methods, and nonhomogeneous hidden Markov models.

- ✔ **Clustering analysis:** In this case, Dr. Lall relies on the tried-and-true methods, including k-nearest neighbor, kernel density, and logspline density estimation.

- ✔ **Machine learning:** Here, Dr. Lall focuses on minimum variance embedding.

Using Spatial Statistics to Predict for Environmental Variation across Space

By their very nature, environmental variables are location-dependent: They change with changes in geospatial location. The purpose of modeling environmental variables with spatial statistics is to enable accurate spatial predictions so that you can use those predictions to solve problems related to the environment.

Spatial statistics is distinguished from natural-resource modeling because it focuses on predicting how changes in space affect environmental phenomenon. Naturally, the time variable is considered, as well, but spatial statistics is all about using statistics to model the inner workings of spatial phenomenon. The difference is in the manner of approach. (For more on spatial statistics, check out Chapter 8.)

In the following sections, I discuss what types of issues you can address with spatial statistical models and the data science that goes into this type of solution. You can also read about a case in which spatial statistics has been used to correlate natural concentrations of arsenic in well water with incidence of cancer.

Addressing environmental issues with spatial predictive analytics

You can use spatial statistics to model environmental variables across space and time so that you can predict changes in environmental variables across space. The following list describes what type of environmental issues are readily addressed using spatial statistical modeling:

- **Epidemiology and environmental human health:** For example, use spatial statistics to model and predict disease patterns and distributions.

- **Meteorology:** Here you could use spatial statistics to model and predict weather phenomenon.

- **Fire science:** You could channel your inner Smokey the Bear and use spatial statistics to model and predict the spread of a fire.

- **Hydraulics:** For example, use spatial statistics to model and predict aquifer conductivity.

- **Ecology:** You could use spatial statistics to model and predict microorganism distribution across a sedimentary lake bottom.

If your goal is to build a model that you can use to predict how change in space will affect environmental variables, you can use spatial statistics to help you do this. In the next section I quickly overview the basics that are involved in spatial statistics.

Describing the data science that's involved

Because spatial statistics involves modeling the x-, y-, z-parameters that comprise spatial datasets, the statistics involved can get rather interesting and unusual. Spatial statistics is, more or less, a marriage of GIS spatial analysis and advanced predictive analytics. The following list describes a few data science processes that are commonly deployed when using statistics to build predictive spatial models:

- **Spatial statistics:** We're back to our old friends krige and kriging, as well as Thomas point processes and variogram, and semivariogram analysis, among other processes. You can find out more about these (and related) topics in Chapter 8.

- **Statistical programming:** Involves probability distributions, time series analyses, regression analyses, and Monte Carlo simulations, among other processes.

✔ **Clustering analysis:** Could include nearest neighbor algorithms, k-means clustering, or kernel density estimations, among other processes.

✔ **GIS technology:** GIS technology pops up a lot in this chapter, but that's to be expected because its spatial analysis and map-making offerings are incredibly flexible.

✔ **Coding requirements:** Programming for a spatial statistics project could entail using R, SPSS, SAS, MATLAB, and SQL, among other programming languages.

Using spatial statistics to address environmental issues

A great example of using spatial statistics to generate predictions for location-dependent environmental variables can be seen in the recent work of Dr. Pierre Goovaerts. Dr. Goovaerts uses advanced statistics, coding, and his authoritative subject-matter expertise in agricultural engineering, soil science, and epidemiology to uncover correlations between spatial disease patterns, mortality, environmental toxin exposure, and socio-demographics.

In one of Dr. Goovaerts recent projects, he used spatial statistics to model and analyze data on groundwater arsenic concentrations, location, geologic properties, weather patterns, topography, and land cover. Through his recent environmental data science studies, he discovered that the incidence of bladder, breast, and prostate cancers is spatially correlated to long-term arsenic exposure.

With respect to data science technologies and methodologies, Dr. Goovaerts commonly implements the following:

✔ **Spatial statistical programming:** Once again, kriging and semivariogram analysis top the list.

✔ **Statistical programming:** Least squares regression model-fitting and Monte Carlo simulations are central to Dr. Goovaerts work. (For more on these techniques, check out Chapter 4.)

✔ **GIS technologies:** If you want map-making functionality and spatial data analysis methodologies, you're going to need GIS technologies.

If you want to find out more about Dr. Goovaerts' work, check out his website at `https://sites.google.com/site/goovaertspierre`.

Chapter 20

Data Science for Driving Growth in E-Commerce

*B*ig data and analytics aren't really new things to most people these days. However, the creative ways in which big data and analytics are being used to transform lives and businesses *are* new. Businesses are quickly catching on to the fact that in this fast-paced era, an organization's survival hinges on its ability to integrate data science and analytics into every major decision that's made — particularly in relation to strategic marketing decision making. In fact, the demand for marketing analytics practitioners has increased by 136 percent in the last three years alone. Marketing analytics professionals use data science and analytics to drive sales growth and user adoption rates for today's *e-commerce business* — a business that sells products or services on the Internet.

These days, even the most traditional, old-fashioned business enterprise has at least some sort of web presence that would qualify as an e-commerce operation. Other e-commerce businesses are 100-percent digital and have no real on-the-ground presence to speak of. Because many businesses use blogging to build a well-branded online space where visitors receive access to insightful or entertaining content in exchange for their website visits and brand loyalty, even an individual blogger who has a website and a strong social presence can be considered an e-commerce business.

In recent years, the practice of using marketing analytics and data science to develop tactical strategies for e-commerce business growth came to be known as *growth hacking* — growth hacking is also referred to as *growth engineering*, or simply just *growth*. Growth hacking is particularly well-suited for startup growth because of the lower-cost, more-innovative methods growth hackers generally employ. In marketing, the word *conversion* describes the scenario in which a marketing effort is successful in getting a user, or prospective user, to take some desired action. Examples of conversions include the act of getting someone to visit your website, subscribe to your newsletter, follow your social media channel, or purchase your product.

In the growth game, the only goals are to get visitors to convert and to move them along in a swift and steady flow through all layers of the sales funnel. This chapter provides you with some simple concepts and methods that you can use to get started in growing your e-commerce business. This chapter gives you only the tip of the growth iceberg. For brevity, I've omitted many of the more advanced and complicated tactics.

True growth hacking is a hybridization of the following fields:

- **Engineering:** In an e-commerce context, this includes systems design, process design, systems thinking, and iterative design.

- **Marketing:** Subcategories of marketing include psychology, branding, and aesthetic design.

- **Business intelligence:** Think *intelligence* as in Central Intelligence Agency, rather than smarts. Subcategories here include metric selection, descriptive analytics, diagnostic analytics, and prescriptive analytics based on simple inference.

- **Data science:** Casting its web rather widely, data science requires math and statistics know-how, web programming chops, the ability to code in Python or R, SQL skills, and subject-matter expertise in e-commerce business and Internet marketing.

In this chapter, I discuss the data science that's involved in growth hacking, and how you can use it to super-charge your online business growth. Just keep in mind that marketing analytics professionals who engage in data science for e-commerce growth may have to wear many hats — for example, Digital Analytics Consultant, Web Analytics Engagement Analyst, Digital Web Marketing Analytics, or Optimization Manager. For simplicity's sake, I refer to all of these roles as *e-commerce data science*.

Here's a look at the data science that's involved in this line of work:

- **Math and statistics requirements:** Practitioners should understand and know how to apply significance testing, time series analysis, trend and seasonal analysis, regression analysis, multivariate regression, segmentation analysis, A/B split testing, and multivariate testing.

✔ **Programming requirements:** Data scientists working in growth should be solid in SQL, as well as web-programming languages like JavaScript, HTML, DHTML, and AJAX. Python and R programming could come in handy for segmentation analysis, data visualization, or building a recommendation engine, although not many growth specialists are required to do this type of work because of the high availability of applications designed specifically for these purposes.

✔ **Subject matter expertise:** Data scientists working in this field must have a deep understanding of e-commerce business, its various structures, its systems, and its channels. They must also understand Internet marketing fundamentals.

Data scientists in e-commerce generally use applications for their analyses, although sometimes they need to use coding to carry out a customized analysis. E-commerce data scientists use data science to formulate highly-focused, results-oriented business strategies. They do *not* focus on exploratory data analysis. In e-commerce data science, your job is to use data in order to better understand users so that you can devise ways to drive growth results. You use algorithms and data visualizations only to achieve these goals. It's all about how you as a data scientist can derive insights from a wide variety of software and web applications — many of which I discuss in the section "Appraising popular web analytics applications," later in this chapter, by the way.

Data scientists in this field are often asked to analyze clickstream data, site performance data, and channel performance data in order to provide decision support on the effectiveness of tactical optimization strategies. They often have to design, develop, and manage *tag deployments* — the placing of code snippets in the header of a web page used to collect data for use in 3rd party analytics applications. Data scientists in this field also work on A/B split testing, multivariate testing, and mouse-click heatmap analytics (all explained later in the section on "Checking out common types of testing in growth").

Advanced data scientists in this field may also be expected to build personalization and recommendation engines. Practitioners need to communicate data insights in a clear, direct, and meaningful manner, using written words, spoken words, and data visualizations. Lastly, any data scientist who works in growth has to have a very solid understanding of e-commerce and Internet marketing.

Making Sense of Data for E-Commerce Growth

Data science in e-commerce serves the same purpose that it does in any other discipline — to derive valuable insights from raw data. In e-commerce, you're looking for data insights that you can use to optimize a brand's marketing return on investment (ROI) and to drive growth in every layer of the sales funnel. How you end up doing that is up to you, but the work of most data scientists in e-commerce involves the following:

✔ **Data analysis:** Simple statistical and mathematical inference. Segmentation analysis gets rather complicated when trying to make sense of e-commerce data. You also use a lot of trend analysis, outlier analysis, and regression analysis.

✔ **Data wrangling:** *Data wrangling* involves using processes and procedures to clean and convert data from one format and structure to another, so that the data is accurate and in the format analytics tools and scripts require for consumption. In growth work, source data is usually captured and generated by analytics applications. Most of the time, you can derive insight within the application, but sometimes you need to export the data so that you can create data mashups, perform custom analyses, and create custom visualizations that aren't available in your out-of-the-box solutions. These situations could demand you use a fair bit of data wrangling to get what you need from the source datasets.

✔ **Data visualization design:** Data graphics in e-commerce are usually very simple. Expect to use a lot of line charts, bar charts, scatter charts, and map-based data visualizations. Data visualizations should be simple and to the point, but the analyses required to derive meaningful insights may take some time.

✔ **Communication:** After you make sense of the data, you have to communicate its meaning in clear, direct, and concise ways that decision makers can easily understand. E-commerce data scientists need to be excellent at communicating data insights via data visualizations, a written narrative, and conversation.

✔ **Custom development work:** In some cases, you may need to design custom scripts for automated custom data analysis and visualization. In other cases, you may have to go so far as to design a personalization and recommendation system, but because you can find a ton of prebuilt applications available for these purposes, the typical e-commerce data scientist position description doesn't include this requirement.

Optimizing E-Commerce Business Systems

Time for a (brief) primer on how you can begin using web analytics, testing tactics, and segmentation and targeting initiatives to ignite growth in all layers of your e-commerce sales funnel. Before getting into the nitty-gritty of these methods, though, you first need to understand the fundamental structure and function of each layer in a sales funnel. In keeping with a logical and systematic approach, I'm breaking down the e-commerce sales funnel into the following five stages — acquisition, activation, retention, referral, and revenue.

Acquisition, activation, retention, referral, and revenue are also referred to as AARRR, the Pirate Metrics. (Say AARRRR out loud a few times and you'll know why it's called the Pirate Metrics.) This growth framework (see Figure 20-1) was originally suggested by famed angel investor and entrepreneur, Dave McClure. The term is now widely used throughout the growth-hacking community.

Figure 20-1: The AARRR of the e-commerce sales funnel.

Here are the functions of each stage of the sales funnel:

- ✔ **Acquisition:** Your brand acquires new users in the form of website visitors. New users are oftentimes acquired via social media marketing, search engine marketing, search engine optimization, content marketing, or partnerships.

- ✔ **Activation:** Acquired users activate, either through email subscription, RSS subscription, or social followings.

- ✔ **Retention:** Activated users take some sort of action — such as accepting an offer or responding to a call to action within your email marketing campaign.

- ✔ **Referral:** Retained users refer new users to your brand's acquisition layer.

- ✔ **Revenue:** Users make revenue-generating purchases.

Angling in on analytics

Web analytics can be described as the practice of generating, collecting, and making sense of Internet data in order to optimize web design and strategy. Configure web analytics applications to monitor and track absolutely all of your growth tactics and strategies, because without this information, you're operating in the dark — and nothing grows in the dark.

Web analytics provide fast and clear results that gauge e-commerce growth strategy effectiveness. You can use web analytics as a diagnostic tool, to get to know your audience, to understand their preferences, to start doing more of what works, and to stop doing the things that clearly don't work. If you want to devise growth strategies that actually grow your business, then you need to make sure you've configured web analytics to track and monitor all stages of the funnel, as well as every touch point between your brand and its prospective customers.

Appraising popular web analytics applications

Data scientists working in growth hacking should be familiar with (and know how to derive insights from) the following web analytics applications:

- ✔ **Google Analytics (`www.google.com/analytics`):** A free, easy-to-use, powerful web analytics tool, Google Analytics is great for monitoring not only the volumes of traffic that come to your website over time, but also the demographics and summary statistics on your visitors, your website referral sources, your visitor flow patterns, real-time visitor behavior analytics, and much more. Google Analytics can show you benchmarking analytics that provide insights about how your website's performance compares to the performance of other websites in your industry.

- ✔ **Adobe Analytics (`www.adobe.com/solutions/digital-analytics/marketing-reports-analytics.html`):** You can use Adobe Analytics for marketing attribution, mobile app performance, social media marketing performance, return-on-investment (ROI) investigation, and real-time visitor monitoring.

- ✔ **IBM Digital Analytics (`www-03.ibm.com/software/products/en/digital-analytics`):** The perfect platform for integrating performance data from all of your business' web channels — from data generated by website guests visiting using personal computers to mobile visitor statistics, and even social media channel performance — IBM Digital Analytics offers powerful analytics capabilities to keep you informed of real-time and historical visitor behaviors, as well as relevant cross-channel interactions. The platform also offers marketing attribution and tag management capabilities.

✔ **Webtrends (**`http://webtrends.com`**):** Offering advanced multi-channel analytics, real-time visitor behavior monitoring, and the technology you need to reclaim lost sales from shopping cart abandonment via email remarketing tactics, Webtrends is a powerhouse web analytics application. It even goes the extra mile by offering a campaign optimization feature that you can use to track, monitor, and optimize your search engine marketing efforts, as well as your search and social advertisement campaigns.

✔ **Google Tag Manager (**`www.google.com/tagmanager`**):** Website tags — code snippets that collect data for use in your 3rd party analytics applications — can help you measure and manage the effectiveness of your Internet marketing campaigns, but the process of deploying tags is error-prone and requires coding. Google Tag Manager is a free tag-management tool that offers a code-free interface and a rules-based system that allows you to easily manage and deploy your website marketing and tracking tags.

✔ **Assorted social analytics tools:** In addition to the more heavy-weight offerings described in this list, you can find many free, easy-to-use social analytics applications to monitor and measure the effectiveness of your social media growth initiatives. These include SumAll (`https://sumall.com`), which is great for tracking Twitter, Facebook, YouTube, Instagram, and Google Analytics metrics (as well as offering analytics tracking options for many different ecommerce platforms, banking platforms, operational management platforms, and more); Facebook Page Insights (`https://www.facebook.com/Your_Facebook_Page_ID/insights/`); Pinterest Analytics (`https://analytics.pinterest.com`); Iconosquare Statistics for Instagram (`http://iconosquare.com`); and Google URL Shortener for link tracking (`https://goo.gl`).

Accessing analytics for acquisitions

Analytics for acquisitions provide a measure and gauge of the effectiveness of your user acquisition tactics. If you want to optimize your brand's channels, to glean a deeper understanding of your audiences, or to evaluate the performance of your growth tactics, then look to user acquisition analytics. In this list, I describe some means by which you can use web analytics to begin boosting your user acquisitions:

✔ **Audience discovery:** By taking a close look at your web analytics and the sources from which your new users are being acquired, you can infer an idea about the interests of users in each of your channels.

✔ **Channel optimization:** After discovering insights about your channel audiences, you can use those insights to optimize your channels — designing your channels and the offerings you extend along them so that they better align with the preferences of each channel audience.

✔ **Optimized social-growth strategies:** Social media networks are brand channels. Each network functions for its own purpose, and the preferences of audience members in different networks tend to differ, even if the niche is the same. For example, content about news events tends to perform well on Twitter, whereas Facebook audiences seek to be entertained and inspired. News content doesn't fare so well on the Facebook network and vice versa. What's more, your specific audiences have their own particular interests and nuances per social network. Use social analytics to deduce the interests of your audiences per social channel, and then you can use that information to optimize your efforts there. You can also use social network analytics to identify the main influencers in your niche so that you can begin forging friendships and strategic alliances.

Applying analytics for activation

User activation analytics provide a measure and gauge of your user activations over time. You can use activation analytics to gauge how your user-activation tactics are performing, allowing you to optimize your user sign-ups, even on a per-channel basis. The following are a few ways in which you can use web analytics to optimize your user activation growth rates:

✔ **Sign-up rate monitoring:** Analytics that reflect the number of new user sign-ups, either in the form of email subscriptions or RSS subscriptions. This metric gives you an idea of how well your website's content is meeting the wants and needs of newly acquired users. These analytics are also a good gauge of the overall effectiveness of your *calls to action —* your prompts that tell users to sign up in exchange for some promised benefit to them.

✔ **Average session duration:** You can easily derive information on average session duration by taking a quick and basic look at your Google Analytics. Average session duration is a good gauge of how compelling your visitors find your website. And the more compelling your site, the more likely it is that your acquired users will convert to active users — and active users to refer their friends and convert to paying customers.

If you're working on growth for a client or employer, then you can access their Google Analytics account by having them add your Google Account as an authorized user of their Google Analytics account. If you're working on growth for your own brand or website, then you must sign-up for a free Google Analytics account (at www.google.com/analytics/) and then install the Google Analytics Tracking code into your site.

Whether you're working on behalf of a client or yourself, you must have your own Google Account. You can get one of those by registering through Google (at https://accounts.google.com/SignUp).

✔ **Website heatmaps for website optimization:** A website *heatmap* is a visual graphic that uses colors to depict the areas of a webpage where visitors are clicking with greatest and least intensity. Applications such as SessionCam (www.sessioncam.com/website-heatmaps) and ClickTale (www.clicktale.com/products/heatmap-suite) offer mouse-click heatmap data visualizations that show you how your customers and user segments are using your website — in other words, what website features and areas are most attractive to users. This information tells you about the effectiveness of your activation tactics and your overall web design. If you see that user attention flow isn't focused toward your call-to-action areas, then you should perhaps redesign your page in a way that helps to redirect user focus.

Your main goal should always be to push users towards the next stage of the sales funnel.

Reviewing analytics for retentions

Retention analytics provide a measure of your user retention tactics. Retention analytics can help you boost customer loyalty or increase the amount of time your users spend interacting with your brand. Boosting user retentions is, in large part, a function of marketing strategy and psychology, but web analytics are also an integral part of maintaining and growing your brand's retention rates. Here's how you can use web analytics to optimize your user retentions growth:

✔ **Email marketing open rates:** Tracking and monitoring *time series* — collections of data on attribute values over time — that capture email open rates can give you an idea of how well your email marketing tactics are performing, in general. For example, if you see a steady decline in open rates, either your subscribers aren't that interested in the topics described in email headlines or you're sending emails too frequently and spamming your users' inboxes — in other words, wearing out your welcome. High email open rates reflect a high level of subscriber loyalty, which is always a good thing.

✔ **RSS view rates:** Tracking and monitoring time series that capture RSS view rates can give you an idea of how well your blog post titles are performing with your RSS subscribers — in other words, how well the blog content topic is matched to your subscribers' interests. This metric can also tell you whether your headline copy is intriguing enough to draw RSS subscribers in for a read. High RSS view rates reflect higher levels of loyalty among your RSS subscribers.

✔ **Customer satisfaction monitoring:** Sentiment analysis is an analysis technique where you apply text mining and data categorization techniques to web data in order to identify the feelings and attitudes of people (and customers) in your networks. Some social analytics applications offer a built-in sentiment analysis feature. You can use one of these applications or code something up yourself. Whatever you choose, be sure to stay on top of what people are saying about your brand across your social media channels because it's vital for the protection and proactive management of your brand's reputation. As they say, "The customer is always right."

Talking about testing your strategies

In growth, you use testing methods to optimize your web design and messaging so that it performs at its absolute best with the audiences to which it's targeted. Although testing and web analytics methods are both intended to optimize performance, testing goes one layer deeper than web analytics. You use web analytics to get a general idea about the interests of your channel audiences and how well your marketing efforts are paying off over time. After you have this information, you can then go in deeper to test variations on live visitors in order to gain empirical evidence about what designs and messaging your visitors actually prefer.

Testing tactics can help you optimize your website design or brand messaging for increased conversions in all layers of the funnel. Testing is also useful when optimizing your landing pages for user activations and revenue conversions. In the following sections, I introduce the testing strategies that are most commonly deployed in growth and discuss how you can use those strategies to optimize your efforts. I also provide you with a few tips on what applications are available to make testing easier and more fun.

Checking out common types of testing in growth

When you use data insights to increase growth for e-commerce businesses, you're likely to run into the three following testing tactics — A/B split testing, multivariate testing, and mouse-click heatmap analytics.

An *A/B split test* is an optimization tactic that you can use to split variations of your website or brand messaging between sets of live audiences in order to gauge responses and decide which of the two variations performs best. A/B split testing is the simplest testing method you can use for website or messaging optimization.

Multivariate testing is, in many ways, similar to the multivariate regression analysis that I discuss in Chapter 4. Like multivariate regression analysis, multivariate testing allows you to uncover relationships, correlations, and causations between variables and outcomes. In the case of multivariate testing, you're testing several conversion factors simultaneously over an extended period of time in order to uncover which factors are responsible for increased conversions. Multivariate testing is more complicated than A/B split testing, but it usually provides quicker and more powerful results.

Lastly, you can use *mouse-click heatmap analytics* to see how visitors are responding to your design and messaging choices. In this type of testing, you use the mouse-click heatmap to help you make optimal website design and messaging choices to ensure that you're doing everything you can to keep your visitors focused and converting.

Landing pages are meant to offer visitors little to no options, except to convert or to exit the page. Because a visitor has so few options on what he can do on a landing page, you don't really need to use multivariate testing or website mouse-click heatmaps. Simple A/B split tests suffice.

Data scientists working in growth hacking should be familiar with (and know how to derive insight from) the following testing applications:

- ✔ **Webtrends (**`http://webtrends.com`**):** Offers a conversion-optimization feature that includes functionality for A/B split testing and multivariate testing.

- ✔ **Optimizely (**`www.optimizely.com`**):** A popular product among the growth-hacking community. You can use Optimizely for multi-page funnel testing, A/B split testing, and multivariate testing, amongst other things.

- ✔ **Visual Website Optimizer (**`https://vwo.com`**):** An excellent tool for A/B split testing and multivariate testing.

Testing for acquisitions

Acquisitions testing provides feedback on how well your content performs with prospective users in your assorted channels. You can use acquisitions testing to help compare your message's performance in each channel, helping you optimize your messaging on a per-channel basis. If you want to optimize the performance of your brand's published images, then you can use acquisition testing to compare image performance across your channels, as well. Lastly, if you want to increase your acquisitions through increases in user referrals, then use testing to help optimize your referrals messaging for the referrals channels. Acquisition testing can help you begin to understand the specific preferences of prospective users on a channel-by-channel basis. You can use A/B split testing to improve your acquisitions in the following ways:

- ✔ **Social messaging optimization:** After you use social analytics to deduce the general interests and preferences of users in each of your social channels, you can then further optimize your brand messaging along those channels by using A/B split testing to compare your headlines and social media messaging within each channel.

✔ **Brand image and messaging optimization:** Compare and optimize the respective performances of images along each of your social channels.

✔ **Optimized referral messaging:** Test the effectiveness of your email messaging at converting new user referrals.

Testing for activations

Activation testing provides feedback on how well your website and its content perform in converting acquired users to active users. The results of activation testing can help you optimize your website and landing pages for maximum sign-ups and subscriptions. Here's how you'd use testing methods to optimize user activation growth:

✔ **Website conversion optimization:** Make sure your website is optimized for user activation conversions. You can use A/B split testing, multivariate testing, or a mouse-click heatmap data visualization to help you optimize your website design.

✔ **Landing pages:** If your landing page has a simple call to action that prompts guests to subscribe to your email list, then you can use A/B split testing for simple design optimization of this page and the call to action messaging.

Testing for retentions

Retentions testing provides feedback on how well your blog-post and email headlines are performing among your base of activated users. If you want to optimize your headlines so that active users want to continue active engagements with your brand, then test the performance of your user-retention tactics. Here's how you can use testing methods to optimize user retention growth:

✔ **Headline optimization:** Use A/B split testing to optimize the headlines of your blog posts and email marketing messages. Test different headline varieties within your different channels, and then use the varieties that perform the best. Email open rates and RSS view rates are ideal metrics to track the performance of each headline variation.

✔ **Conversion rate optimization:** Use A/B split testing on the messaging within your emails to decide which messaging variety more effectively gets your activated users to engage with your brand. The more effective your email messaging is at getting activated users to take a desired action, the greater your user retention rates.

Testing for revenue growth

Revenue testing gauges the performance of revenue-generating landing pages, e-commerce pages, and brand messaging. Revenue testing methods can help you optimize your landing and e-commerce pages for sales conversions. Here's how you can use testing methods to optimize revenue growth:

- ✔ **Website conversion optimization:** You can use A/B split testing, multivariate testing, or a mouse-click heatmap data visualization to help optimize your sales page and shopping cart design for revenue-generating conversions.

- ✔ **Landing page optimization:** If you have a landing page with a simple call to action that prompts guests to make a purchase, then you can use A/B split testing for design optimization.

Segmenting and targeting for success

The purpose of segmenting your channels and audiences is so that you can exact-target your messaging and offerings for optimal conversions, according to the specific interests and preferences of each user segment. If your goal is to optimize your marketing return on investment by exact-targeting customized messages to entire swathes of your audience at one time, then you can use segmentation analysis to group together audience members by shared attributes and then customize your messaging to those target audiences on a group-by-group basis. In the following sections, I tell you what applications can help you make user segmentation easier and how you can use segmentation and targeting tactics to grow the layers of your sales funnel.

Segmenting for faster and easier e-commerce growth

Data scientists working in growth hacking should be familiar with and know how to derive insight from the following user segmentation and targeting applications:

- ✔ **Google Analytics Segment Builder:** Google Analytics (www.google.com/analytics) contains a Segment Builder feature that makes it easier for you to set up filters when you configure your segments within the application. You can use the tool to segment users by demographic data, such as age, gender, referral source, nationality, and so on. (For more on the Segment Builder, check out the Google Analytics Help page at https://support.google.com/analytics/answer/3124493.)

- ✔ **Adobe Analytics (www.adobe.com/solutions/digital-analytics/marketing-reports-analytics.html):** You can use Adobe Analytics for advanced user segmentation and customer churn analysis — or analysis to identify reasons for and preempt customer loss.

Customer churn is a term that describes the loss, or churn, of existing customers. *Customer churn analysis* is a set of analytical techniques that are designed to identify, monitor, and issue alerts on indicators that signify when customers are likely to churn. With the information that's generated in customer churn analysis, businesses can take preemptive measures to retain at-risk customers.

✔ **Webtrends (**`http://webtrends.com`**):** Webtrends' Visitor Segmentation and Scoring offers real-time customer segmentation features that help you isolate, target, and engage your highest-value visitors. The Conversion Optimization solution also offers advanced segmenting and targeting functionality that you can use to optimize your website, landing pages, and overall customer experience.

✔ **Optimizely (**`www.optimizely.com`**):** In addition to its testing functionality, you can also use Optimizely for visitor segmentation, targeting, and geo-targeting.

✔ **IBM Product Recommendations (**`www-01.ibm.com/software/marketing-solutions/products-recommendation-solution`**):** This solution utilizes IBM Digital Analytics, customer-segmentation, and product-segmentation methods to make optimal product recommendations to visitors of e-commerce websites. IBM Product Recommendations Solutions can help you upsell or cross-sell your offerings.

Segmenting and targeting for acquisitions

You can optimize your acquisition efforts to meet the exact preferences and interests of your prospective users. If you want to maximize your user-acquisition return on investment, then you can use segmenting and targeting to group your prospective users and channels by interest and style preferences, and then use those groupings to send out exact-targeted messaging to prospective users en masse. Acquisitions segmentation and targeting helps you build your channels by providing you solid facts about the preferences of particular segments. After you have your prospective users grouped by preference, then it's just a matter of marketing to those preferences and avoiding messaging that's unfavorable within the segments.

Prospective user and channel segmentation and targeting is the low-lying fruit of acquisitions growth because after you figure out what works with each segment, it's just a matter of continuing to provide that content in order to make your user acquisition numbers grow. Here's how you can use segmentation and targeting tactics to optimize your user acquisitions (which is the same goal as the tactics discussed in the section "Accessing analytics for acquisitions," earlier in this chapter):

✔ **Audience discovery:** By performing segmentation analysis on your website visitor data, you can successfully group your website visitors in certain and distinctive classes according to their shared characteristics.

This approach is far more definitive than the simple inference-based method used for analytics, but the purpose is the same — to use visitor data to better understand who your audiences are, what they're interested in, and how you can best target your messaging and offerings to appeal to them.

✔ **Social media channel optimization:** You can use the insights you've gleaned via segmentation analysis to better understand and cater to the distinct preferences of your social media network audiences.

Targeting for activations

You can increase your user activations by understanding and responding to the interests and preferences of your website users. If you want to optimize your website and its content for increased user activations, then segmentation analysis can help you get a better understanding of your audiences' interests. Here's how you can use segmentation and targeting tactics to optimize your user activation growth:

✔ **Audience discovery:** You can perform segmentation analysis of your website visitor data in order to understand and substantively group users according to their types and preferences. These groupings help you develop more strategically targeted messages to pique the interests of people in your audience segments.

✔ **Strategic channel messaging:** After you have a solid understanding of your user segments and their preferences, you can use this information to help you develop strategic, highly-targeted messaging that performs well within each of the separate segments. This targeted approach can lead to increased social media followings and increased website subscriptions.

Segmenting and targeting for retentions

You can increase your user retentions by understanding and responding to the interests and preferences of your website users. To help increase user retention by reducing customer churn, you can deploy user segmentation and targeting strategies. Simply segment your customer-churn data into *cohorts* — subsets that are grouped according to similarities in some shared characteristic — and then analyze those cohorts to uncover trends and deduce the factors that contribute to churn within each of the groups. After you understand why particular segments of users are churning, you can take preemptive measures to stop that churn before you lose the customers for good.

Segmenting and targeting for revenues

You can increase your brand's revenues by understanding and responding to the interests and preferences of your e-commerce customers. User segmentation and targeting strategies can help you increase revenues and sales volumes. Here's how:

- **Landing and e-commerce page optimization:** You can use segmentation analysis on your website visitor data to better understand visitor behavior patterns per customer category, where a customer category could be defined by age, race, gender, income, referral source, or geographic region. After you distinguish clear user segments, and the preferences thereof, then you can use that information to create separate, customized landing or e-commerce pages that are targeted for optimal sales conversions within the segments.

- **Recommendation engines:** Whether you build them yourself or use a recommender application instead, recommendation systems use collaborative filtering or content-based filtering to segment customers according to shared characteristics. It's useful to segment customers in this way so that you can exact-target offers per customers' known preferences, in order to upsell and cross-sell your brand's offerings.

Chapter 21

Using Data Science to Describe and Predict Criminal Activity

*I*n recent years, data science has been increasingly incorporated into criminological methodologies in a practice that's been referred to as *predictive policing*. Predictive policing offers promising results, and law enforcement decision makers have high hopes that they can use predictive intelligence to help them formulate more effective tactical strategies. Judges hope to use predictive insights for support when deciding when to grant bail to suspects. Police agencies want to use the technology for improved offender monitoring. Consequently, there's a very high demand for crime analysts who are skilled at using data science to build descriptive and predictive information products to support the decisions of law enforcement officials.

To practice data science in criminal analysis, you need to be skilled in GIS, data visualization, coding, and basic math and statistics. If you want to go deeper into descriptive, predictive, or resource modeling, then you need strong skills in spatial statistics. To practice as a data scientist in crime analysis, you also need a strong subject-matter expertise in the criminal justice field.

Criminal data science practitioners aren't replacements for crime analysts — rather, they enhance the work that crime analysts do. Crime analysts are responsible for analyzing and reporting crime data trends as they happen to keep law enforcement officials and public citizens aware so that they can take proactive measures to prevent future criminal activity. Crime analysts work with law enforcement officials to develop strategies and tactics to attack and reduce criminal activity. Data scientists in crime analysis, however, assume a more technical role in the data analysis. They use advanced math, statistics, and coding to uncover spatial and temporal trends hidden deep within crime datasets. Data scientists in crime analysis work to describe, predict, and model resources for the prevention of criminal activity.

Two distinct types of data analysis are relevant to criminology — temporal data analysis and spatial data analysis. *Temporal data analysis* involves the analysis of tabular datasets that contain temporally relevant but not geo-referenced data. *Spatial data analysis* involves analyzing geo-referenced datasets without regard to time. Spatial analysis can also involve analyzing tabular data that's included within geo-referenced spatial datasets. It may even involve analyzing temporal data that pertains to the locations in question — which is known as *spatio-temporal data analysis*.

Temporal Analysis for Crime Prevention and Monitoring

The temporal analysis of crime data produces analytics that describe patterns in criminal activity based on time. You can analyze temporal crime data to develop prescriptive analytics, either through traditional crime analysis means or through a data science approach. Knowing how to produce prescriptive analytics from temporal crime data allows you to provide decision-support to law enforcement agencies that want to optimize their tactical crime fighting.

For purposes of this discussion, consider *temporal data* to be tabular data that's earmarked with date/time entries for each record in the set. You use temporal data analysis to make inferences and draw correlations that you can use to monitor and predict what crimes are happening when and why. In crime analysis, an example of a temporal dataset would be a dataset that describes the counts of different types of crimes that have been committed, broken into count per day and recorded on a daily basis for an entire month.

To be successful at deriving simple, yet useful, insights from temporal crime data, you need only a basic skill level in data science. You should know how to draw fundamental statistical and mathematical inferences, how to spot and investigate outliers, how to analyze patterns in time series, and how to draw correlations or causations through regression techniques. When deriving insights from temporal crime data, you generally produce decision-support products in the form of tabular data reports and simple data visualizations — such as bar charts, line charts, and heat map charts.

Spatial Crime Prediction and Monitoring

Spatial data is tabular data that's earmarked with spatial coordinate information for each record in the dataset. Many times, spatial datasets also have a field that indicates a date/time attribute for each of the records in the set — making it *spatio-temporal data.* If you want to create crime maps or uncover location-based trends in crime data, use spatial data analysis. You can also use spatial analysis methods to make location-based inferences that help you monitor and predict what crimes will occur where, when, and why. In the following sections, I show how you can use GIS technologies, data modeling, and advanced spatial statistics to build information products for the prediction and monitoring of criminal activity.

Crime mapping with GIS technology

One of the most common forms of data insight that's used in law enforcement is the crime map. A *crime map* is a spatial map that visualizes where crimes have been committed during any given time interval. In olden days, you might have drawn this type of map out with pencil and paper, but nowadays, you do the job using a GIS software, such as ArcGIS Desktop or QGIS.

Although crime mapping has become increasingly sophisticated while advances have been made in spatial technologies, the purpose has remained the same — to provide law enforcement decision makers and personnel with location information that describes on-the-ground criminal activities so that they can use that information to optimize their efforts in protecting public safety. GIS software can help you make crime maps that can be used as a descriptive analytic or as a source for simple inference-based predictions. (For much more about map-making and basic spatial analysis, check out Chapter 13.)

Going one step further with location-allocation analysis

Location allocation is a form of predictive spatial analytics that you can use for location optimization from complex spatial data models. For example, in law enforcement, location optimization can predict optimal locations for police stations so that dispatched officers can travel to an emergency in any part of the city within a five-minute response-time window. To help your agency predict the best locations to position officers so that they can arrive immediately at any emergency in any part of town, use location-allocation analysis.

You can most easily do a location-allocation analysis by using the ArcGIS for Desktop Network Analyst add-on to carry out a maximum coverage analysis. (Check out ArcGIS for Desktop at `www.esri.com/software/arcgis/arcgis-for-desktop`.) In this form of analysis, you input data about existing facilities, *demand points* — points that represent places in the study area that exhibit a demand for law enforcement resources— and any spatial barriers that would block or severely impede law enforcement response times. The model outputs information about the optimal locations to place officers for the fastest, most well-distributed response times. Packages such as the Network Analyst add-on are easy to use, which is one of the feature benefits that might have you choose ArcGIS over open-source QGIS. Figure 21-1 shows map results that are derived from a location-allocation analysis.

Figure 21-1:
A map product derived from location-allocation analysis.

Using complex spatial statistics to better understand crime

You can use your skills in GIS, mathematics, data modeling, and spatial statistics in many ways to build descriptive and predictive information products that support the decision making of law enforcement officials. Proprietary spatial analysis software applications have greatly simplified this work by providing special add-on tools specifically designed for spatial analysis of crime data. In addition, free open-source applications such as the CrimeStatIII program (`www.icpsr.umich.edu/crimestat`) are available to help you carry out more advanced forms of statistical analysis. In the following sections, I introduce how you can use your data science skills to derive descriptive and predictive spatial data insights that help law enforcement agencies optimize their tactical response planning.

Delving into descriptive methods

You can incorporate descriptive spatial statistics into crime analysis in order to produce analytics you can then use to understand and monitor the location-based attributes of ongoing criminal activities. You can use descriptive spatial statistics to provide your law enforcement agency with up-to-date information on the location, intensity, and size of criminal activity hot spots, as well as to derive important information about the characteristics of local areas that are positioned between these hot-spots.

This list includes types of approaches that are helpful when using spatial statistics for descriptive methods in crime analysis:

- ✔ **Clustering:** Use methods such as nearest neighbor algorithms (hierarchical and non-hierarchical) and the k-means algorithm to identify and analyze criminal hotspots, to describe the properties of inter-incident distances, or to describe spatial autocorrelation that exists between dense areas of criminal activity. To learn more about clustering methods, be sure to check out Chapters 5 and 6 of this book.

  Spatial autocorrelation is a term that refers to the natural phenomenon that when things are closer to one another in physical location, they exhibit more average similarity than things that are far away from one another. More is covered on this in Chapter 8 on spatial autocorrelation and other spatial statistics.

- ✔ **Advanced spatial mathematics:** You can use spatial mathematical metrics, such as the Euclidian metric or the Manhattan metric (otherwise known as the taxicab metric) to describe the distances between criminal incidents or sets of incidents. The *Euclidean metric* is a measure of the distance between points plotted on a Euclidean plane. The *taxicab metric* is a measure of the distance between points, where distance is calculated as the sum of the absolute value of the differences between two points' Cartesian coordinates.

- ✔ **Descriptive statistics:** Use statistics to generate a description about the location distribution of criminal activities — including information on the directional mean and mean center of criminal incidents.

Building predictive spatial models for crime analysis

You can incorporate predictive statistical models into crime analysis methods to produce analytics that describe and predict where and what kinds of criminal activity are likely to occur.

Predictive spatial models can help you predict the behavior, location, or criminal activities of repeat offenders. You can also apply statistical methods to spatio-temporal data to ascertain causative or correlative variables relevant to crime and law enforcement.

The following list includes types of approaches that are helpful in spatial predictive modeling for crime analysis:

- ✓ **Clustering:** You can use kernel density estimation methods to quantify the spatial density of criminal activities and to generate comparative measures between the densities of criminal activity relative to the base population of the affected area.

  Kernel density estimation (KDE) is a smoothing method that works by placing a *kernel* — or, a weighting function that is useful for quantifying density — on each data point in the data set, and then summing the kernels to generate a kernel density estimate for the overall region.

- ✓ **Advanced spatial statistics:** One example of this would be to use regression analysis to establish how one or more independent crime variables directly cause, or correlate with, a dependent crime variable. Lastly, advanced spatial statistics are used to make behavioral predictions for repeat offenders and to predict future criminal activity based on historical records on criminal behavior and information about present conditions.

Modeling travel demand in criminal activity

Modeling the travel demand of criminal activity allows you to describe and predict the travel patterns of criminals so that law enforcement can use this information in tactical response planning. If you want to predict the most likely route that a criminal will take between the location from where he or she starts out and the location where that person actually commit the crime, then use crime travel modeling.

Travel demand modeling is actually the brainchild of civil engineers and was developed to facilitate improved transportation planning. Although you can use four different approaches in travel demand modeling — trip-based, integrated trip-based, tour-based, and activity schedule-based —, the trip-based approach (see Figure 21-2) is most relevant to crime analysis. The trip-based approach is broken into the following four steps:

1. **Trip generation.**

   Model the *trip production* (the quantity of crime trips that originate in a *zone of origination* — a spatial region, like a neighborhood or subdivision) and the *trip attractions* (the quantity of crime trips that end in the *zone of destination* — the spatial region where the criminal act is executed).

2. Trip distribution.

Incorporate a *trip matrix* — a matrix of rows and columns that covers a study area and depicts the patterns of trips across it— and a *gravity model* — a model that describes and predicts the locational flow of objects across space — to quantify the count of crime trips that occur between each zone of origination and each zone of destination.

3. Modal split.

A *modal split* is the portion of travelers that uses particular trip paths across a study area. For travel demand modeling, you'd generate a count of the number of trips for each zone-of-origination/zone-of-destination pair that occurs via each available route. The choice between routes can be modeled statistical or mathematical.

4. Network assignment.

Assign probability and predict the most likely routes that a criminal would take when traveling from a particular zone of origination to a particular zone of destination across the network of potential travel paths.

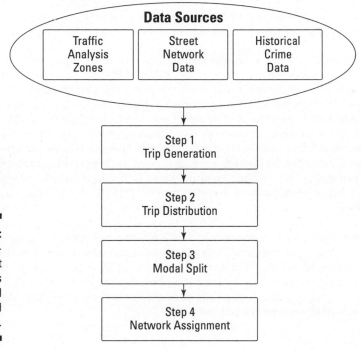

Figure 21-2:
A schematic that represents the travel demand model.

Probing the Problems with Data Science for Crime Analysis

Although data science for crime analysis has a promising future, it's not without its limitations. The field is still young, and it has a long way to go before the bugs are worked out. Currently, the approach is subject to significant criticism for both legal and technical reasons.

Caving in on civil rights

The legal systems of western nations such as the U.S. are fundamentally structured around the basic notion that people have the right to life, liberty, and the pursuit of property. More specifically, the U.S. Constitution's Fourth Amendment explicitly declares that people have a right "to be secure . . . against unreasonable searches and seizures, shall not be violated . . . but upon probable cause." Because predictive policing methods have become more popular, a consternation has arisen among informed U.S. citizens. People are concerned that predictive policing represents an encroachment on their Fourth Amendment rights.

To see how this rights violation could occur, imagine that you've developed a predictive model that estimates a car theft will occur on the afternoon of January 15th at the corner of Apple Street and Winslow Boulevard. Because your predictions have proven accurate in the past, the agency dispatches Officer Bob to police the area at said time and day. While out policing the area, Officer Bob sees and recognizes Citizen Daniel. Officer Bob had arrested Citizen Daniel five years earlier for burglary charges. Officer Bob testified against Citizen Daniel and knows that he was subsequently convicted. Citizen Daniel is also a racial minority, and Officer Bob finds himself being suspicious on that basis alone (known as *racial profiling*, this is illegal, but it happens all the time).

Officer Bob, on said street corner, has a predictive report that says a theft crime is about to occur, and he's in the presence of a man of a racial minority whom he knows has a history of committing theft crimes. Officer Bob decides that the predictive report, combined with what he knows about Citizen Daniel, is enough to justify probable cause, so he performs search and seizure upon Daniel's person.

The conundrum arises when one considers whether a predictive report combined with knowledge of past criminal activity is sufficient to support probable cause. Even if the predictive report were guaranteed to be accurate — which it's not — couldn't this decision to search Citizen Daniel just be mostly racial profiling on the part of Officer Bob? What if Officer Bob is just using the predictive report as a justification so that he can harass and degrade Citizen Daniel because Daniel is a minority and Officer Bob hates minorities? In that case, Officer Bob would certainly be violating Daniel's Fourth Amendment rights. But because Officer Bob has the predictive policing report, who's to say why Officer Bob acts in the way that he does? Maybe he acts in good faith — but maybe not.

Predictive policing practices open a gray area in which officers can abuse power and violate civil rights without being held liable. A significant portion of the U.S. population is against the use of predictive policing measures for this reason, but the approach has technical problems, as well.

Taking on technical limitations

Data science for crime analysis is a special breed, and as such, it's subject to certain problems that may not generally be an issue in other domains of application. In law enforcement, criminal perpetrators are acting according to their own intellects and free will. A brief analogy is the best way to describe the problem.

Imagine that you build a crime travel demand model. Based on the zone of origination, this model predicts that Criminal Carl will almost certainly travel on Ventura Avenue or Central Road when he goes to pick up his next shipment of drugs. In fact, the model predicts these same two routes for all drug criminals who depart from the same zone of origination as Criminal Carl.

Based on this prediction, the Agency sets up two units, one on Ventura Avenue and one on Central Road, in hopes of catching Criminal Carl after the buy. Criminal Carl, of course, doesn't know about all of these plans. He and his buddy Steve travel Ventura Avenue, purchase their drugs, and then return back along the same route. It's nighttime so Steve isn't so worried about wearing his seatbelt since he figures no one could see that anyway. As Criminal Carl and Steve make their way back, Officer Irene begins to tail them and look for a reason to pull them over; Steve's seatbelt infraction is just cause. When Officer Irene talks to the men, she can tell they're high, so she has probable cause to search the vehicle. Criminal Carl and Steve go to jail on drug charges, and when they're released, they tell their criminal friends all the details about what happened.

The Agency uses this model to catch six more drug offenders in rapid time, on either Ventura Avenue or Central Road. Each time they make an arrest, the offenders go out and tell their criminal associates the details of how they got caught. After six busts on these two roads within a relatively short time period, local drug criminals begin to catch on to the fact that these roads are being watched. After word is out about this fact, no criminal will take these streets anymore. The criminals change their patterns in random ways to avert police, thus making your predictive model obsolete.

This kind of common pattern makes it ineffective to use predictive models to reduce crime rates. After criminals deduce the factors that put them at risk, they avoid those factors and randomly assume a different approach so that they can perpetrate their crimes without being caught. Most of the time, agencies continually have to change their analysis strategies to try to keep up with the criminals, but the criminals are almost always one step ahead.

This is a more severe version of an issue that arises in many applications, whenever the underlying process is subject to change without notice. Models must always be kept up to date.

Part VI
The Part of Tens

In this part . . .

✔ Find out all about some fantastic open data resources

✔ Explore some great (free) data science resources and applications

Chapter 22

Ten Phenomenal Resources for Open Data

*O*pen data is part of a larger trend toward a less restrictive, more open understanding of the idea of intellectual property, a trend that's been gaining tremendous popularity over the past decade. *Open data* is data that's been made publically available and that's permitted to be used, reused, built upon, and shared with others. Open data is part of the open movement. Beyond open data, this so-called *open movement* also includes open-source software, open hardware, open-content creative work, open access to scientific journals, and open science — all committed to the notion that content (including raw data from experiments) should be shared freely.

The distinguishing feature of open licenses is that they have copyleft instead of copyright. With *copyleft,* the only restriction is that the source of the work must be identified, sometimes with the caveat that derivative works can't be copyrighted with a more restrictive license than the original. If the second condition is in force, successfully commercializing the work itself becomes difficult, although people often find plenty of other indirect, creative avenues of commercialization.

Be aware that sometimes work that's labeled as open may not actually fit the accepted definition. You're responsible to check the licensing rights and restrictions of the open data you use.

People often confuse *open* licenses with Creative Commons licenses. *Creative Commons* is a not-for-profit organization that's dedicated to encouraging and spreading creative works by offering a legal framework through which usage permissions can be granted and obtained, so that sharing parties are safe from legal risks when building upon and using work and knowledge that's been openly shared. Some Creative Commons licenses are open and some explicitly forbid derivative works and/or commercialization.

As part of more recent open government initiatives, governments around the world began releasing open government data. Governments generally provide this data so that it can be used by volunteer analysts and *civic hackers* — programmers who work collaboratively to build open-source solutions that use open data to solve social problems — in an effort to benefit society at large. In 2013, the G8 nations (France, the United States, the United Kingdom, Russia, Germany, Japan, Italy, and Canada) signed a charter committing themselves to open data, prioritizing the areas of national statistics, election results, government budgets, and national maps.

The open government movement promotes government transparency and accountability, nurtures a well-informed electorate, and encourages public engagement. To put it in computing terms, open government facilitates a read/write relationship between a government and its citizenry.

Digging through Data.gov

The Data.gov program (at www.data.gov) was started by the Obama administration to provide open access to non-classified U.S. government data. Data.gov data is being produced by all departments in the Executive branch — the White House and all Cabinet-level departments — as well as datasets from other levels of government. By mid-2014, you could search for over 100,000 datasets by using the Data.gov search. The website is an unparalleled resource if you're looking for U.S. government-derived data on the following indicators:

- ✔ **Economic:** Find data on finance, education, jobs and skills, agriculture, manufacturing, and business.

- ✔ **Environmental:** Looking for data on energy, climate, geospatial, oceans, and global development? Look no further.

- ✔ **STEM industry:** Your go-to place for anything science-, technology-, engineering-, and mathematics-related — data on energy science and research, for example.

- ✔ **Quality of life:** Here you can find data on weather patterns, health, and public safety.

- ✔ **Legal:** If your interests go in a more legalistic direction, Data.gov can help you track down data on law and ethics.

Data.gov's data policy makes federal data derived from this source extremely safe to use. The policy says that "U.S. Federal data available through Data.gov is offered free and without restriction. Data and content created by government employees within the scope of their employment are not subject to domestic copyright protection." And because it comes in countless formats — including XLS, CSV, HTML, JSON, XML, and geospatial — you can almost certainly find something that you can use.

Datasets aren't the only thing that are open on Data.gov. You can also find over 60 open-source application programming interfaces (APIs) available on the platform. You can use these APIs to create tools and apps that pull data from government departments listed in the Data.gov data catalog. The catalog itself uses the popular open-source CKAN API. (CKAN here is short for *C*omprehensive *K*nowledge *A*rchive *N*etwork) Even the code used to generate the Data.gov website is open source and is published on GitHub (at `http://github.com/`), in case you're interested in digging into that.

Data.gov allocates hundreds of thousands of dollars in prizes per year for app development competitions. If you're an app developer and you're looking for a fun side project that has the potential to provide you financial rewards, while also offering you an opportunity to make a positive impact on society, then check out the Data.gov competitions. Popular apps developed in these competitions include an interactive global hunger map and an app that calculates and tracks bus fares, routes, and connections in Albuquerque, New Mexico in real-time.

Checking Out Canada Open Data

For many decades, Canada has been a world leader for its data collection and publication practices. Both *The Economist* and the Public Policy Forum have repeatedly named Statistics Canada — Canada's federal department for statistics — as the best statistical organization in the world.

If you take a look at the Canada Open Data website (`http://open.canada.ca`), the nation's strong commitment to data is overwhelmingly evident. At the Canada Open Data website, you can find over 200,000 datasets. Among the 25 most popular offerings on the Canada Open Data site are datasets that cover the following indicators:

- ✔ **Environmental:** Such as natural disasters and fuel consumption ratings

- ✔ **Citizenship:** Permanent resident applications, permanent resident counts, foreign student entry counts, and so on

- ✔ **Quality of life:** For example, cost-of-living trends, automobile collisions, and disease surveillance

Canada Open Data issues its open data under an *open government license* — a usage license that's issued by a government organization in order to specify the requirements that must be met in order to lawfully use or reuse the open data that the organization has released. Canada Open Data releases data under the Open Government License – Canada — you're required to acknowledge the source every time you use the data, as well as provide backlinks to the Open Government License – Canada page at `http://open.canada.ca/open-government-licence-canada`.

Diving into data.gov.uk

The United Kingdom got off to a late start in the open government movement. data.gov.uk (`http://data.gov.uk`) was started in 2010, and by mid-2014, only about 20,000 datasets were yet available. Like Data.gov (discussed in the section "Digging through Data.gov," earlier in this chapter), data.gov.uk is also powered by the CKAN data catalog.

Although data.gov.uk is still playing catch-up, it has an impressive collection of Ordnance Survey maps old enough — 50 years or more — to be out of copyright. If you're looking for world-renowned, free-to-use survey maps, data.gov.uk is an incredible place for you to explore. Beyond its stellar survey maps, data.gov.uk is a great source for data on the following indicators:

- **Environmental:** data.gov.uk's most prolific theme
- **Government spending**
- **Societal**
- **Health**
- **Education**
- **Business and economic**

Interestingly, the dataset most frequently downloaded from data.gov.uk is a dataset that covers the Bona Vacantia division — the government division charged with tracking the complicated processes involved in determining the proper inheritance of British estates.

Like the Canada Open Data website (see the preceding section), data.gov.uk uses an Open Government License, which means you're required to acknowledge the data source every time you use it, as well as provide backlinks to the data.gov.uk Open Government License page at `www.nationalarchives.gov.uk/doc/open-government-licence`.

Although data.gov.uk is still young, it's growing quickly, so check back often. If you can't find what you're looking for, the data.gov.uk website offers functionality through which you can specifically request the datasets that you want to see.

Checking Out U.S. Census Bureau Data

Then U.S. Census is held every ten years, and since 2010, the data has been made freely available at `www.census.gov`. Statistics are available down to the level of the census block — which aggregates by 30-person counts, on average. The demographics data provided by the U.S. Census Bureau can be extremely helpful if you're doing marketing or advertising research and need to target your audience according to the following classifications:

- ✔ Age
- ✔ Average annual income
- ✔ Household size
- ✔ Gender or race
- ✔ Level of education

In addition to its census counts on people in the U.S., the U.S. Census Bureau conducts a census of businesses. You can use this business census data as a source for practical industry research to tell you information such as the number of businesses, the number of employees, and the size of payroll per industry per state or metropolitan area.

Lastly, the U.S. Census Bureau carries out an annual American Community Survey to track demographics with a statistically representative sample of the population during non-census years. You can check this data if you need specific data about what has happened during a particular year or set of years.

Some census blocks have a population density that's far greater than average. When you use data from these blocks, remember that the block data has been aggregated over a person count that's greater than the average 30-person count of census blocks.

With respect to features and functionality, the U.S. Census Bureau has a lot to offer. You can use QuickFacts (`http://quickfacts.census.gov/qfd`) to quickly source and pull government data from the U.S. Federal, State, County, or Municipal level. Also, the U.S. Census offers Census Explorer (`www.census.gov/censusexplorer`), a great feature that you can use to create and display web-based interactive charts or maps of census data. Although you can find all of this data by going through the Data.gov website (which you can read about in the section "Digging through Data.gov," earlier in this chapter), these extra features and functions make Census.gov worth a visit.

Knowing NASA Data

Since its inception in 1958, NASA has made public all of its non-classified project data. Because they've been in the open-data game so long, NASA has tons of data! NASA datasets have been growing even faster with recent improvements in satellite and communication technology. In fact, NASA now generates four terabytes of new earth-science data per day — that's equivalent to over a million MP3 files. Many of NASA's projects have accumulated data into the petabyte range.

NASA's open data portal is called data.NASA (`http://data.nasa.gov`). This portal is a source of all kinds of wonderful data, including data about

- ✔ Astronomy and space (of course!)
- ✔ Climate
- ✔ Life sciences
- ✔ Geology
- ✔ Engineering

Some examples from its hundreds of datasets include detailed data on the color of the Earth's oceans, a database of every lunar sample and where it's stored, and the Great Images in NASA (GRIN) collection of historically significant photographs.

Wrangling World Bank Data

The World Bank is an international financial institution run by the United Nations. It provides loans to developing countries to pay for capital investment that hopefully will lead to poverty reduction and some surplus so that the recipient nations can repay the loan amounts over time. Because World Bank officers need to make well-informed decisions about which countries would be more likely to repay their loans, they've gathered an enormous amount of data on member nations. They've made this data available to the public at the World Bank Open Data page (`http://data.worldbank.org`).

If you're looking for data to buttress your argument in a really interesting data-journalism piece that's supported by global statistics, the World Bank should be your go-to source. No matter the scope of your project, if you need data about what's happening in developing nations, the World Bank is the place to go. You can use the website to download entire datasets or simply view the data visualizations online. You can also use the World Bank's Open Data API to access what you need.

World Bank Open Data supplies data on the following indicators (and many, many more):

- **Agriculture & rural development:** Here you'll find data on major contract awards, contributions to financial intermediary funds, forest area, and rural population size data.

- **Economy & growth:** For the Big Picture — data on gross domestic product (GDP), gross capital formation, and agricultural value-added data, for example — no source is more exhaustive than World Bank Open Data.

- **Environment:** Data here can tell you all about methane emissions, nitrous oxide emissions, and water pollution.

- **Science and technology:** Great for tracking patent applications and trademark applications data.

- **Financial sector:** Research the health (or lack thereof) of a national economy by looking at a nation's bank capital-to-assets ratio, foreign direct investment, market capitalization, and new or supplemental project data.

- **Poverty income:** For a clearer sense of how a country's poorer population is faring, analyze the data associated with gross national income (GNI) per capita, income shares, and the poverty gap.

World Bank Data also includes *microdata* — sample surveys of households and businesses in developing countries. You can use microdata to explore variations in your datasets.

Getting to Know Knoema Data

Knoema (pronounced *no-mah*) purports to be the largest repository of public data on the web. The Knoema platform houses a staggering 500+ databases, in addition to its 150 million *time series* — 150 million collections of data on attribute values over time, in other words. Knoema includes, but isn't limited to, all of these data sources:

- **Government data from industrial nations:** Data from Data.gov, Canada Open Data, data.gov.uk, and Eurostat.

✔ **National public data from developing nations:** Data from countries such as India and Kenya.

✔ **United Nations data:** Includes data from the Food and Agriculture Organization, the World Health Organization, and many other UN organizations.

✔ **International organization data:** There's more to the international scene than the United Nations, so if you're looking for data from organizations such as the International Monetary Fund and the Organization for Economic Co-operation and Development, Knoema is where you want to be.

✔ **Corporate data from global corporations:** Knoema offers data made public by private corporations such as British Petroleum, BASF, and so on.

Knoema is an outstanding resource if you're looking for international data on agriculture, crime statistics, demographics, economy, education, energy, environment, food security, foreign trade, health, land use, national defense, poverty, research and development, telecommunications, tourism, transportation, or water.

In addition to being an incredible data source, Knoema is also a multi-faceted tasking platform. You can use the Knoema platform to make dashboards that automatically track all of your favorite datasets. You can use the platform's data visualization tools to quickly and easily see your data in a tabular or map format. You can use the Knoema Data Atlas (http://knoema.com/atlas) to drill down among categories and/or geographic regions and quickly access the specific datasets you need. As an individual, you can upload your own data and use Knoema as a free hosting service. Above and beyond all of this, Knoema even offers the Knoema Market — a place where you can go to get paid just for being part of data-driven projects. Check it out at http://knoema. com/market.

Although a lot of Knoema's data is pretty general, you can still find some surprisingly specific data, as well. If you're having a hard time locating data on a very specific topic, you might have luck finding it on the Knoema platform. Figure 22-1 illustrates just how specific Knoema data can be.

Figure 22-1:
The index
of insect
records in
Knoema's
search.

Queuing Up with Quandl Data

Quandl (www.quandl.com) is a Toronto-based website that aims to be a search engine for numeric data. Unlike most search engines, however, its database isn't automatically generated by spiders that crawl the web. Rather, it focuses on linked data that's updated via *crowdsourcing* — updated manually via human curators, in other words.

Because most financial data is in numeric format, Quandl is an excellent tool for staying up to date on the latest business informatics. As you can see in Figure 22-2, a search for *Apple* returns over 4,700 datasets from 11 different sources with time series at the daily, weekly, monthly, quarterly, or annual level. Many of these results are related to the United Nations' agricultural data. If you're looking for data on Apple Computers, you can narrow the scope of your search by replacing the *Apple* search term with the company's stock abbreviation *AAPL*.

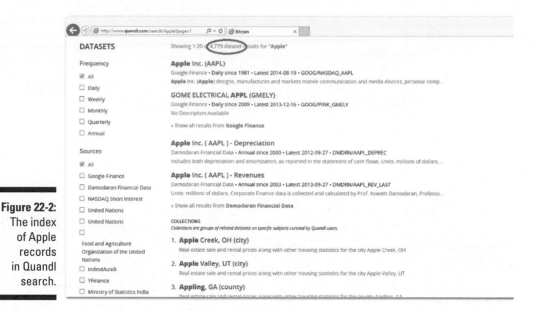

The Quandl database includes links to over 10 million datasets (although they use a generous metric in declaring what distinguishes one dataset from another). Quandl links to 2.1 million UN datasets and many other sources, including datasets in the Open Financial Data Project, the central banks, real estate organizations, and well-known think tanks.

You can browse Quandl data and get instant charts based on what you find. If you sign up for a free registered account, then you can download as much data as you want or use the Quandl application programming interface (API). The Quandl API includes wrappers to accommodate platforms such as Java, Python, Julia, R, MATLAB, Excel, and Stata, among others.

Exploring Exversion Data

Modeled after Github — the cloud-hosted platform across which programmers can collaboratively share and review code—, Exversion aims to provide the same collaborative functionality around data that GitHub provides around code. The Exversion platform offers version control functionality and hosting services to which you can upload and share your data. To illustrate how Exversion works, imagine a platform that would allow you to first *fork* (or copy) a dataset and then make the changes you want. Exversion would be there to keep track of what has changed from the original set and every change that you make to it. Exversion also allows users to rate, review, and comment on datasets.

Datasets hosted on the Exversion platform are either provided by a user or created by a spider that crawls and indexes open data to make it searchable from a single application programming interface (API). Like GitHub, with a free user account, all the data you upload to Exversion is public. If you're willing to pay for an account, then you can create your own private data repositories. Also, with the paid account, you get the option to share your data with selected users for collaborative projects.

When you work on collaborative projects, version control becomes vitally important. Instead of learning this lesson the hard way, just start your project on a version-enabled application or platform — this approach will save you from a lot of problems in the future.

Exversion is extremely useful in the data-cleanup stage. Most developers are familiar with data-cleanup hassles. Imagine you want to use a particular dataset, but in order to do so, you must put tabs in all the right places to make the columns line up correctly. Meanwhile, the other 100 developers out there working with that dataset are doing the exact same thing. In contrast, if you download, clean, and then upload the data to Exversion, other developers can use it and don't have to spend their time doing the same work later. In this way, everyone can benefit from each other's work, and each individual person can spend more time analyzing data and less time cleaning it.

Mapping OpenStreetMap Spatial Data

OpenStreetMap (OSM) is an open, crowd-sourced alternative to commercial mapping products such as Google Maps and ESRI ArcGIS Online. In OSM, users create, upload, or digitize geographic data into the central repository.

The OSM platform is quite robust. Governments and private companies have started contributing to, and pulling from, the shared datasets. Even corporations as big as Apple are relying on OSM data. Currently, OSM has over 1 million registered users. To illustrate how a person can create data in OSM, imagine that someone links the GPS systems on her mobile phone to the OSM application. Because of this authorization, OSM can automatically trace the routes of roads while the person travels. Later, this person (or another OSM user) can go into the OSM online platform to verify and label the routes.

The data in OSM isn't stored as maps, but as geometric and text representations — points, lines, polygons, and map annotation — so all of OSM's data can be quickly downloaded from the website and easily assembled into a cartographic representation via a desktop application. (For more on map-making and GIS, see Chapter 13.)

Chapter 23

Ten (or So) Free Data Science Tools and Applications

- -

- -

*B*ecause visualizations are a vitally important part of the data scientist's toolkit, it should come as no surprise that you can use quite a few free web-based tools to make visualizations in data science. (Check out Chapter 11 for links to a few.) With such tools, you can leverage the brain's capacity to quickly absorb visual information. Because data visualizations are a very effective means of communicating data insights, many tool and application developers work hard to ensure that the platforms they design are simple enough for even beginners to use. These simple applications can sometimes be useful to more advanced data scientists, but at other times, data science experts simply need more technical tools to help them delve deeper into datasets.

In this chapter, I present ten free web-based applications that you can use to do data science tasks that are more advanced than the ones described in Chapter 11. You can download and install many of these applications on your personal computer, and most of the downloadable applications are available for multiple operating systems.

Always make sure that you read and understand the licensing requirements of any app you use. Protect yourself by determining how you're allowed to use the products you create with that app.

Making Custom Web-Based Data Visualizations with Free R Packages

I discuss some very easy-to-use web apps for data visualization in Chapter 11, so you may be wondering why I'm presenting yet another set of the packages and tools useful for creating really cool data visualizations. Here's the simple answer: The tools that I present in this section require you to code using the R statistical programming language — a programming language I present in Chapter 15. Although you may not have much fun coding things up yourself, with these packages and tools, you can create results that are more customized for your needs. In the following sections, I discuss using Shiny, rCharts, and rMaps to create really neat looking web-based data visualizations.

Getting Shiny by RStudio

No too long ago, you needed to know how to use a statistics-capable programming language like R if you wanted to do any kind of serious data analysis. And if you needed to make interactive web visualizations, you'd have to know how to code in languages like JavaScript or PHP. Of course, if you wanted to do both simultaneously, then you'd have to know how to code in an additional two or three more programming languages. In other words, web-based data visualization based on statistical analyses was a cumbersome task.

The good news is that things have changed. Due to the work of a few dedicated developers, the walls between analysis and presentation have crumbled. After the 2012 launch of RStudio's Shiny package (http://shiny.rstudio.com), both statistical analysis and web-based data visualization can be carried out in the same framework.

RStudio — already, by far, the most popular integrated development environment (IDE) for R — developed the Shiny package to allow R users to create web apps. Web apps made in Shiny run on a web server and are *interactive* — with them, you can interact with the data visualization to move sliders, select check boxes, or click the data itself. Because these apps run on a server, they're considered *live* — when you make changes to the underlying data, those changes are automatically reflected in the appearance of the data visualization. Web apps created in Shiny are also *reactive* — in other words, their output updates instantly in response to a user interaction, without the user having to click a Submit button.

If you want to quickly use a few lines of code to instantly generate a web-based data visualization application, then use R's Shiny package. What's more, if you want to customize your web-based data visualization app to be more aesthetically appealing, you can do that by simply editing the HTML, CSS, and JavaScript that underlies the Shiny application.

Because Shiny produces server-side web apps, you need a server host and the know-how to host your web app on a server before you can make useful web apps by using the package.

Shiny runs a public web server called ShinyApps.io (www.shinyapps.io). You can use that server to host an app for free, or you can pay to host there if your requirements are more resource-intensive. The most basic level of service costs $39 per month and promises you 250 hours of application run time per month.

Charting with rCharts

Although R has always been famous for its beautiful static visualizations, only just recently has it been possible to use R to produce web-based interactive data visualizations.

Things changed dramatically with the advent of rCharts (http:// rcharts.io). rCharts is an open-source package for R that takes your data and parameters as input and then quickly converts those to a JavaScript code block output. Code block outputs from rCharts can use one of many popular JavaScript data visualization libraries, including NVD3, Highcharts, Rickshaw, xCharts, Polychart, and Morris.

To see some examples of data visualizations created by using rCharts, check out the rCharts Gallery at http://rcharts.io/gallery. This gallery includes simple data graphics such as standard bar charts and scatterplots, as well as more complex data graphics such as chord diagrams and hive plots.

Mapping with rMaps

rMaps (http://rmaps.github.io) is the brother of rCharts. Both of these open-source R packages were crafted by Ramnath Vaidyanathan. Using rMaps, you can create animated or interactive choropleths, heatmaps, or even maps that contain annotated location droplets (such as those found in the JavaScript mapping libraries Leaflet, CrossLet, and Data Maps).

rMaps allows you to create a spatial data visualization that contains interactive sliders that users can move to select the data range they want to see.

If you're an R user and you're accustomed to using the simple R Markdown syntax to create web pages, you'll be happy to know that you can easily embed both rCharts and rMaps in R Markdown.

If you prefer Python to R, Python users aren't being left out on this trend of creating interactive web-based visualizations within one platform. Python users can use server-side web app tools such as Flask — a less–user-friendly, but more powerful tool than Shiny — and the Bokeh and Mpld3 modules to create client-side JavaScript versions of Python visualizations. The Plotly tool has a Python application programming interface (API) — as well as ones for R, MATLAB, and Julia — that you can use to create web-based interactive visualizations directly from your Python IDE or command line. (Check out Flask at `http://flask.pocoo.org`, Bokeh at `http://bokeh.pydata.org`, Mpld3 at `http://mpld3.github.io`, and Plotly at `https://plot.ly`.)

Checking Out More Scraping, Collecting, and Handling Tools

Whether you need data to support a business analysis or an upcoming journalism piece, web-scraping can help you track down interesting and unique data sources. In *web-scraping* you set up automated programs and then let them scour the web for the data you need. I talk a lot about the general ideas behind web-scraping in Chapter 18, but in the following sections, I want to elaborate a bit more on the free tools that you can use to scrape data or images, including import.io, ImageQuilts, and DataWrangler.

Scraping data with import.io

Have you ever tried to copy and paste a table from the web into a Microsoft Office document and then not been able to get the columns to line up correctly? Frustrating, right? This is exactly the pain point that import.io was designed to address.

import.io — pronounced "import-eye-oh" — is a free desktop application that you can use to painlessly copy, paste, clean, and format any part of a web page with only a few clicks of the mouse. You can even use import.io to automatically crawl and extract data from multi-page lists. (Check out import.io at `https://import.io/`.)

Using import.io, you can scrape data from a simple or complicated series of web pages:

- ✔ **Simple:** Access the web pages through simple hyperlinks that appear on Page 1, Page 2, Page 3.

- ✔ **Complicated:** Fill in a form or choose from a drop-down list, then submit your scraping request to the tool.

import.io's most impressive feature is its capability to observe your mouse clicks to learn what you want, and then offer you ways that it can automatically complete your tasks for you. Although import.io learns and suggests tasks, it doesn't take action on those tasks until after you've marked the suggestion as correct. Consequently, these human-augmented interactions lower the risk that the machine will draw an incorrect conclusion due to over-guessing.

Collecting images with ImageQuilts

ImageQuilts (`http://imagequilts.com`) is a Chrome extension developed in part by the legendary Edward Tufte, one of the first great pioneers in data visualization — he popularized the use of the data-to-ink ratio to judge the effectiveness of charts.

The task ImageQuilts performs is deceptively simple to describe but very complex to implement. ImageQuilts makes collages of tens of images and pieces them all together into one "quilt" that's comprised of multiple rows of equal height. This task can be complex because the source images are almost never the same height. ImageQuilts scrapes and resizes the images before stitching them together into one output image. The image quilt shown in Figure 23-1 was derived from a "Labeled for Reuse" Google Images search of the term *data science*.

ImageQuilts even allows you to choose the order of images or to randomize them. You can use the tool to drag and drop any image to any place, remove an image, zoom all images at the same time, or zoom each image individually. You can even use the tool to covert between image colors — from color to grayscale or inverted color (which is handy for making contact sheets of negatives, if you're one of those rare people who still processes analog photography).

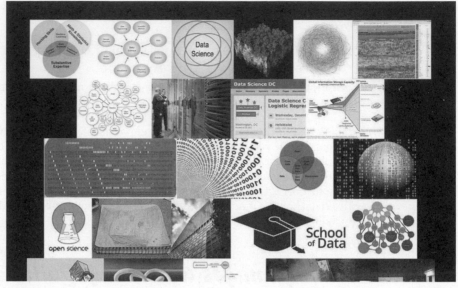

Figure 23-1:
An
ImageQuilts
output from
the Google
Images
search
term *data
science.*

Wrangling data with DataWrangler

DataWrangler (`http://vis.stanford.edu/wrangler`) is an online tool
that's supported by the University of Washington Interactive Data Lab (at
the time DataWrangler was developed, this group was called the Stanford
Visualization Group). This same group developed Lyra, an interactive data
visualization environment that you can use to create complex visualizations
without programming experience.

If your goal is to *sculpt* your dataset — or clean things up by moving things
around like a sculptor would (split this part in two, slice off that bit and move
it over there, push this down so that everything below it gets shifted to the
right, and so on) — DataWrangler is the tool for you.

You can do manipulations with DataWrangler similar to what you can do in
Excel using Visual Basic. For example, you can use DataWrangler or Excel
with Visual Basic to copy, paste, and format information from lists on the
Internet.

DataWrangler even suggests actions based on your dataset and can repeat
complex actions across entire datasets — actions such as eliminating
skipped rows, splitting data from one column into two, or turning a header

into column data. DataWrangler can also show you where your dataset is missing data.

Missing data can indicate a formatting error that needs to be cleaned up.

Checking Out More Data Exploration Tools

Throughout this book, I talk a lot about free tools that you can use to visualize your data. And although visualization can help clarify and communicate your data's meaning, you need to make sure that the data insights you're communicating are correct — that requires great care and attention in the data analysis phase. In the following sections, I introduce you to a few free tools that you can use for some advanced data analysis tasks.

Talking about Tableau Public

Tableau Public (`www.tableausoftware.com/public`) is a free desktop application that aims to be a complete package for chart-making. If the name sounds familiar, it may be because Tableau Public is just the free version of the popular Tableau Desktop program. As part of the freeware limitation, the application doesn't let you save files locally to your computer. All of your work must be uploaded to Tableau Public's cloud server, unless you purchase the software.

Tableau Public creates three levels of document — the worksheet, the dashboard, and the story. In the worksheet, you can create individual charts from data you've imported from Access, Excel, or a text-format `.csv` file. You can then use Tableau to easily do things such as choose between different data graphic types or drag columns onto different axes or subgroups.

You have to deal with a bit of a learning curve when working with the flow of the application and its nomenclature — for example, *dimensions* are categorical data and *measures* are numeric data.

Tableau offers many different default chart types — bar charts, scatterplots, line charts, bubble charts, Gantt charts, and even geographical maps. Tableau Public can even look at the type of data you have and suggest types of charts that you can use to best represent it. For example, imagine you have two dimensions and one measure. In this situation, a bar chart is a popular choice because you have two categories of data and only one numeric measure for those two categories. But if you have two dimensions and two measures, a scatterplot might be a good option because the scatterplot data graphic allows you to visualize two sets of numerical data for two categories of data.

You can use a Tableau dashboard to combine charts with text annotations or with other data charts. You can also use the dashboard to add interactive filters, such as checkboxes or sliders, so that users can interact with your data to visualize only certain time series or categories. With a Tableau story, you can combine several dashboards into a sort of slideshow presentation that shows a linear story revealed through your data.

You can use Tableau Public's online gallery to share all of the worksheets, dashboards, and stories that you generate within the application. You can also embed them into websites that link back to the Tableau Public cloud server.

Getting up to speed in Gephi

Remember back in school when you were taught how to use graph paper to do math and then draw *graphs* of the results? Well, apparently that nomenclature is incorrect. Those things with an *x*-axis and *y*-axis are actually called *charts*. Graphs are actually *network topologies* — the same type of network topologies I talk about in Chapter 9.

If this book is your first introduction to network topologies, welcome to this weird and wonderful world. You're in for a voyage of discovery. Gephi (http://gephi.github.io) is an open-source software package you can use to create graph layouts and then manipulate them to get the clearest and most effective results. The kinds of connection-based visualizations you can create in Gephi are very useful in all types of network analyses — from social media data analysis to an analysis of protein interactions or horizontal gene transfers between bacteria.

To illustrate a network analysis, imagine that you want to analyze the interconnectedness of people in your social networks. You can use Gephi to quickly and easily present the different aspects of interconnectedness between your Facebook friends. So, imagine that you're friends with Alice. You and Alice share 10 of the same friends on Facebook, but Alice also has an additional 200 friends with whom you're not connected. One of the friends that you and Alice share is named Bob. You and Bob share 20 of the same friends on Facebook also, but Bob has only 5 friends in common with Alice.

On the basis of shared friends, you can easily surmise that you and Bob are the most similar, but you can use Gephi to visually graph the friend links between yourself, Alice, and Bob.

To take another example, imagine you have a graph that shows which characters appear in the same chapter as which other characters in Victor Hugo's immense novel *Les Misérables*. (Actually, you don't have to imagine it; Figure 23-2 shows just such a graph, created in the Gephi application.) The larger bubbles indicate that these characters appear most often, and the more lines attached to a bubble, the more he or she co-occurs with others — the big bubble in the center-left is, of course, Jean Valjean.

When you use Gephi, the application automatically colors your data into different clusters. Looking to the upper-left of Figure 23-2, the cluster of characters in blue (the somewhat-darker color in this black-and-white image) are characters who mostly appear only with each other (they're the friends of Fantine, such as Félix Tholomyès — if you've only seen the musical, they don't appear in that production). These characters are connected to the rest

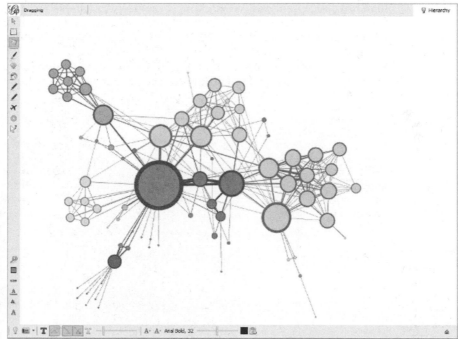

Figure 23-2:
A moderate-sized graph on characters in the book *Les Misérables.*

of the book's characters through only one character, Fantine. If a group of characters appear only together and never with any other characters, they'd be in a separate cluster of their own and not attached to the rest of the graph in any way.

To take one final example, check out Figure 23-3, which shows a graph of the United States power grid and the degrees of interconnectedness between thousands of power-generation and power-distribution facilities. This type of graph is commonly referred to as a *hairball graph,* for obvious reasons. You can make it less dense and more visually clear, but making those kinds of adjustments is as much of an art as it is a science. The best way to learn is through practice, trial, and error.

Machine learning with the WEKA suite

Machine learning is the class of artificial intelligence that's dedicated to developing and applying algorithms to data, so that the algorithms can automatically learn and detect patterns in large datasets. Waikato Environment for Knowledge Analysis (WEKA; `www.cs.waikato.ac.nz/ml/weka`) is a popular suite of tools that is useful for machine learning tools. It was written in Java and developed at the University of Waikato, New Zealand.

WEKA is a standalone application that you can use to analyze patterns in your datasets and then visualize those patterns in all sorts of interesting

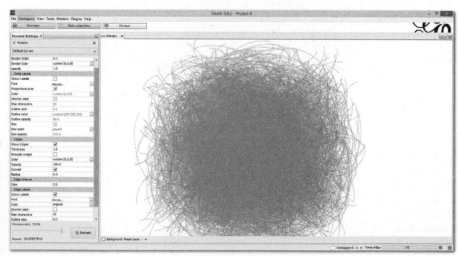

Figure 23-3:
A Gephi hairball graph of the U.S. power grid.

ways. For advanced users, WEKA's true value is derived from its suite of machine-learning algorithms that you can use to cluster or categorize your data. WEKA even allows you to run different machine-learning algorithms in parallel to see which ones perform most efficiently. WEKA can be run through a graphical user interface (GUI) or by command line. Thanks to the very well-written Weka Wiki documentation, the learning curve for WEKA isn't as steep as you might expect for a piece of software this powerful.

Checking Out More Web-Based Visualization Tools

As I mention earlier in this chapter, Chapter 11 highlights a lot of free web apps that you can use to easily generate unique and interesting data visualizations. As neat as those tools are, two more are worth your time. These tools are a little more sophisticated than many of the ones I cover in Chapter 11, but with that sophistication comes more customizable and adaptable outputs.

Getting a little Weave up your sleeve

Web-Based Analysis and Visualization Environment, or *Weave*, is the brain-child of Dr. Georges Grinstein at the University of Massachusetts Lowell. Weave is an open-source, collaborative tool that uses Adobe Flash to display data visualizations. (Check it out at www.oicweave.org.)

Because Weave relies on Adobe Flash, you can't access it with all browsers, particularly those on Apple mobile devices — iPad, iPhone, and so on.

The Weave package is Java software designed to be run on a server with a database engine like MySQL or Oracle, although it can be run on a desktop computer so long as a local host server (such as Apache Tomcat) and database software are both installed. Weave offers an excellent Wiki (http://info.iweave.com/projects/weave/wiki) that explains all aspects of the program, including installation on Mac, Linux, or Windows systems.

You can most easily install Weave on the Windows OS because of Weave's single installer that installs the desktop middleware, as well as the server and database dependencies. For the installer to be able to install all of this, though, you need to first install the free Adobe Air run-time environment on your machine.

You can use Weaver to automatically access countless open datasets or simply upload your own, as well as generate multiple interactive visualizations (such as charts and maps) that allow your users to efficiently explore even the most complex datasets.

Weave is the perfect tool to create visualizations that allow your audience to see and explore the interrelatedness between subsets of your data. Also, if you update your underlying data source, your Weave data visualizations update in real-time, as well.

Figure 23-4 shows a demo visualization on Weave's own server. It depicts every county in the United States, with many columns of data from which to choose. In this example, the map shows county-level obesity data on employed women who are 16 years of age and older. The chart at the bottom-left shows a correlation between obesity and unemployment in this group.

Figure 23-4: A figure of a chart, map, and data table in Weave.

Checking out Knoema's data visualization offerings

Knoema (http://knoema.com) is an excellent open data source, as I spell out in Chapter 22, but I would be telling only half the story if I didn't also mention Knoema's open-source data visualization tools. With these tools, you can create visualizations that enable your audience to easily explore data, drill down on geographic areas or on different indicators, and automatically produce data-driven timelines. Using Knoema, you can quickly export all results into PowerPoint files (.ppt), Excel files (.xls), PDF files (.pdf),

JPEG images (`.jpg`), or PNG images (`.png`), or even embed them on your website.

If you embed the data visualizations in a web page of your website, those visualizations automatically update if you make changes to the underlying dataset.

Figure 23-5 shows a chart and a table that were quickly, easily, and automatically generated with just two mouse clicks in Knoema. After creating charts and tables in Knoema, you can export the data, further explore it, save it, or embed it in an external website.

Figure 23-5:
An example of data tables and charts in Knoema.

You can use Knoema to make your own dashboards, as well, either from your own data or from open data in Knoema's repository. Figures 23-6 and 23-7 show two dashboards that I quickly created using Knoema's Eurostat data on capital and financial accounts.

Figure 23-6:
A map of
Eurostat
data in
Knoema.

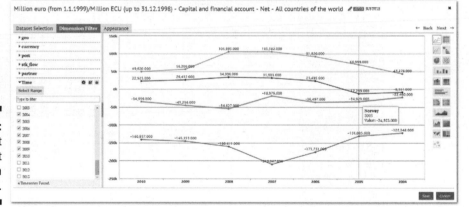

Figure 23-7:
A line chart
of Eurostat
data in
Knoema.

Index

• Q •

• R •

About the Author

Lillian Pierson, P.E. is an entrepreneurial data scientist and professional environmental engineer. She's the founder of Data-Mania (www.data-mania.com), a start-up that focuses mainly on web analytics, data-driven growth services, data journalism, and data science training services. Apart from her technical and entrepreneurial work, as a (data) journalist, Pierson has been covering the topics of data science, analytics, and statistics for prominent organizations like John Wiley & Sons, Inc.; IBM; and UBM. Be sure to check out Pierson's data blog at the Data-Mania website.

When Lillian isn't working at the computer, she's generally out exploring and experiencing the beauties of the foreign places and cultures in which she lives. As a datapreneur, Pierson lives somewhat of a nomadic lifestyle. Between international events, travel for work, and seasonal migrations, she tends to travel often and far. She's currently residing on the island of Koh Samui, in the southern seas of Thailand. She plans to make a permanent, seasonal home of the island.

Dedication

I dedicate this book to my parents — Nan Rawson, Russ Pierson, and Scott Carruth. I know and understand the supreme advantage (and responsibility) I've inherited through the gifts they so generously shared with me. I am eternally grateful.

Author's Acknowledgments

I extend a huge thanks to all the people who've helped me produce this book. Many thanks to David Taylor for all the time, energy, contributions, and input you've provided me for this book project. Also, I want to extend a tremendous thank you to Dr. Pierre Goovaerts for his generous contribution of time and expertise to supplement the book's discussion on spatial statistics. Thanks so much to Shlomo Argamon, for your technical edits. Lastly, I extend a huge thanks to Paul Levesque, Andy Cummings, Kyle Looper, and the rest of the editorial and production staff at Wiley.

Publisher's Acknowledgments

Acquisitions Editor: Kyle Looper,
    Andy Cummings

Senior Project Editor: Paul Levesque

Copy Editor: Laura K. Miller

Technical Editor: Shlomo Argamon

Editorial Assistant: Claire Brock

Sr. Editorial Assistant: Cherie Case

Project Coordinator: Sheree Montgomery,
    Vinitha Vikraman

Cover Image: ©iStockphoto.com/denisovd

Apple & Mac

iPad For Dummies,
6th Edition
978-1-118-72306-7

iPhone For Dummies,
7th Edition
978-1-118-69083-3

Macs All-in-One
For Dummies, 4th Edition
978-1-118-82210-4

OS X Mavericks
For Dummies
978-1-118-69188-5

Blogging & Social Media

Facebook For Dummies,
5th Edition
978-1-118-63312-0

Social Media Engagement
For Dummies
978-1-118-53019-1

WordPress For Dummies,
6th Edition
978-1-118-79161-5

Business

Stock Investing
For Dummies, 4th Edition
978-1-118-37678-2

Investing For Dummies,
6th Edition
978-0-470-90545-6

Personal Finance
For Dummies, 7th Edition
978-1-118-11785-9

QuickBooks 2014
For Dummies
978-1-118-72005-9

Small Business Marketing
Kit For Dummies,
3rd Edition
978-1-118-31183-7

Careers

Job Interviews
For Dummies, 4th Edition
978-1-118-11290-8

Job Searching with Social
Media For Dummies,
2nd Edition
978-1-118-67856-5

Personal Branding
For Dummies
978-1-118-11792-7

Resumes For Dummies,
6th Edition
978-0-470-87361-8

Starting an Etsy Business
For Dummies, 2nd Edition
978-1-118-59024-9

Diet & Nutrition

Belly Fat Diet For Dummies
978-1-118-34585-6

Mediterranean Diet
For Dummies
978-1-118-71525-3

Nutrition For Dummies,
5th Edition
978-0-470-93231-5

Digital Photography

Digital SLR Photography
All-in-One For Dummies,
2nd Edition
978-1-118-59082-9

Digital SLR Video &
Filmmaking For Dummies
978-1-118-36598-4

Photoshop Elements 12
For Dummies
978-1-118-72714-0

Gardening

Herb Gardening
For Dummies, 2nd Edition
978-0-470-61778-6

Gardening with Free-Range
Chickens For Dummies
978-1-118-54754-0

Health

Boosting Your Immunity
For Dummies
978-1-118-40200-9

Diabetes For Dummies,
4th Edition
978-1-118-29447-5

Living Paleo For Dummies
978-1-118-29405-5

Big Data

Big Data For Dummies
978-1-118-50422-2

Data Visualization
For Dummies
978-1-118-50289-1

Hadoop For Dummies
978-1-118-60755-8

Language &
Foreign Language

500 Spanish Verbs
For Dummies
978-1-118-02382-2

English Grammar
For Dummies, 2nd Edition
978-0-470-54664-2

French All-in-One
For Dummies
978-1-118-22815-9

German Essentials
For Dummies
978-1-118-18422-6

Italian For Dummies,
2nd Edition
978-1-118-00465-4

Available in print and e-book formats.

Available wherever books are sold. **For more information or to order direct visit www.dummies.com**

Math & Science

Algebra I For Dummies,
2nd Edition
978-0-470-55964-2

Anatomy and Physiology
For Dummies, 2nd Edition
978-0-470-92326-9

Astronomy For Dummies,
3rd Edition
978-1-118-37697-3

Biology For Dummies,
2nd Edition
978-0-470-59875-7

Chemistry For Dummies,
2nd Edition
978-1-118-00730-3

1001 Algebra II Practice
Problems For Dummies
978-1-118-44662-1

Microsoft Office

Excel 2013 For Dummies
978-1-118-51012-4

Office 2013 All-in-One
For Dummies
978-1-118-51636-2

PowerPoint 2013
For Dummies
978-1-118-50253-2

Word 2013 For Dummies
978-1-118-49123-2

Music

Blues Harmonica
For Dummies
978-1-118-25269-7

Guitar For Dummies,
3rd Edition
978-1-118-11554-1

iPod & iTunes
For Dummies, 10th Edition
978-1-118-50864-0

Programming

Beginning Programming
with C For Dummies
978-1-118-73763-7

Excel VBA Programming
For Dummies, 3rd Edition
978-1-118-49037-2

Java For Dummies,
6th Edition
978-1-118-40780-6

Religion & Inspiration

The Bible For Dummies
978-0-7645-5296-0

Buddhism For Dummies,
2nd Edition
978-1-118-02379-2

Catholicism For Dummies,
2nd Edition
978-1-118-07778-8

Self-Help & Relationships

Beating Sugar Addiction
For Dummies
978-1-118-54645-1

Meditation For Dummies,
3rd Edition
978-1-118-29144-3

Seniors

Laptops For Seniors
For Dummies, 3rd Edition
978-1-118-71105-7

Computers For Seniors
For Dummies, 3rd Edition
978-1-118-11553-4

iPad For Seniors
For Dummies, 6th Edition
978-1-118-72826-0

Social Security
For Dummies
978-1-118-20573-0

Smartphones & Tablets

Android Phones
For Dummies, 2nd Edition
978-1-118-72030-1

Nexus Tablets
For Dummies
978-1-118-77243-0

Samsung Galaxy S 4
For Dummies
978-1-118-64222-1

Samsung Galaxy Tabs
For Dummies
978-1-118-77294-2

Test Prep

ACT For Dummies,
5th Edition
978-1-118-01259-8

ASVAB For Dummies,
3rd Edition
978-0-470-63760-9

GRE For Dummies,
7th Edition
978-0-470-88921-3

Officer Candidate Tests
For Dummies
978-0-470-59876-4

Physician's Assistant Exam
For Dummies
978-1-118-11556-5

Series 7 Exam For Dummies
978-0-470-09932-2

Windows 8

Windows 8.1 All-in-One
For Dummies
978-1-118-82087-2

Windows 8.1 For Dummies
978-1-118-82121-3

Windows 8.1 For Dummies,
Book + DVD Bundle
978-1-118-82107-7

Available in print and e-book formats.

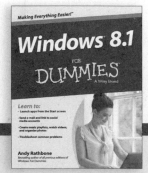

Available wherever books are sold. **For more information or to order direct visit www.dummies.com**

Take Dummies with you everywhere you go!

Whether you are excited about e-books, want more from the web, must have your mobile apps, or are swept up in social media, Dummies makes everything easier.

Leverage the Power

For Dummies is the global leader in the reference category and one of the most trusted and highly regarded brands in the world. No longer just focused on books, customers now have access to the For Dummies content they need in the format they want. Let us help you develop a solution that will fit your brand and help you connect with your customers.

Advertising & Sponsorships

Connect with an engaged audience on a powerful multimedia site, and position your message alongside expert how-to content.

Targeted ads · Video · Email marketing · Microsites · Sweepstakes sponsorship

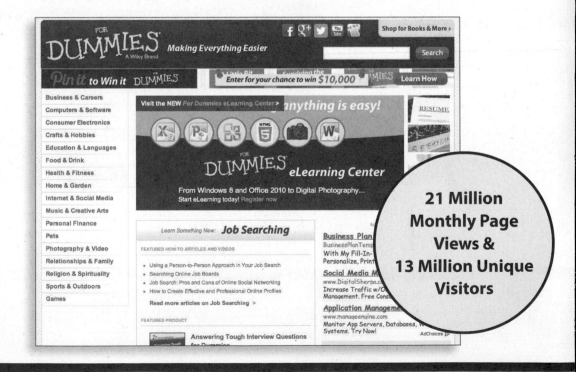